Digital Forensics and Investigations

T0320295

Digital Forensics and Investigations

People, Processes, and Technologies to Defend the Enterprise

Jason Sachowski

CRC Press
Taylor & Francis Group
Boca Raton London New York

CRC Press is an imprint of the
Taylor & Francis Group, an **informa** business

CRC Press
Taylor & Francis Group
6000 Broken Sound Parkway NW, Suite 300
Boca Raton, FL 33487-2742

First issued in paperback 2020

© 2018 by Taylor & Francis Group, LLC
CRC Press is an imprint of Taylor & Francis Group, an Informa business

No claim to original U.S. Government works

ISBN-13: 978-1-138-72093-0 (hbk)
ISBN-13: 978-0-367-77865-1 (pbk)

Visit the Taylor & Francis Web site at
http://www.taylorandfrancis.com

and the CRC Press Web site at
http://www.crcpress.com

Contents

SECTION II ENHANCING DIGITAL FORENSIC CAPABILITIES

SECTION III INTEGRATING DIGITAL FORENSIC CAPABILITIES

SECTION IV APPENDIXES

SECTION V TEMPLATES

Preface

At the beginning of all experimental work stands the choice of the appropriate technique of investigation.

—Walter Rudolf Hess

Acknowledgments

I would like to most of all thank my wife and my children for showing me that no matter what I do in my lifetime, they will always be my greatest success.

Thank you to my parents for providing me with countless opportunities to become who I am today and for encouraging me to keep pushing my boundaries.

Thank you to my colleagues for allowing me the honor to work with you and for the infinite wisdom and knowledge you have given me.

Lastly, thank you to Blair for opening doors.

About the Author

Jason Sachowski has over 13 years of experience in digital forensic investigations, secure software development, and information security architecture. He currently manages a team delivering Digital Forensic, Electronic Discovery, and Data Loss Assessments for The Bank of Nova Scotia, commonly known as Scotiabank, Canada's third largest and most international bank.

Throughout his career, Sachowski has led and conducted hundreds of digital forensic investigations involving enterprise servers, network logs, smart phones, and database systems. Complementary to his technical experiences and skills, he has also developed and maintained processes and procedures, managed large information security budgets, and governed the negotiation of third-party contracts.

In addition to his professional career, Sachowski is also the author of the book *Implementing Digital Forensic Readiness: From Reactive to Proactive Process*, he serves as a contributing author and content moderator for *Dark Reading* online publications, is a subject matter expert for the professional development of information security certifications, and volunteers as an advocate for CyberBullying prevention and CyberSecurity awareness.

Sachowski holds several Information Security and Digital Forensic certifications including: Certified Information Systems Security Professional—Information Systems Security Architecture Professional (CISSP—ISSAP), Certified Cyber Forensics Professional (CCFP), Certified Secure Software Lifecycle Professional (CSSLP), Systems Security Certified Practitioner (SSCP), and EnCase Certified Examiner (EnCE).

Introduction

Since the digital forensic profession was formalized as a scientific discipline decades ago, its principles, methodologies, and techniques have remained consistent despite the evolution of technology and can ultimately be applied to any form of digital data. Within a corporate environment, digital forensic practitioners are often relied upon to maintain the legal admissibility and forensic viability of digital evidence in support of a broad range of different business functions.

Why This Book

For the most part, where digital forensic education and training is provided today, focus is commonly placed on the "hands-on" and "how to" aspects of the discipline; such as how to forensically acquire a hard drive. Understandably, academics will primarily concentrate on the technical execution of digital forensics because it universally translates across every industry and geo-location where the discipline is practiced.

In some cases, the nontechnical side of digital forensics can be overlooked as an importance contributor to achieving true synergies in a business environment. Taking a step back, the importance of realizing a seamless integration among the people, process, and technology areas of digital forensics is essential in establishing a holistic approach to defending an enterprise.

This book was written from the business perspective of the digital forensics profession that examines all three areas of enterprise's digital forensic capabilities required to successfully integrate with other key business functions, including

- Focusing on the implementation aspects of a digital forensic program within an enterprise
- Encompassing the administrative, technical, and physical components required for enterprise digital forensic capabilities
- Detailing the people, process, and technology requirements for integrating digital forensic capabilities throughout the enterprise

Who Will Benefit from This Book

This book was written from a nontechnical, business perspective to provide readers with realistic methodologies and strategies to how the people, process, and technology aspects of digital forensics are integrated throughout an enterprise to support different business operations.

While this book does cover the fundamental principles, methodologies, and techniques of digital forensics, it largely focuses on outlining how the people, process, and technology areas are used to defend the enterprise through integrating digital forensic capabilities with key business functions.

The information contained in this book has been written to benefit people who

- Are employed, both directly and indirectly, in the digital forensic profession and are working to expand their organization's digital forensic capabilities
- Are employed in the information security profession and are interested in either (1) becoming directly involved in the digital forensic profession or (2) enhancing their organization's defenses
- An academic scholar pursuing nontechnical, business knowledge about digital forensics to provide them with education to become employed in the digital forensic profession

Who Will Not Benefit from This Book

This book is not designed to provide readers with the technical knowledge about digital forensics; including the "hands-on" and "how to" aspects of the discipline such as how to forensically acquire a hard drive.

How This Book Is Organized

This book is organized into five thematic sections:

- *Part 1: Enabling Digital Forensics* outlines the fundamental principles, methodologies, and techniques applied unanimously throughout the digital forensic discipline.
- *Part 2: Enhancing Digital Forensics* analyses additional considerations for enabling and enhancing digital forensic capabilities throughout an enterprise environment.
- *Part 3: Integrating Digital Forensics* addresses best practices for integrating the people, process, and technologies components of digital forensics across an enterprise environment.
- *Part 4: Appendixes* provides supplementary content that expand topics and subject areas discussed in throughout other sections of this book.
- *Part 5: Templates* supply structured templates and forms used in support of the digital forensic and business functions/processes covered throughout.

ENABLING DIGITAL FORENSICS

1

The use of technology in criminal activities has evolved significantly over the past 50 years. With this evolution, the digital forensic profession was born through the work of pioneers who strived to expand their interest in technology advancement into what is now a well-established and recognized professional discipline.

Because of their work, digital forensics has become a profession that strictly follows forensic science disciplines consisting of the best practices of proven methodologies, techniques, and principles. Applying these best practices and the ability to make use of them within an organization provides an additional defense-in-depth layer to ensure that digital evidence is forensically viable in a court of law. In other words, digital forensics is the application of science to law.

Organizations that demonstrate a good understanding of the requirements for implementing digital forensic capabilities within their environment are much better equipped to gather and process digital evidence in line with the legal requirements for prosecuting criminals. However, if these requirements are ignored or otherwise not followed, not only do organizations run the risk of digital evidence being either compromised, lost, or overlooked, but also that it will not be admissible in a court of law based on concerns about integrity or authenticity.

Even though legal prosecution might not be the end goal, such as cases where an employee has violated a corporate policy, there is always the potential that some form of disciplinary action will take place, such as employment termination. In all cases, it is fundamentally important that organizations consistently follow the digital forensic best practices because evidence used during an investigation may wind up in a court of law.

In this section, we will look at the principles, methodologies, and techniques applied unanimously throughout the digital forensic discipline, and the best practices that organizations must adhere to.

Chapter 1

Introduction to Digital Forensics

The profession now commonly referred to as *digital forensics* was once made up of unstructured processes; custom, home-grown toolsets; and knowledge based on the collective work of hobbyists. Over the past 50 years, the digital forensic profession evolved alongside advancements in technology to become a mature discipline where a common body of knowledge (CBK)[1] made up of proven scientific principles, methodologies, and techniques brought about a level of standardization and formal structure to the profession.

A Brief History of Forensics and Technology

Technology, or all sorts, has evolved throughout human history. The beginning of digital forensics dates to the 1970s when crimes involving technology were first committed (refer to Chapter 4 titled *"Laws, Standards, and Regulations"* for a history of crime and technology).

Throughout the history of digital forensics, there were specific eras where the efforts and work of key individuals evolved digital forensics into the mature scientific discipline it is today. Like other forms of human and industrial history, it's beneficial to learn about the events that happened beforehand that have paved the path for where we are today.

Preface (1960–1980)

From the 1960s forward until the mid-1980s, computer systems were predominantly used to perform data-processing operations and were not typically connected to other systems outside of an organization. System administrators were largely responsible for securing their own systems, work which comprised primarily of system audits to ensure the efficiency and accuracy of the data-processing functions. When it came time to investigate a computer system for legal issues, law enforcement would turn to skilled system administrators who used common system administration tools, such as data recovery and backup utilities, to gather and process electronically stored information (ESI).[2]

Most technology-related investigations performed during this time were rudimentary at best, because there was a misunderstanding of goals; absence of structure (i.e., laws, principles); and lack of tools, processes, and training. This era is considered the *ad hoc* era of digital forensics.

Infancy (1980–1995)

When the personal computer (PC) made its debut, there was a sudden burst of interest in computer systems that incited hobbyists to get a better understanding of how the internal components of these technologies worked. Among these hobbyists were individuals from law enforcement, government agencies, and corporations who started sharing what they had learned about technology and what information could be extracted. These individuals are considered the pioneers of computer forensics, as the field was initially known.

It was during this era that government agencies came to realize that the skilled individuals who were assisting them with technology-related investigations needed better and more formalized training, better structure in the processes they followed, and better tools. In one stream, development of software-based programs, like Maresware or AccessData, emerged with capabilities to facilitate specific digital forensic activities (i.e., forensic imaging). In another stream of work, several agencies built small groups of specialized and trained individuals who would be used to gather evidence from computer systems to be used in legal proceedings. One of the earliest groups created was the Federal Bureau of Investigation (FBI) Computer Analysis Response Team (CART), established in 1984.

This structure is primarily attributed to the collective efforts of the pioneers who brought about a new level of acceptable procedures, specialty-built tools, and improved education and training. This era is when ad hoc efforts transitioned into a *structured* state to address technology-related investigations.

Childhood (1995–2005)

Starting in 1995, new technical working groups (TWG) and scientific working groups (SWG) followed the lead of the FBI CART with the goal of creating a CBK of principles, methodologies, and techniques that could standardize and bring about further formal structure to computer forensics. Work done by the Scientific Working Group on Digital Evidence (SWGDE), in collaboration with the International Organization on Computer Evidence (IOCE) and G8 High Tech Crime Subcommittee, resulted in the first publication of digital forensic principles, which proved to be a major step forward in formalizing digital forensics as a science.

In the 2000s, digital forensics was recognized as a science having established structured procedures and making significant advancements in education and training. With the technology explosion, such as the Internet and mobile devices, the term *computer forensics* was becoming increasingly more difficult to use because of how digital evidence was now distributed across multiple interconnected technologies. Recognizing this, the Digital Forensic Research Workshop (DFRWS) proposed in 2001 to update the descriptor *computer forensics* into the term *digital forensics*. This proposal initiated an expansion of new specializations, such as *network forensics* and *mobile forensics*, which led to increased scrutiny over the previously established digital forensics principles.

This era saw the establishment of more structure in processes, education, and technologies. It was during this time when the formalization of digital forensics as a professional discipline occurred as result of establishing a consistent set of scientific principles, methodologies, and techniques.

Adolescence (2005–2015)

In 2008 the American Academy of Forensic Sciences (AAFS) responded to the scrutiny by creating the Digital and Multimedia Sciences (DMS) section, which led to major advancements by providing a common foundation by which groups can share knowledge and resolve digital-forensic challenges.

With the expanding scope of digital forensics, both academic curriculum and professional certification programs were offered to educate, train, and accredit professional knowledge and experience in the field. Likewise, digital forensic tools underwent a major evolution away from the home-grown applications into feature-robust and enterprise-capable commercial software suites that not only supported digital forensics, but also provided functionality to the fields of incident response, electronic discovery (eDiscovery), and information governance.

Today, what started out as the pastime of hobbyists has arrived at a point of convergence between various law enforcement agencies, organizations large and small, and several intelligence agencies where well-established best practices universally follow consistent and scientifically proven principles, methodologies, and techniques. This era is defined as enhancing the structure of digital forensics into an *enterprise* state.

Thoughts for the Future

Digital forensics has made significant advancements over the past 50 years to become the mature scientific discipline it is today. Predicting the future is a gambler's game; but if history has taught us anything, it is that technology and digital forensics will continue to evolve in parallel to each other.

One thing for certain is that the digital-forensic CBK will continue to develop and mature. At the end of the day, practitioners of the future will be better educated and trained because they have decades of knowledge from every individual who has contributed before them. On the other hand, future technology advancements will respectively introduce unique challenges that the digital-forensic community will need to address. Two examples of where the future of digital forensics will see development are cloud and quantum computing.

Cloud Computing

Over the past several years, *cloud computing* has made significant shifts in how organizations have transformed their business operations. Generally, there is no limit to the type of business services that can moved into cloud environments, which means that the applications and data reside on systems external to the business itself. This presents a challenge to digital forensics, as organizations do not have physical access to the computer systems that might need to be seized and searched as part of an investigation.

In 2014 the National Institute of Standards and Technology (NIST) released a draft publication entitled *NIST Cloud Computing Forensic Science Challenges* based on the research performed by the NIST Cloud Computing Forensic Science Working Group. The document pulls together a list of challenges faced by digital forensic practitioners when managing incidents and investigations in a cloud-computing ecosystem. The goal of this publication is to put structure around conducting digital forensics involving cloud-based systems and to establish consistent principles, methodologies, and techniques.

For example, challenges identified by NIST working group specific to cloud-computing ecosystems include, but are not limited to:

- Recovery of deleted data in shared environments
- Evidence correlation across multiple cloud service providers (CSP)
- Segregation of electronically stored information (ESI) in multitenant systems
- Competence and trustworthiness of CSP as an effective and immediate first responder
- Jurisdiction over interconnected devices anywhere around the world

The full list of challenges are in *NIST Cloud Computing Forensic Science Challenges*, available on the NIST website (http://csrc.nist.gov/publications/drafts/nistir-8006/draft_nistir_8006.pdf).

Quantum Computing

Currently, despite much theory and experimentation, quantum computing is still in its infancy, and the topic of *quantum forensics* has received minimal attention from research communities. From research completed so far, there are theories of potential impact in the capability to conduct live forensics on a quantum system, leaving practitioners with the only option to conduct forensic analysis postmortem.

Discussed further in Chapter 2 titled "*Investigative Process Methodologies,*" data that exists within a live, or dynamic, state can provide practitioners with a great deal of potential evidence; however, it is extremely volatile. This means that if criminals gained access to a quantum system to commit their crimes, there could be minimal artifacts recoverable for use in any type of investigation.

Addressing concerns about the impact quantum computing could have on live forensics, organizations will need to invest resources into understanding their potential to extract the maximum amount of evidence from recoverable data elements.

Evolutionary Cycle of Digital Forensics

Digital forensics has become the scientific discipline it is today because of the work done by those involved in computer forensics in the 1970s. Driving structure and maturity in the profession is the product of influences both tactical, such as technology advancements, and strategic, such as the creation of global working groups dedicated to digital forensics.

Making a prediction as to what the future holds for digital forensics is not a trivial question. If we have learned anything about how the past has shaped digital forensics into what it is today, the best and most educated prediction is that history will repeat itself. This does not mean that the digital forensics profession will revert back to the way it was in the 1970s; rather, that maturity of the discipline will be subject to continuous improvement that follows a cyclical methodology like the one illustrated in Figure 1.1 below.

Ad Hoc Phase

The ad hoc phase between the 1970s and the mid-1980s is an example of a starting point in the continuous improvement of digital forensics. Otherwise referred to as the preforensics or protoforensics era, this phase is characterized by the absence of structure; ambiguous goals; and an overall lack of tools, processes, and training.

Looking at the history of digital forensics and crime, discussed in Chapter 4 titled "*Laws, Standards, and Regulations,*" it is evident that both technological advancements and legal precedence are the major contributors for evolution within the digital forensic profession. Generally, the term *ad hoc* refers to something new that has been created (i.e., technology, law) and, because of this, the approach is disorganized or not theory driven. This is not to say that we ignore everything that

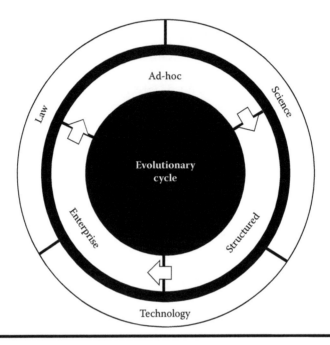

Figure 1.1   Digital forensics evolutionary cycle.

came previously and start anew, but that with new developments in technology, there is a need to circle back to ensure structure is provided in terms of digital forensic capabilities.

Structured Phase

The structured phase from the mid-1980s through the 1990s is an example of the next period in the evolution of digital forensics. This phase is characterized by the development of complex solutions, which brings harmony and structure to processes and tools that were identified as challenges faced during the ad hoc phase. Elements specifically addressed during this phase include:

- ▪ Establishment of policy-based programs (i.e., laws, regulations)
- ▪ Definition and coordination of processes that align with established policies
- ▪ Requirement for forensically sound[3] tools

Foremost, for investigative processes to be clearly defined and documented there needs to be policies in place, such as laws and regulations, to establish a foundation for investigation. In turn, these policies drive the need to legitimize processes and tools to ensure they are consistently applied to ensure repeatable and —reproducible outcomes. Ultimately, if the tools used cannot consistently reproduce results, its legitimacy can be called into question and the forensic viability of evidence gathered or processed cannot be guaranteed. For processes and tools to produce credible evidence that is forensically sound requires it be:

- Verifiable as authentic to its original source data
- Collected and preserved in a manner that preserves its integrity
- Analyzed using tools and techniques that maintain its integrity

At the end of this phase, the formal structure brings digital forensic processes and tools in line with the scientific principles, methodologies, and techniques required for achieving a state of maturity.

Enterprise Phase

The *enterprise* phase in the 2000s is an example of the final era in the maturity of digital forensics. This phase is characterized by the recognition of processes and tools to be a science that involves the real-time collection of evidence; the general acceptance for the development of effective tools and processes; and the application of formally structured principles, methodologies, and techniques

Ultimately, this phase of the digital forensic evolution came about from the need to automate digital forensic processes. Not only does this automation support the ability to perform proactive evidence collection, but it also allows for methodologies and techniques to be consistently applied that maintain standards set out by the legal system to ensure the legal admissibility of evidence.

The evolution of digital forensics is cyclical when it comes to maturing existing scientific principles, methodologies, and techniques for new technologies and standards (i.e., laws and regulations). However, at the same time the evolution of digital forensics is linear in the sense that the scientific principles, methodologies, and techniques are maturing, the continued development and contribution to the digital forensic CBK persists.

Technical and Scientific Working Groups

Throughout the evolution of digital forensics, several different working groups were created to develop a CBK of principles, methodologies, and techniques that could standardize and bring formal structure to computer/digital forensics. Over the years, more than 30 different working groups have been established. Each of these groups have played, and continue to play, a large role in the development of standards and guidelines, facilitating the research and development of forensic science, and several other disciplines related to law enforcement and security.

As early as 1984, law enforcement agencies developed programs to examine digital evidence. As mentioned earlier, one of the earliest groups created was CART by the FBI in 1984, established to address the growing need for a structured and programmatic approach to handling the challenges of digital evidence. Even though CART was unique to the FBI, its basic functions and general organization were replicated by many foreign law enforcement agencies.

In the early 1990s, scientists gathered to form technical working groups (TWG) during the structured phase of digital forensics. Predominantly, these TWGs were of short duration and usually had a single deliverable, such as guidebooks. While not directly related to the digital forensic profession, the FBI created the first TWG, a group of scientists meeting to discuss the challenges being faced by the introduction of DNA evidence into the legal system. Finalized in 1993, the work completed by the Technical Working Group for DNA Analysis Methods (TWGDAM) created guidelines for proficiency testing and quality assurance, which gave DNA evidence a solid scientific foundation when presented in a court of law. At the same time, the U.S. Department of Justice's (DOJ) National Institute of Justice (NIJ) recognized the work being done by the FBI's working group and decided to borrow their model to further expand on it. The NIJ created several of its own TWGs to address the technical needs of the U.S. criminal justice system and to recommend initiatives the NIG should fund. Instead of limiting membership to scientists, the NIJ invited experts and professionals—including practitioners, engineers, attorneys, academics, and other agencies—to broaden the range of knowledge and experience of those contributing to the TWGs.

International Organization on Computer Evidence (IOCE)

In 1995 the International Organization on Computer Evidence (IOCE) was created to provide international law enforcement agencies a forum to collaborate and exchange information about computer crime investigations and other forensics issues involving technology. In response to the G8 Communique and action plans of December 1997, working groups from around the world—including Canada, Europe, and the United States—began developing international standards for the handling and recovery of digital evidence. The standardized international principles for the recovery of digital evidence are governed by the following attributes:

- Consistency with all legal systems
- Allowance for the use of a common language
- Durability
- Ability to cross international boundaries
- Ability to instill confidence in the integrity of evidence
- Applicability to all forensic evidence
- Applicability at every level, including that of individual, agency, and country

At the International Hi-Tech Crime and Forensics Conference (IHCFC) in 1999, the IOCE proposed the following principles that were unanimously approved by member countries:

- Upon seizing digital evidence, actions taken should not change that evidence.
- When it is necessary for a person to access original digital evidence, that person must be forensically competent.
- All activity relating to the seizure, access, storage, or transfer of digital evidence must be fully documented, preserved, and available for review.
- An individual is responsible for all actions taken with respect to digital evidence while the digital evidence is in their possession.
- Any agency that is responsible for seizing, accessing, storing, or transferring digital evidence is responsible for compliance with these principles.

G8 High-Tech Crime Subcommittee

In 1997 the G8 States (France, Germany, Italy, the United Kingdom, Japan, the United States, Canada, and Russia) established the Subgroup of High-Tech Crime. The goal of this subcommittee was "to ensure that law enforcement agencies can quickly respond to serious cyber-threats and incidents" by guaranteeing that no criminal receives safe havens anywhere in the world. From the work of the G8 Subgroup, the *Principles On Transborder Access to Stored Computer Data— Data Principles on Accessing Data Stored in a Foreign State* were approved by the G8 Group containing the following series of principles to combat computer crime, which should be applied when law enforcement agencies are investigating technology-related crimes in other countries:

- Preservation of stored data in a computer system
  - Each state shall ensure its ability to secure rapid preservation of data that is stored in a computer in particular data held by third parties such as service providers, and that is subject to short retention practices or is otherwise particularly vulnerable to loss or modification, for the purpose of seeking its access, search, copying, seizure or disclosure, and ensure that preservation is possible even if necessary only to assist another State.
  - A State may request another State to secure rapid preservation of data stored in a computer system located in that other State.
  - Upon receiving a request from another State, the requested State shall take all appropriate means, in accordance with its national law, to preserve such data expeditiously. Such preservation shall be for a reasonable time to permit the making of a formal request for the access, search, copying, seizure or disclosure of such data.

- ■ Expedited mutual legal assistance
  - – Upon receiving a formal request for access, search, copying, seizure or disclosure of data, including data that has been preserved, the requested State shall, in accordance with its national law, execute the request as expeditiously as possible, by:
    - • Responding pursuant to traditional legal assistance procedure
    - • Ratifying or endorsing any judicial or other legal authorization that was granted in the requesting State and, pursuant to traditional legal assistance procedures, disclosing any data seized to the requesting State
    - • Using any other method of assistance permitted by the law of the requested State
  - – Each State shall, in appropriate circumstances, accept and respond to legal assistance requests made under these Principles by expedited but reliable means of communications, including voice, fax or e-mail, with written confirmation to follow where required.
- ■ Transborder access to stored data not requiring legal assistance
  - – Notwithstanding anything in these Principles, a State need not obtain authorization from another State when it is acting in accordance with its national law for the purpose of:
    - • Accessing publicly available (open source) data, regardless of where the data is geographically located
    - • Accessing, searching, copying, or seizing data stored in a computer system located in another State, if acting in accordance with the lawful and voluntary consent of a person who has the lawful authority to disclose to it that data. The searching State should consider notifying the searched State, if such notification is permitted by national law and the data reveals a violation of criminal law or otherwise appears to be of interest to the searched State.

Scientific Working Group on Digital Evidence (SWGDE)

In 1998 the Technical Working Group on Digital Evidence (TWGDE) held their first meeting, consisting of members from several government and law enforcement agencies. With rapid adoption of the work generated by the TWGDE, the name was changed to the Scientific Working Group on Digital Evidence (SWGDE) to distinguish the group's long-term focus on forensic science to continue developing and standardizing forensic protocols and analytical practices. The SWGDE, functioning as the US-based representation for IOCE efforts, is responsible for "the development of cross-disciplinary guidelines and standards for the recovery, preservation, and examination of digital evidence, including audio, imaging, and electronic devices." The standards and principles defined by the SWGDE are as follows:

- *Principle 1*: In order to ensure that digital evidence is collected, preserved, examined, or transferred in a manner safeguarding the accuracy and reliability of the evidence, law enforcement and forensic organizations must establish and maintain an effective quality system. Standard Operating Procedures (SOPs) are documented quality-control guidelines that must be supported by proper case records and use broadly accepted procedures, equipment, and materials.
  - *Standards and Criteria 1.1:* All agencies that seize and/or examine digital evidence must maintain an appropriate SOP document. All elements of an agency's policies and procedures concerning digital evidence must be clearly set forth in this SOP document, which must be issued under the agency's management authority.
  - *Standards and Criteria 1.2*: Agency management must review the SOPs on an annual basis to ensure their continued suitability and effectiveness.
  - *Standards and Criteria 1.3*: Procedures used must be generally accepted in the field or supported by data gathered and recorded in a scientific manner.
  - *Standards and Criteria 1.4*: The agency must maintain written copies of appropriate technical procedures.
  - *Standards and Criteria 1.5*: The agency must use hardware and software that is appropriate and effective for the seizure or examination procedure.
  - *Standards and Criteria 1.6*: All activity relating to the seizure, storage, examination, or transfer of digital evidence must be recorded in writing and be available for review and testimony.
  - *Standards and Criteria 1.7*: Any action that has the potential to alter, damage, or destroy any aspect of original evidence must be performed by qualified persons in a forensically sound manner

Principles of Digital Forensics

Digital forensics is the application of science to law, and, subsequently, must follow the scientific principles, methodologies, and technique required for admissibility in a court of law. Even if legal prosecution is not the end goal of an investigation, such as corporate policy violations, there may be a requirement for legal action at some point. Therefore, it is important to handle all potential digital evidence in a manner that guarantees it will remain admissible in a court of law.

Evidence Exchange

One of the main goals in conducting a forensic investigation is to establish factual conclusions that are based on credible evidence. According to the *Locard's Exchange Principle*, illustrated in Figure 1.2, anyone or anything entering a crime scene takes

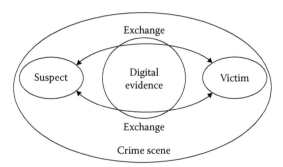

Figure 1.2   Locard's Exchange Principle.

something in with them and leaves something behind when they leave. The *Locard's Exchange Principle* states that with contact between entities, there will be an exchange.

In the physical world, an example of this exchange can occur where a perpetrator might inadvertently leave their fingerprints or traces of blood at the crime scene. Alternatively, another example could be where a perpetrator might take a crucial piece of evidence away from the crime scene, such as a knife, to make the job of identifying evidence more challenging. In both examples, these exchanges produce tangible forms of evidence that demonstrate both class and individual characteristics. Evidence that possesses class characteristics, otherwise referred to as class evidence, have features that group items by type, such as hair color. On its own, this type of evidence does not provide conclusive identification of a perpetrator and individualizing characteristics. What individualizes evidence, such as hair color, are those characteristics that possess unique qualities that differentiate one from another and help to narrow down the group to a single item. Using the analogy of hair color, examples of individual characteristics can include, but are not limited to, length, style (e.g., straight, wavy), or highlights.

In the digital world, evidence exists in a logical state that is intangible in comparison to physical evidence. However, exchanges like those in the physical world can persist and are equally as relevant in the digital world. Email communication and web browsing are clear examples of how these exchanges occur within the digital world. If a threatening email message is sent, the individual's computer will contain artifacts of this, as will the email servers used to transmit the message between people. Practitioners can identify and gather a copious amount of evidence relating to this threatening email in the form of access logs, email logs, and other artifacts within computer systems.

Forensic Soundness

Evidence can make or break an investigation. Equally important in both the physical and digital worlds, it is critical that evidence is handling in a way that will not raise questions when later presented in a court of law.

Forensically sound is a term used to qualify and, in some cases, justify the use of a technology or methodology. Likewise, *forensic soundness* occurs when ESI,[2] as digital evidence, remains complete and materially unaltered as a result of using a technology or methodology. This means that during every digital investigation, proper forensic techniques are used following consistent methodologies that are based on established scientific principles.

While Chapter 2 titled *"Investigative Process Methodologies"* discusses this further, the below principles must be followed to achieve forensic soundness specific to digital evidence:

- *Minimally Handle the Original*: Digital forensic process should be minimally applied to original data sources. Instead, a forensic image of ESI should be taken and used to perform investigative processes and techniques.
- *Account for Any Change*: In some instances, digital evidence can change from its original state. When change occurs, it should be documented to note the nature, extent, and reason for the change.
- *Comply with the Rules of Evidence*: Throughout an investigation, applicable rules of evidence (ex. laws and regulations) should be considered. Refer to Chapter 4 titled *"Laws, Standards, and Regulations"* for additional information.
- *Avoid Exceeding One's Knowledge*: Do not undertake any activity or task that is beyond your current level of knowledge and skill.

Perhaps one of the biggest causes for why digital evidence does not maintain forensic soundness is human error. To guarantee forensic soundness, digital evidence must be gathered, processed, and maintained following principles, methodologies, and techniques that do not alter its state at any time; thus, demonstrating the evidence is authentic and has integrity.

Authenticity and Integrity

The goal for maintaining the authenticity of digital evidence is to demonstrate that it is the same data as what was originally seized. From a technical perspective, there are times when digital evidence cannot be compared to its original state; such as with random access memory (RAM) that is constantly in a state of change. For these occurrences, point- in-time snapshots are taken that demonstrate the state of the technology at that moment. From a legal perspective, authentication means satisfying the legal systems that the:

- Content of the record has remained unchanged
- Information in the record does in fact originate from its original source
- Extraneous information about the record is accurate (i.e., timestamp)

Supporting the need to establish authenticity, the goal for maintaining the integrity of digital evidence is to demonstrate that it has not been changed since the time it was first gathered. In digital forensics, verifying integrity involves comparing the digital fingerprint of digital evidence when it is first gathered and subsequently throughout its lifecycle. Currently, the most common means of generating a digital fingerprint in digital forensics is to use a one-way cryptographic hash algorithm such as the Message Digest Algorithm family (i.e., MD5, MD6)[4] or the Secure Hashing Algorithm family (i.e., SHA-1, SHA-2, SHA-3).[5]

> In 2004–2005, experts identified that the MD5 and SHA-1 algorithms contained flaws where two unique inputs, having distinctively different properties and characteristic, would result in the same computational hash value being outputted.
>
> Dubbed a "hash collision," this meant that the same computational hash value could be engineered in a way that multiple pieces of digital evidence could return the same hash value. Naturally, this raised concerns in the digital forensic community about the impact it would have on the legal admissibility of digital evidence.
>
> In 2009 during the matter of United States vs. Joseph Schmidt III, the court rules that chance of a hash collision is not significant and is not an issue. Specifically, a digital fingerprint of a file still produces a digital algorithm that uniquely identified that file.
>
> This ruling meant that the integrity of digital evidence that was done using either the MD5 or SHA-1 algorithms can be relied upon as legally admissible.

The uniqueness of these cryptographic algorithms makes them an important technique for documenting the integrity of digital evidence. While the potential for "hash collisions" exists, the use of the Message Digest Algorithm family or Secure Hashing Algorithm family remains an acceptable way of demonstrating the authenticity and integrity of digital evidence.

Chain of Custody

Perhaps the most important aspect of maintaining authenticity and integrity is documenting the continuity of possession for digital evidence. This chain of custody is used to demonstrate the transfer of ownership over digital evidence between entities and can be used to validate the integrity of evidence being presented in court. Without a chain of custody in place, arguments can be made that evidence has been tampered, altered, or improperly handled, which can lead to potential evidence contamination of other consequences. It is best to keep the number of custody transfers to a minimum, as these individuals can be called upon to provide testimony on the handling of evidence during the time they controlled it.

A sample template that can be used as a chain-of-custody form has been provided in the Templates section of this book.

Summary

Digital forensics is the application of science to law and must follow established and scientifically proven principles, methodologies, and techniques required to legally admit evidence in a court of law. If history has taught us anything, it is that the advancement in technology will stand as the catalyst to new and evolved digital forensic principles, methodologies, and techniques.

Glossary

1. **Common body of knowledge (CBK)** is the complete concepts, terms, and activities that make up a professional domain.
2. **Electronically stored information (ESI)** is information created, manipulated, communicated, stored, and best utilized in digital form and requiring the use of computer hardware and software.
3. **Forensically sound** qualifies and, in some cases, justifies the use of a forensic technology or methodology.
4. **Message Digest Algorithm family** is a suite of one-way cryptographic hashing algorithms that is commonly used to verify data integrity through the creation of a unique digital fingerprint of differing length based on version used.
5. **Secure Hashing Algorithm family** is a suite of one-way cryptographic hashing algorithms that is commonly used to verify data integrity through the creation of a unique digital fingerprint of differing length based on version used.

Chapter 2

Investigative Process Methodologies

In Chapter 1, we learned that digital forensics is built on an extensive common body of knowledge (CBK)[1] of well-established and proven scientific principles, methodologies, and techniques. With the evolution of digital forensics throughout the years, there were consistent advancements being made in education, technologies, and processes, which painted a picture that bypassing, switching, or not following proper processes could result in missed, incomplete, or inadmissible evidence. From this realization, practitioners developed process models that would function as a framework for digital forensics processes to be consistently applied.

Existing Process Models

When technology was first involved with criminal activities, practitioners did not follow any guiding principles, methodologies, and techniques while collecting and processing digital evidence. It was only in the 1980s when law enforcement agencies realized that there was a need to have an established set of processes that could be consistently followed to support their forensic investigations and guarantee the legal admissibility of digital evidence.

Since then, there have been several authors who have taken on the task of developing and proposing a process model by which practitioners can follow, as assurance that evidence has been collected, processed, and preserved following repeatable methodologies and techniques. Over the years, several different process models were proposed to formalize the digital forensic discipline and transform ad hoc tasks and activities into tested and proven methodologies.

Displayed in Table 2.1 below is a list of different process methodologies that have been developed and proposed for digital forensic investigations. It is important to note that while this listing may not be complete, the inclusion of a process methodology does not suggest it is better or recommended over other methodologies that were not included in the table.

Table 2.1   Investigative Process Models

ID	Year	Author(s)	Model Name	Stages
P01	1995	Pollitt	Computer Forensic Investigative Process	4
P02	2001	U.S. Department of Justice	Computer Forensic Process Model	4
P03	2001	Palmer	Digital Forensic Research Workshop Investigative Model (Generic Investigation Process)	6
P04	2001	Lee et al.	Scientific Crime Scene Investigation Model	4
P05	2002	Reith et al.	Abstract Model of the Digital Forensic Procedures	9
P06	2003	Carrier and Spafford	Integrated Digital Investigation Process	5
P07	2003	Stephenson	End-to-End Digital Investigation	9
P08	2004	Baryamureeba and Tushabe	Enhanced Integrated Digital Investigation Process	5
P09	2004	Ciardhuáin	Extended Model of Cybercrime Investigation	13
P10	2004	Beebe and Clark	Hierarchical, Objective-Based Framework for the Digital Investigations Process	6
P11	2004	Carrier and Spafford	Event-Based Digital Forensic Investigation Framework	5
P12	2006	Kent et al.	Four-Step Forensic Process	4
P13	2006	Kohn et al.	Framework for a Digital Forensic Investigation	3

ID	Year	Author(s)	Model Name	Stages
P14	2006	K. Roger et al.	Computer Forensic Field Triage Process Model	12
P15	2006	Ieong	FORZA: Digital Forensics Investigation Framework	6
P16	2006	Venter	Process Flows for Cyber Forensics Training and Operations	3
P17	2007	Freiling and Schwittay	Common Process Model for Incident and Computer Forensics	3
P18	2007	Bem and Huebner	Dual Data Analysis Process	4
P19	2008	Selamat et al.	Digital Forensic Investigations Framework	5
P20	2009	Perumal	Digital Forensic Model Based on Malaysian Investigation Process	7
P21	2010	Pilli et al.	Generic Framework for Network Forensics	9
P22	2011	Yusoff	Generic Computer Forensic Investigation Model	5
P23	2011	Agarwal et al.	Systematic Digital Forensic Investigation Model	11
P24	2012	Adams et al.	Advanced Data Acquisition Model (ADAM)	3

When each of the process models listed above was being created, the author(s) developed them to serve a purpose, whether be to function as a generalized approach that could be universally adopted or to address specific requirements (i.e., law enforcement). One of the biggest challenges with digital forensics, unlike some other areas of forensic science, is that there is such a broad scope of where it is used—such as governments, law enforcement, or corporations—that no process model addresses the unique requirements of those working in other environments. This makes it difficult to have the collective digital forensic community adopt a prescriptive process methodology that is applied for all investigations.

Appendix A: Investigative Process Models further dissects each of the preceding process models to better understand the tasks performed during each phase, and to demonstrate both the uniqueness and commonalities within each phase.

Mapping Out Process Models

As stated previously, there is no one-best process model that can be universally adopted as the methodology for all digital forensic investigations. Primarily, this is attributed to influences of the author(s) involved before and during the development of their respective process models. Most notable is the existence of non-parallel characteristics used throughout their proposed methodology, such as the interchangeable use of procedures, processes, phases, functions, tasks, and steps.

Illustrated in Figure 2.1, the stages of each process model, referenced by an identification (ID) number, have been compared to understand where

Investigative phase	P01	P02	P03	P04	P05	P06	P07	P08	P09	P10	P11	P12	P13	P14	P15	P16	P17	P18	P19	P20	P21	P22	P23	P24	TOTAL
Access																		☑							1
Acquisition	☑																	☑			☑		☑		4
Admission	☑																								1
Analysis		☑	☑		☑		☑			☑		☑					☑	☑	☑	☑		☑	☑		13
Approach strategy					☑																				1
Archive storage																			☑						1
Attribution																				☑					1
Authorization								☑												☑					2
Awareness								☑																	1
Case specific analysis													☑												1
Chain of evidence construction							☑																		1
Chronology timeline analysis													☑												1
Collection		☑	☑		☑	☑	☑		☑		☑						☑		☑			☑			10
Collect evidence and evidence information														☑											1
Corroboration							☑																		1
Communication shielding																						☑			1
Debrief scene & record seizure information														☑											1
Deployment						☑		☑	☑																3
Detection																				☑					1
Digital crime investigation						☑			☑																2
Dissemination of information								☑										☑							2
Documentation of scene																						☑			1
Dynamite								☑																	1
Evaluation	☑																								1
Event deconfliction						☑																			1
Event normalization						☑																			1
Examination		☑	☑		☑		☑				☑						☑		☑			☑			8
Hypothesis creation							☑																		1
Identification	☑		☑	☑	☑													☑							5
Incident closure									☑																1
Incident response									☑											☑					2
Individualization				☑																					1
Initial planning																							☑		1
Inspect and prepare scene														☑											1
Internet Investigation													☑												1
Investigation												☑							☑						2
Notification								☑																	1
Onsite planning																							☑		1
Physical crime investigation						☑			☑																2
Planning								☑					☑						☑						3
Preanalysis																☑									1
Pre-Process																					☑				1
Postanalysis																☑									1
Postprocess																					☑				1
Preliminary correlation							☑																		1
Preparation				☑				☑		☑							☑		☑			☑			6
Presentation		☑	☑			☑		☑	☑	☑							☑		☑	☑		☑			10
Preservation		☑	☑																☑	☑	☑	☑			6
Proof and defense							☑												☑						2
Readiness				☑			☑		☑																3
Recognition		☑																					☑		2
Reconnaissance																			☑						1
Reconstruction				☑																					1
Report	☑											☑				☑	☑								4
Result																		☑				☑			2
Returning evidence				☑																					1
Review						☑		☑																	2
Search and identify					☑																				1
Second level correlation						☑																			1
Securing the scene																							☑		1
Survey																						☑			1
Timeline analysis							☑																		1
Traceback							☑																		1
Transport and storage						☑																			1
Triage													☑												1
User usage profile investigation													☑												1

Figure 2.1 Process model comparison table.

commonalities exist. Important to note that the FORZA: Digital Forensics Investigation Framework (2006) was not included in this comparison because of the significant differences in using layers and roles, instead of stages, for describing the investigative workflow.

With all investigative process models mapped out in Table 2.1 and illustrated in Figure 2.2, it is evident that while there are obvious differences, there remain similarities with respect to some the stages included throughout. Not getting caught

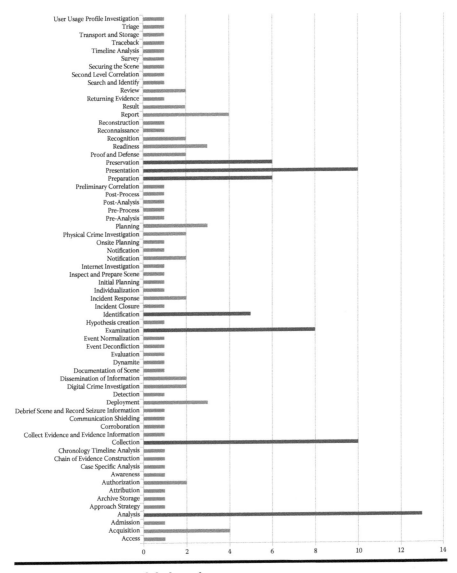

Figure 2.2   Process model phase frequency.

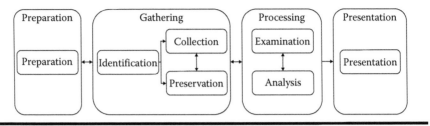

Figure 2.3   High-level digital forensic process model.

up in the subtle differences in the naming conventions for stages used between each process model, or the purpose for why it was originally created, the most commonly used stages among all methodologies are:

- *Preparation,* including activities to ensure equipment and personnel are prepared
- *Identification* involving the detection of an incident or event
- *Collection,* using approved techniques to retrieve relevant data
- *Preservation,* establishing proper evidence gathering and chain of custody
- *Examination,* evaluating digital evidence to reveal data and reduce volumes
- *Analysis,* examining the context and content of digital evidence to determine relevancy
- *Presentation,* including preparing reporting documentation

Seeing how these seven stages are commonly referenced across all process models lends to the hypothesis that a more generalized approach can be used for digital forensic investigations. For the purposes of describing the activities and tasks performed during a digital forensic investigation, the stage illustrated in Figure 2.3 will be applied:

- *Preparation* involves activities to ensure that administrative, technical, and physical provisions are in place.
- *Gathering* involves following proven techniques to identify, collect, and preserve evidence.
- *Processing* reveals data and reduce volumes based on the contextual and content relevancy.
- *Presentation* includes preparing reporting documentation.

The Process Methodology Workflow

Assessment of the digital forensic process methodology in this section follows the High-Level Digital Forensic Process Model outlined in Figure 2.3 above.

Phase 1: Preparation

As the first phase of the investigative workflow, *preparation* is essential for the successful execution of the activities completed as part of the remaining phases. If the activities included as part of this phase are not completed, whether insufficiently finished or does not contain adequate detail, there is a higher risk that activities performed later will be negatively impacted resulting on inadmissibility of evidence in a court of law.

Processes and Procedures

Before digital forensic capabilities can be realized, there needs to be approved documentation that establishes a baseline of standards, guidelines, and techniques to follow. Combined with the documentation created through the organization's information security governance framework, standard operating procedures (SOP) are the backbone for performing digital forensics throughout the workflow. Further discussion about digital forensics processes, procedures, and how an organization's information security governance framework complements digital forensics, can be found in Chapter 6 titled "*The Business of Digital Forensic.*"

Education, Training, and Awareness

No two organizations are the same (i.e., size, location, industry), which means that when it comes to building a digital forensic team, there will be different requirements for resourcing. Regardless of these factors, one consistent aspect of digital forensics across all organizations is the need to follow and apply the established scientific principles, methodologies, and techniques. Doing so demands that all people in an organization have proper and adequate knowledge of and training in digital forensics, depending on their role in supporting digital forensic capabilities.

Detailed discussion about the different levels of education, training, and awareness an organization should require of their people can be found in Chapter 3 titled "*Education, Training, and Awareness.*"

Technology and Toolsets

In many cases, a dedicated lab environment is where digital forensic investigations are performed and digital evidence is stored. As a starting point, a forensic lab environment must be both physically and logically secured to guarantee forensic soundness. When the lab has been built, the team can begin acquiring their forensic "toolkit," which will be made up of a series of hardware equipment and software tools, that will be used to gather and process digital evidence. Further discussion about different tools and technologies valuable to digital forensics can be found in Chapter 6 titled "*The Business of Digital Forensics.*"

Phase 2: Gathering

This second phase of the investigative workflow consists of the activities and tasks involved in the identification, collection, and preservation of digital evidence. The work done in this phase is perhaps the most important of all in the investigative workflow because it is critical in establishing the meaningfulness, relevancy, and legal admissibility of evidence for the remainder of the investigation.

Identification

Evidence exists in both the physical and logical sense. Locating it, in either form, requires practitioners to complete a specific series of activities and tasks that must be followed in a sequence. When it comes to electronically stored information (ESI),[2] it is important to know the physical data sources involved, such as peripherals or computer systems, as they can influence the existence and state of digital evidence.

After a source of digital evidence has been identified, it is critical that proper evidence-handling techniques are applied always. If proper techniques are not followed, there is greater risk that the authenticity and integrity of that evidence will be jeopardized, and it can no longer be used to establish factual conclusions. Throughout this phase, appropriate SOPs are required to provide practitioners with consistent and repeatable processes to guarantee evidence will remain forensically sound[3] and legally admissible.

As previously noted, no two organizations are the same (i.e., size, location, industry), and the SOPs used to identify evidence is subjective to each environment. Regardless, the following topics are fundamental to identifying evidence to minimize the potential for (human) errors or oversight.

Securing the Scene

Although the primary focus of digital forensics is on ESI, it is important to remember that evidence can and likely will exist in both the physical and digital sense.

For example, when law enforcement agencies arrive at a crime scene, their first step is to establish a perimeter around the scene to control and preserve potential evidence. By taking the necessary steps to secure a physical crime scene, first responders can then start documenting the state of physical evidence and provide a level of assurance that evidence will be secured from tampering, corruption, or loss.

The same methodology of establishing a crime scene perimeter applies to the digital world as it does to the physical world. However, in the digital world determining how wide to "cast the net" around a crime scene can be more of a challenge because of the dynamic nature of technology. In some cases, even after we draw the line around a digital crime scene, evidence can be identified which then expands the scope of the investigation and changes the scale of the perimeter.

The best strategy for dealing with this is to initially set the crime scene perimeter wider and work to narrow it down by ruling out the existence of evidence. We know from Chapter 1 that Locard's Exchange Principle states that anyone or anything entering a crime scene takes something in with them and leaves something behind when they leave. Going one step further, consider the concept that everything in a crime scene has a relationship and that a small change to one thing can result in a big difference to another, a phenomena known as the butterfly effect.

An analogy for combining these concepts could be that of a spider web whereby placing the event at the center, there are several ways to move outward and identify evidence. As we move away from the center (event), there will be several interconnected paths that have, whether directly or indirectly, played a part in the actual event. As we move further away from the center, there is greater opportunity to identify additional evidence relevant to the event. At the same time, some paths could result in a conclusion that no evidence exists, therefore eliminating that path and reducing the size of the crime scene.

Regardless of whether the crime scene is physical or digital, whoever is responsible for securing the scene and establishing the perimeter needs to be trained and have the knowledge necessary to make educated decisions.

Documenting the Scene

Now that a crime scene perimeter has been defined, practitioners must record details about the crime scene. In the physical world, this means answering questions, such as:

- What items are physically located within the crime scene?
- Where are these items physically located within the crime scene?
- What state/condition are these items currently in (i.e., connected, powered down)?

An approach to answering these questions and providing a means for reconstruction after the crime scene has been released is to either record a video or photograph the crime scene before it is disturbed or evidence is seized. Best practices when shooting video or taking photographs to document a crime scene include:

- Providing a complete view of the physical environment, including floor-to-ceiling and wall-to-wall
- Capturing individual perspectives of dedicated work areas (as needed), such as cabinets, shelves, garbage cans
- Showing wired connections between computer systems and peripherals or other devices, such as printers or switches

- Recording ports, slots, and plugs on the computer systems that are open, empty, or unused
- Picturing processes, documents, etc., that are actively visible on the monitor. It is important not to press any keys or buttons that could result in triggering the system to perform some action (i.e., logic bomb[4]).

In addition to photographs and videos, details about the crime scene must also be documented in a notebook. A dedicated notebook, or logbook, should be used by every digital forensic practitioner as a means of maintaining an accurate record of events, actions taken, and interactions involving their investigations. Similar to how law enforcement agencies document their interactions in a logbook, forensic practitioners need to write down their efforts on the presumption that the investigation could eventually end up in court.

At a minimum, information recorded in a practitioner's dedicated notebook should include the full date and time, the practitioner's full name, and the practitioner's badge number (if applicable). As a best practice, notes should be taken in chronological order. If the logbook does not have page numbers, then this will need to be added to each page to reference the sequence of events.

Lastly, there should be no whitespace (empty space) available that would allow for additional notes to be made after the practitioner has finished their documentation. Best practices to prevent this from happening is to fill in all blank space with solid lines so that unauthorized supplementary information cannot be added.

A sample template that can be used as a dedicated notebook can be found in the Templates section of this book.

Search and Seizure

At this point in the investigation, the crime scene has been secured and documented. This means that practitioners can now start work searching for and seizing potential evidence. As items are being assessed as potential evidence, it is important to remember that the goal in this stage is not to seize everything just because it is within the boundaries of the crime scene. Rather, the goal is to make educated decisions about the relevance an item has before it is seized. Making these educated decisions requires practitioners have the knowledge and experience necessary to determine what is evidence, or what is not evidence, and then document the reason for these decisions.

Much like with the initial activities, documentation continues to be of importance as evidence is being seized. The reality is that the act of seizing evidence is the point where a chain of custody begins and must be maintained to establish the authenticity and integrity of the evidence. From the point where evidence is seized and its chain of custody is established, this documentation must accompany the evidence for its evidentiary lifetime.

Seizing evidence in the digital world can be more of a challenge because of the dynamic nature of technology and the different locations or formats that it can exist within, such as network device configurations or physical badge reader logs. There might come a time when evidence is identified in a location that is not covered in existing processes and procedures. If this does happen, what is most important is ensuring that educated and trained practitioners are involved in the seizure activities to apply the fundamental principles, methodologies, and techniques of digital forensics.

A sample template that can be used as a chain of custody form can be found in the Templates section of this book.

Collection and Preservation

While the collection and preservation of digital evidence are distinctly represented within this phase, the activities performed within each are closely related in objectives. Digital evidence is volatile by nature because of how technology is inherently dynamic. Therefore, when gathering digital evidence practitioners must ensure the original state of ESI,[2] as identified through the investigation, is preserved using tools and techniques that follow the forensic principles and methodologies.

Traditionally, digital evidence could be identified within technologies that allowed for practitioners to physically seize the device and return to a secure and controlled forensic lab where an exact, bit-level duplicate of the evidence could be generated for further processing. However, with the increasing volumes of digital evidence being encountered, across more types of technologies than traditional hard drives (i.e., random access memory [RAM], network devices), there are challenges being faced in regards to collecting and preserving data within an isolated lab environment. For example, where an organization spans internationally and potential digital evidence exists among disperse technology, having it seized and returned to an isolated lab environment is becoming less efficient. Alternatively, modern forensics tools and technologies allow practitioners to conduct remote gathering of digital evidence while following the same principles, methodologies, and techniques as would be the case in a lab environment.

Regardless of what techniques are used to produce a forensically sound duplicate of gathered digital evidence, it must be the result of a method that ensures authenticity and integrity to guarantee its admissibility in a court of law. Most commonly, establishing the authenticity and integrity of digital evidence is done using a one-way cryptographic hash algorithm such as the Message Digest Algorithm family (i.e., MD5, MD6)[5] or the Secure Hashing Algorithm family (i.e., SHA-1, SHA-2, SHA-3).[6] The uniqueness of these cryptographic algorithms makes them an important technique for documenting the authenticity and integrity of digital evidence.

Order of Volatility

Because of technology's dynamic nature, gathering of digital evidence in a specific state, at a specific point in time, can only be done once. Therefore, it is essential that practitioners follow a consistent process methodology that provides them guidance on the order to which different types of digital evidence must be gathered. Fundamentally, there are two types of digital evidence:

■ Volatile data is any ESI that is temporarily stored and lost when power is removed. Examples of volatile data include, but are not limited to, network connections, running processes, open files, and login sessions.
■ Non-volatile data is any ESI that is persistently stored and preserved in a specific state when power is lost. Examples of non-volatile data include, but are not limited to, configuration files, dump files, slack space, and data files.

Generally, the more volatile ESI is within a given system the more challenging it is to forensically gather it. Therefore, it is critical that practitioners have the knowledge and expertise necessary to make informed decisions about what ESI should be preserved as part of an investigation. Ideally, deciding whether to collect ESI as digital evidence comes with the inherent risk that the longer it takes to make the decision, the greater the possibility that the ESI will be lost or changed. Illustrated in Table 2.2 is the order of volatility for digital evidence, ordered from most volatile to least volatile, including its lifespan and types of ESI that can be collected from it.

Table 2. 2   Order of Volatility

Lifespan	Storage Type	Data Type
As short as a single clock cycle	CPU Storage	Registers
		Caches
	Video	RAM
Until host is shut down	System Storage	RAM
	Kernel Tables	Network Connections
		Login Sessions
		Running Processes
		Open Files
		Network Configurations
		System Date/Time

Lifespan	Storage Type	Data Type
Until overwritten or erased	Nonvolatile Data	Paging/Swap Files
		Temporary/Cache Files
		Configuration/Log Files
		Hibernation Files
		Dump Files
		Registry
		Account Information
		Data Files
		Slack Space
	Removable Media	Floppy Disks
		Tapes
		Optical Disc (read/write only)
Until physically destroyed		Optical Disc (write only)
	Outputs	Paper Printouts

Phase 3: Processing

Within this third phase, activities performed include the examination and analysis of evidence to determine its relevancy to subsequently reduce data volumes. Throughout this phase, maintaining the established authenticity and integrity of evidence is essential for guaranteeing a forensically sound investigation. For the most part, tools and equipment used to support this phase of the investigative workflow provide automated capabilities to validate and verify the one-way cryptographic hash algorithm created when the digital evidence was seized. This technique allows practitioners to prove beyond reasonable doubt that their interactions with evidence did not in any way impact the integrity and authenticity of the evidence.

Traditionally, processing digital evidence is done inside a secure lab environment. Within this controlled environment, practitioners have a higher level of assurance that digital evidence is being properly handled so that it does not become susceptible to unauthorized access or exposed to elements that could otherwise contaminate it. However, with the increasing volumes of digital evidence being encountered, across more types of technologies than traditional hard drives (e.g., mobile phones), there are challenges in regards to storing and processing this amount of data within an isolated lab environment. Additionally, where an organization spans internationally and practitioners located around the world need access to gathered digital evidence, having it located within the confines of an isolated lab environment is becoming less efficient. Alternatively, evidence storage networks, designed to streamline investigations and support collaboration across multiple locations, are being built. They follow the least privilege access[7] methodology to house the sheer volumes of ESI, while continuing to uphold the integrity, authenticity, and chain of custody for digital evidence. Detailed discussions about digital forensic lab environments and digital evidence storage networks can be found in Chapter 10 titled "*Digital Evidence Management.*"

Within the volumes of ESI being gathered, there will be a combination of digital evidence that is easy to see while there will be others that tend to hide in plain sight, such as deleted files or encrypted content. For the most part, tools and equipment offer a suite of capabilities to help practitioners parse through digital evidence to examine each individual data element to understand its true nature so that when it comes time to start analyzing, the analytical work of practitioners will not be as challenging. Detailed discussion about antiforensics can be found in Chapter 9 titled "*Combatting Antiforensics.*"

As the investigation starts to focus on analyzing digital evidence to start making sense of it, the investigation starts to move away from the scientific foundation and into the realm of art and perception. On one hand, if practitioners rely too much on subjective points of view based on experience, they could potentially overlook evidence. On the other hand, if they rely too much on technology as the catchall way to find all evidence, they could be lead to wrong or incomplete conclusions. It is not that practitioners conjure up some form of magic when they are determining what constitutes order (evidence) versus chaos (clutter), it is that this phase of the investigative workflow is more an art than it is a science. Essentially, analytics is a practitioner's ability to sort through masses of data, find hidden patterns and correlations, and extract relevance and meaning to establish facts. One part of this equation lies within the use of technology that helps to automate the examination and analysis of digital evidence, but practitioners cannot solely rely on technology to solve problems. The other part of the equation is building and refining analytical skills through professional education, training, and past experiences. Detailed discussion about the different levels of education, training, and awareness an organization should require of their people can be found in Chapter 3.

Phase 4: Presentation

As discussed previously, documentation is a critical element of every investigation that needs to start at the beginning of an investigation and be carried on throughout, until completion of the case. Even though the need for different types of documentation varies during an investigation (i.e., chain of custody, dedicated notebook), it must always be complete, accurate, and as comprehensive as possible. In this last phase of the investigative workflow, practitioners must piece together all their documentation in a final report, such as documentation demonstrating the processes, techniques, tools, equipment, and interactions used to maintain the authenticity, reliability, and trustworthiness of digital evidence.

There are times when the investigation can fall apart because of a poorly written final report. The purpose of the final investigative report is to communicate the findings and factual conclusions after the investigation. In the end, if key decision-makers, such as upper management or judges, cannot grasp what is being communicated throughout the report, then no matter what the evidence concludes, it won't be effective in the legal case.

Some items to consider when writing a final investigative report include:

- Structure and layout should flow naturally and logically
- Content should be clear and concise to accurately demonstrate a chronology of events
- Use of jargon, slang, and technical terminology should be limited or avoided. Where used, a glossary should be included to define terms in a layperson's language.
- Where acronyms and abbreviations are used, they must be written out in full expression on the first use.
- Because final reports are written after the fact, meaning after an investigation, content should be communicated in the past tense, but can change tense where conclusions or recommendations are being made.
- Format a final report not only for distribution within the organization, but also with the mindset that it may be used as testimony in a court of law.

A template for creating written formal reports has been provided as a reference in the Templates section of this book.

Summary

With the formalization of digital forensics as a science, several authors proposed process models as a means of establishing a consistent methodology for applying proven principles and techniques to meet investigative needs. Despite the subtle difference in naming conventions for the phases included in these process models, the underlying fundamental workflow and concepts remain consistent as demonstrated in the process methodology workflow.

Glossary

1. **Common body of knowledge (CBK)** is the complete concepts, terms, and activities that make up a professional domain.
2. **Electronically stored information (ESI)** is information created, manipulated, communicated, stored, and best utilized in digital form, requiring the use of computer hardware and software.

3. **Forensically sound** qualifies and, in some cases, justifies the use of a forensic technology or methodology.
4. **Logic bomb** is a set of hidden instructions incorporated into a program so that when/if a condition is satisfied they will be carried out.
5. **Message Digest Algorithm family** is a suite of one-way cryptographic hashing algorithms that are used to verify data integrity through the creation of a unique digital fingerprint of differing length based on version used.
6. **Secure Hashing Algorithm family** is a suite of one-way cryptographic hashing algorithms that are used to verify data integrity through the creation of a unique digital fingerprint of differing length based on version used.
7. **Least privilege access** is the practice of limiting subject access to objects at the minimal level required to allow normal operations and functions.

Chapter 3

Education, Training, and Awareness

From what was discussed in Chapter 1, the evolution of digital forensics over the years has established a common body of knowledge (CBK)[1] from which educational programs, including training and awareness, have been created. Within a corporate environment, it is important that varying levels of digital forensic education is made available to all stakeholders involved with digital forensics, so that they have an appropriate level of knowledge to execute their job functions, in accordance with digital forensic principles, methodologies, or techniques. Without implementing adequate levels of education, the people factor becomes the biggest shortfall in an organization's digital forensic lifecycle.

Organizational Roles and Responsibilities

In a corporate environment, there are many people involved in supporting their organization's digital forensics lifecycle, spanning beyond digital forensic practitioners. These people, such as system support personnel and management, all have different roles and responsibilities when it comes to their involvement in digital forensics. Overall, every role a person plays is equally important in ensuring that the organization's digital forensic capabilities operate within the established principles, methodologies, and techniques, so that evidence will be admissible in a court of law.

The need for different roles within the digital forensic lifecycle not only guarantees admissibility of evidence, but also supports and maintains a separation of duty.[2] Fundamentally, the ability to create distinct roles with respect to digital forensics is subjective to factors such as the size or structure of the organization. Depending on the ability to create these distinct roles, there will be individuals located throughout the organization who play different roles and have varying involvement throughout the digital forensic lifecycle.

Naturally, the responsibilities carried with each role differ because of how the individuals in them interact and are (in)directly involved in the digital forensic lifecycle. For example, the following are different types of roles whose support in an organizational environment is a necessity for the digital forensic lifecycle:

■ *Executive sponsor* is an individual within the executive management team, such as a vice president (VP) or senior vice president (SVP), who is ultimately responsible for an organization's digital forensic program.
■ *Director* is an individual responsible for overseeing the funding and resourcing, including people and technology, of the digital forensic program.
■ *Team* is the group directly responsible for the digital forensic program. Within the team, there can be a series of subroles depending on the size and arrangement of the organization, including:
   – *Manager* or *team lead* is an individual responsible for providing task delegation and leadership to team members
   – *Members* are individuals who are responsible for the execution and delivery of activities and tasks specific to the organization's digital forensic program
   – *Stakeholders* are business lines, other teams, individuals, or organizations, both internal and external to your organization, that are impacted or have an impact on the digital forensic program.

The Digital Forensic Team

In the example roles identified in the preceding section, the digital forensic team is a role played by several individuals who are the core individuals responsible for execution of the activities and tasks of a digital forensic program. Titles used to describe different roles specific to the digital forensics team can be subjective and are commonly used interchangeably.

Roles

Regardless of the title used, individuals who have a direct role on the digital forensic team are much more involved in applying and adhering to the scientific principles, methodologies, and techniques of the profession, in contrast to the organizational roles outlined previously. For example, the following are titles commonly used for the different roles within a digital forensic team:

■ *Technician* is a role that is responsible for identification, collection, and preservation of evidence at a crime scene, as outlined in the *gathering* phase of the investigative process workflow. In some cases, this role is responsible for gathering and processing volatile data from live systems as evidence. These individuals must be adequately trained in the proper evidence-handling techniques to establish the chain of custody, and guarantee the integrity and authenticity of evidence are preserved. Additionally, it is critical that these individuals have the knowledge and expertise necessary to make informed decisions about the order in which volatile data should be gathered and process.

■ *Examiner* and *analyst* are titles commonly used interchangeably to describe individuals who are responsible for the examination and analysis of evidence after it has been gathered, as illustrated in the *processing* phase of the investigative process workflow. In cases where the role of a technician does not exist, this role will also be responsible for the gathering, processing, and handling of evidence as described previously. In addition to the knowledge and experience required for a technician's role, individuals in this role must also be educated and trained in the use of tools and techniques to interpret the context and content of evidence to determine its relevancy to an investigation. Not only do these individuals need to be strong technically, so that they can accurately decipher the meaning of evidence, but they also need to have a sharp analytical mindset that allows them to established links between evidence to draw factual conclusions.

■ *Investigator* is another example of a title that is used interchangeably. Most often, this title is used in place of analyst/examiner and inherits the same scope of responsibilities. However, the responsibilities of this role go beyond just processing evidence and include duties such as working with internal (i.e., IT support) and external (i.e., law enforcement) entities to identify new pieces of evidence relevant to the investigation. Depending on the organization, individuals who occupy this role might also assume the responsibilities of the technician and analyst/examiner as noted previously. With the use of this title, it is important to note that in some jurisdictions, the use of the investigator title requires those individuals to have a private investigator license to validate that they meet the minimum requirements for maintaining their education and experience in the field of practice.

■ *Team lead* is any individual who provides members of the digital forensic team with direction, instruction, and guidance on how to execute their responsibilities. In some cases, this role may not exist because the size of the digital forensic team—or organization—does not warrant having it. Where this role does exist, even though the scope of responsibility for these individuals does not directly include the gathering or processing of evidence, they can be used to assist in performing an investigation when needed. Because there is this possibility, team leads need to be educated and have experience in performing the activities and tasks across all roles of the digital forensic team.

■ *Managers*, like team leads, also provide the digital forensic team with direction, instruction, and guidance on how to execute their responsibilities. Also, like the role of team lead, a manager role may not exist in an organization because it is not warranted due to the size of the team. However, a notable difference in comparison to the team lead is that the manager role has expanded leadership responsibilities for the overall success of the digital forensic team, including resourcing and funding. While these individuals do not have direct involvement with the day-to-day execution of the digital forensic program, it is expected that they are educated and knowledgeable in how to consistently uphold the scientific principles, methodologies, and techniques of digital forensics.

Refer to Chapter 2 titled *"Investigative Process Methodologies"* for more details about the investigative workflow and the order of volatility.

Titles

Just how some of the roles noted previously are used interchangeably to illustrate the different roles within the digital forensic team, the following titles were not in the previous list because of the subtle differences in how they represent an individual's achievement in (non)technical skills, as discussed in the following section:

- *Practitioner* is an individual who is actively engaged and occupied in the field of digital forensics. These individuals are recognized as a result of their documented qualifications (i.e., diploma or degree) and possess both the technical and nontechnical skills to directly support an organization's digital forensic program.
- *Specialist* is any individual who is highly skilled and concentrates on one (or more) focus areas of digital forensics. An argument could be made that the digital forensic discipline as a whole can be viewed as a focus area, but given how broad it has become (i.e., computer systems, gaming consoles, mobile devices), using this title is better suited to describe a specific area of digital forensics, such as malware forensics, cloud computing, or eDiscovery.
- *Professional* is an individual who has a paid occupation in the digital forensic discipline. Not only are these individuals highly skilled and possessing formal education in the technical execution of digital forensics, but in some occupations (i.e., enterprise environment) also have significant nontechnical, business skills, as described later in this chapter.
- *Expert* is an individual who has been authoritatively recognized for their knowledge and experience in digital forensics. With the adjective "authoritative" applied to this title, it suggests that this title is respectively held by those individuals who have established themselves in a court of law.

These three titles do not articulate a function or responsibility; therefore, they are not used to illustrate a role with the digital forensic team. Generally, they are more often used to describe individuals who have gained extensive knowledge and experience in digital forensics.

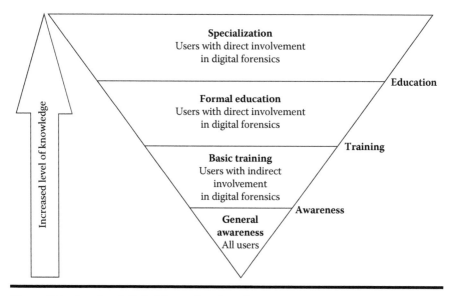

Figure 3.1   Levels of digital forensic education.

Types of Training and Awareness

With every role outlined in the previous section, there is a need for different training and awareness that aligns to the defined responsibilities. However, it is not expected that every role will have the same type of education because the knowledge required for each roles varies. Illustrated in Figure 3.1, the types of education start at the bottom of the pyramid and move upwards as training and awareness becomes more in-depth and specialized. The following sections describe the different types of education that organizations should consider effective ways to communicate principles, methodologies, and techniques to all stakeholders.

General Awareness

The lowest level of education is awareness, which covers content in a generalized way. The purpose of this type of education is to ensure people have foundational knowledge without getting too detailed or specialized. With this type of education, it is not expected that people will be competent in the field of digital forensics. Instead, they will possess general information about organizational policies, standards, and guidelines, so that they can indirectly contribute to digital forensics.

Awareness training should be mandatory for all stakeholders and completed regularly, such as annually, to ensure up-to-date knowledge is maintained. Additionally, when a new stakeholder has been identified, such as new employees, they should be expected to complete the awareness training immediately.

Examples of topics and subjects that should be included as part of a digital forensic awareness program include, but is not limited to, the following:

- Business code of conduct
- Information security awareness
- Data protection and privacy

Basic Training

With this type of education, people are taught more in-depth content so that they have fundamental knowledge and are competent in digital forensic principles, methodologies, and techniques. Essentially, the difference between this training and general awareness is that the knowledge gained here is intended to teach people the skills necessary to directly support the organization's digital forensic program.

Education provided at this level would not be the equivalent of a formal education program at an academic institutions (i.e., university, college). This level of education can be achieved through the creation of an in-house training course that offers quality information but not to the extent that formal college or university courses offer.

Information communicated at this level is more detailed than general awareness because it must provide the knowledge required by a certain role. Depending on the individual's role, knowledge on different principles, methodologies, and techniques would be required to maintain a specific standard of competency.

Examples of topics and subjects that should be included as part of basic digital forensic knowledge include, but is not limited to:

- *Logging and retention*, which relates to the practice of recording events and preserving them, as per the organizational governance framework, to facilitate digital forensic investigations. Refer to Chapter 10 titled "*Digital Evidence Management*" for further discussion about requirements for handling potential digital evidence.
- *Incident handling and response*, which relates to the process of managing the occurrence of security events throughout the enterprise. Refer to Chapter 12 titled "*Incident Management and Response*" for detailed information about integrating digital forensic capabilities into incident handling and response capabilities.

Formal Education

At the highest level of training, a working and practical knowledge of all digital forensics must be gained. Individuals who require this level of knowledge are those who must have the skills and competencies to guarantee that all principles, methodologies, and techniques are consistently applied and upheld in the organization's digital forensic program.

Working directly in digital forensics requires individuals to have a significant training and technical skills so that they can comprehend and consistently apply the well-established scientific fundamentals. The information provided at this level of education is detailed, and individuals must acquire strong working and practical knowledge.

Professional Certifications and Accreditations

Following the completion of a formalized education program, individuals can choose to become certified or accredited. Internationally, there are many professional organizations that have established certification and accreditation curriculums specific to digital forensics. Predominantly, these certifications are provided by professional organizations with an industry-wide perspective on the digital forensic profession; however, there are a small number of certifications provided by organizations that create and sell digital forensic technologies.

It is important to keep in mind that while professional certification provides assurance that an individual meets the required level of knowledge in digital forensics, these accreditations do not provide the in-depth level of education that formal academic program teach.

Refer to Appendix B: Education and Professional Certifications for a list of higher/postsecondary institutes that offer formal digital forensic education programs and for a list of digital forensic certifications.

Specializations

Not too long ago, digital forensics was still looked at as a niche field falling within the realm of information security. However, today those who practice digital forensics can be viewed as generalists within a broad discipline. As technology advances and becomes more engrained in an organization's core business functions, such entities are integrating their digital forensic capabilities across key business operations. For this reason, it is more common for individuals to expand their knowledge in digital forensics and apply it to other disciplines throughout an enterprise environment, such as:

- *Electronic discovery (eDiscovery)*, which relates to the discovery, preservation, processing, and production of electronically stored information (ESI)[3] in support of compliance or litigation matters.
- *Incident management and response*, which relates to reducing business impact by managing the occurrence of computer security events.

Further information about how digital forensics integrates into the above business operations can be found in Section 3, Integrating Digital Forensic Capabilities.

An Educational Roadmap

Ask around and most likely you will get different perspectives about what "education" means. To some, it means graduating from college or university to earn a degree, diploma, or certificate. To others, it means attending training sessions put on by some third party, such as a vendor. And yet, there are those who prefer the self-taught methods using resources at their fingertips (i.e., books, webinars).

A common question posed to those people already in the field of digital forensics is "What type of knowledge and training is needed to get into the field?" The reality is that there is no single best way to get a digital forensic education, acquire new skills, or keep current with skills you already have. Rather than setting out a development plan that people should follow on their educational roadmap, the following sections provide building blocks for different types and levels of education a person can gain.

The intention of the following sections is to provide people with the generalized subject areas for which continuous education and training will provide them with a catalyst for growing themselves within the digital forensic profession. While the following subject areas contribute to understanding digital forensic principles, methodologies, and techniques, it is important to remember that these topics are subjective to an organizational setting and do not necessarily reflect the knowledge or experience required in law enforcement or other industries.

Technical Knowledge

When developing a digital forensic skill set, the most common type of training provided through education programs (i.e., academic institutes, books) is the technical components. Within this context, the word "technical" is not used as reference specifically to information technology, but rather to the practical execution of digital forensics, which includes putting into practices its principles, methodologies, and techniques.

Introductory

Entering the field of digital forensics means starting out somewhere. There are volumes of resources, such as books, that provide people with an excellent way of building a foundation to their educational roadmap. As a sample, the following subject areas are essential knowledge for all digital forensic practitioners to have:

- *Investigation principles* are the values that, as a digital forensic practitioner, must be consistently followed and applied throughout the investigative process methodologies, including, but not limited to, forensic soundness, evidence authenticity and integrity, and chain of custody. Refer to Chapter 1 for further details about the principles of digital forensics.

■ *Evidence management* includes the technical, administrative, and physical controls necessary to safeguard digital evidence before, during, and after a digital forensic investigation.

■ *Computer systems* are made up of interconnected hardware components that share a central storage system and any number of peripheral devices, such as printers, scanners, etc.

■ *Operating systems (OS)* are software programs that are perhaps one of the most important components of a computer system. Essentially, an OS is a collection of software that manages hardware and performed basic tasks, such as controlling peripheral devices, managing input devices (i.e., keyboards), and scheduling tasks. Recognizing that there are several types of OS software available in the market today (i.e., Microsoft Windows, Apple macOS, Linux, Unix), at a minimum a digital forensic practitioner should understand the more popular platforms that are commonly used by consumers and those that are present throughout their organizations.

■ *File systems* are the methods and structures used by an OS to organize, track, and retrieve data. Recognizing that there are several types of file systems used today (i.e., FAT12/16/32, NTFS, ext2/3/4, iOS), at a minimum a practitioner should understand the more popular platforms that are commonly used by consumers and those that are present throughout their organizations.

■ *Networking protocols* are the mechanisms by which devices, such as systems, define rules and conventions for communicating with each other.

■ Scripting is an interpreted programming language designed for integrating and communicating with other programming languages in support of task automation. Recognizing that there are several scripting languages (i.e., BATCH, VBScript, Perl, Python), a practitioner should understand at least one scripting language.

■ *Legal studies* include knowledge of the precedence set forth by the rules, standards, and directives of legal systems. Refer to Chapter 4 titled *"Laws, Standards, and Regulations"* for further details about the application of law to forensic science.

As a practitioner, understanding these subject areas is considered foundational knowledge required for the technical execution of digital forensic principles, methodologies, and techniques throughout the investigative process workflow, which is discussed further in Chapter 2 titled *"Investigative Process Methodologies."*

Intermediate

With foundational knowledge acquired, practitioners can decide to further their education by expanding the scope of knowledge beyond those directly linked to the execution of digital forensics. The following are examples of subject areas where knowledge gained will enhance a digital forensic practitioner's educational roadmap:

- *Cryptography*, while one of its purposes is to protect the confidentiality of information, it has also been used as a means of hiding data and communications. Knowledge of cryptography's use for security and antiforensics is valuable to examine and analyze digital evidence. Refer to Chapter 9 titled *"Combatting Antiforensics"* for further information about the use of cryptography for data hiding.
- *Mobile devices* have proliferated in the past decade, which has allowed for a growth in the mobile workforce community and supported the concept of "always connected, always available." Recognizing that there are countless manufacturers that have their own proprietary devices (i.e., Apple, Blackberry, Samsung), at a minimum a practitioner should understand the platforms used predominantly throughout their organizations.
- *Cyber and security investigations* can encompass a broad scope of digital evidence that must be gathered and process from systems and applications located throughout the Internet. Refer to Chapter 14 titled *"Information Security and Cybersecurity"* for further information on different types of security investigations. Also, understanding the different laws, standards, and regulations that govern accessing or gathering evidence is important. Refer to Chapter 4 titled *"Laws, Standards, and Regulations"* for further information about the application of law to forensic science.
- *Incident response* is the structured approach by which organizations address and manage computer security events. Digital forensics practitioners are a key stakeholder throughout the entire methodology. Refer to Chapter 12 titled *"Incident Management and Response"* for further information about integrating digital forensics into the incident management methodology.
- *Electronic discovery*, or eDiscovery, refers to the use of a structured approach by which organizations identify, gather, and process ESI for producing evidence per legal or compliance requests. Refer to Chapter 13 titled *"Electronic Discovery and Litigation Support"* for further information about integrating digital forensics into eDiscovery methodology.
- *Cloud computing* is changing the landscape of how business operations are conducted and how digital evidence is gathered and processed. It is important to be proactive in developing strategies for adapting and expanding an organization's digital forensic capabilities into these environments.
- *Network forensics*, a subdiscipline of digital forensics, consists of monitoring and analyzing the network traffic and communications of computer systems and devices for the purposes of gathering evidence. Similar to random access memory (RAM), network forensics largely involves volatile data that is only

available for a short period of time. The ability to forensically gather digital evidence from networks can help to corroborate and correlate digital evidence from other devices and computer systems.

■ *Malware reverse engineering*, as related to digital forensics, is the process of analyzing computer systems to identify malicious software, establish conclusions for how it got there, and determine what changes it caused on host system. Building these skills requires learning and using a variety of systems and network tools designed to isolate, disassemble, and analyze the properties of malware.

Advanced

Leveraging what was learned previously, advanced education further expands subject areas into the application of digital forensics in the execution of other disciplines and professions. The following are subject areas that can elevate a digital forensic practitioner's education to the highest level of technical and practical execution:

■ *Systems development*, also referred to as applications development, describes the process for planning, creating, testing, and deploying information systems. Knowledge about the systems development lifecycle (SDLC) is important for practitioners to understand the ways in which systems and applications interact with data.

■ *Security architecture* compliments enterprise architecture by focusing on the necessities and potential risk involved in certain scenarios or environments throughout the organization. Enterprise architecture is the practice of following a comprehensive approach when conducting analysis, design, planning, and implementation for the successful development and execution of an enterprise strategy. It is valuable for a practitioner to know how and where the implementation of administrative, technical, and physical security control can create greater capabilities for digital forensics.

Refer to Chapter 14 titled *"Information Security and Cybersecurity"* for further information on integrating digital forensics with enterprise security capabilities.

Nontechnical Knowledge

For the most part, academic institutions focus more on the technical aspects of digital forensics to provide practitioners with the knowledge and skills necessary to directly support their role and responsibilities. However, it is equally important to balance these technical skills with nontechnical (soft) skills. Within this complimentary set of nontechnical skills comes varying levels of knowledge that, depending on a student's educational roadmap, can elevate a career to the next level.

Introductory

We already know that getting into the digital forensic profession means starting out somewhere. While there are resources available to provide people with knowledge about nontechnical (soft) skills, perfecting them comes with practice and experience over time. For example, the following subject areas are foundational knowledge for all digital forensic practitioners to have:

- *Time management* is about planning and controlling time spent to effectively accomplish a task or goal. With respect to digital forensics, this means being able to prioritize the tasks and activities required to work through the investigative process methodology and establish fact-based conclusions.
- *Analytical skill* is the ability to extract meaning and relevance from the masses of data to find the hidden patterns and unexpected correlations so that fact-based conclusions can be made. While learning about analytical styles can be gained academically, perfecting these skills requires a practitioner to continuously refine and improve their capabilities.
- *Technical writing*, in regard to digital forensics, is any form of writing that is used to communicate in a clear and concise manner the findings and conclusions of a digital forensic investigation. It is important to avoid the overuse of technical jargon or slang that can create confusion among nontechnical readers.
- *Communication skills* are essential to have in any career and are complimentary to technical writing skills. This means being able to illustrate complex technical information in a natural, logical business language that is simple to understand.
- *Critical thinking* is a person's ability to remain objective when analyzing digital evidence during an investigation. Possessing this skill is essential for upholding a standard of professional conduct and ethics; refer to Chapter 5 titled *'Ethics and Professional Conduct'* for further discussion.

Intermediate

Continuing to build and develop the foundational nontechnical skills outlined previously, a practitioner determined to enhance their educational roadmap can seek to expand skills into new subject areas. As mentioned previously, acquiring a new skill is not a one-and-done process but more of a continuous development plan. In addition to refining and improving existing skills, the following are examples of subject areas where knowledge gained will expand a digital forensic practitioner's educational tool bag:

- *Interrogation* is a form of interviewing used to obtain information from people during an investigation. This is a skill that can range from simple techniques, such as building rapport, to more advanced techniques, such as deciphering (non)verbal cues. This is another skill that requires ongoing development, and it is a skill that can elevate a person to the next level of their nontechnical career.

■ *Interpersonal skills* are the skills that are used to interact with people. This skill can be viewed as beneficial in two ways: the first is in demonstrating leadership and professionalism, which is useful as a means for getting the job done; and the second is complimentary to interrogation (i.e., rapport building) to obtain useful information.

■ *Leadership* within an organization could be viewed as either taking on any form of leadership role, such as a team lead or manager, or being able to effectively communicate the importance of digital forensics throughout the organization. Learning how to lead both people and the future of a digital forensic program is essential knowledge if the education roadmap is to elevate into a director or executive sponsor role.

■ *Project management* is the application of knowledge, skills, methodologies, and techniques in completing defined activities to meet predefined requirements. Having relationships to time management, possessing this skill expands a practitioner's ability to effectively execute (multiple) investigations by consistently following the same investigative-process methodology.

Advanced

When an educational roadmap is intended to grow someone into the role of director, or eventually into executive sponsorship, focus turns away from skills directly related to digital forensics and more onto subject areas that are intended to bring about heightened business-centric proficiencies. In addition to refining and improving existing skills, the following are examples of subject areas where knowledge gained can move a digital forensic practitioner into a management role:

■ *Conflict resolution* is how two or more parties find a solution to a disagreement. This skill is better suited for a leadership role (i.e., team lead or director) as other skills, such as negotiation and interrogation, are more beneficial to other digital forensics roles (i.e., investigator).

■ *Budget management* involves adhering to corporate protocols to analyze, organize, and provide oversight to the costs and expenditures of the digital forensics program. Knowledge in this subject area is critical for ensuring sustained delivery of operations and continued growth.

■ *Resource management* involves the deployment and allocation of people when and where required. In the context of a digital forensics program, this skill builds on the previous leadership knowledge into more of a management role.

■ *Strategic mindset* demonstrates that you are aware of the importance for organization to have digital forensic capabilities. This proactive approach includes the aptitude for establishing and maintaining strategic relationships, building and nurturing strategic relationships, and applying previous skills toward strategic influencing.

Of the skills outlined previously, both technical and nontechnical (soft) knowledge are building blocks for the experience required as part of their educational roadmap. However, although all organizations are different, and some of the intermediate or advanced topics may or may not be applicable in a specific environment, this does not mean these items are to be disqualified from someone's educational roadmap. Progressing through the educational roadmap is not a simple task; it requires people to invest in themselves by dedicating their time and effort into furthering their career.

As people gain new knowledge and experience as they progress through their educational roadmap, they will be better equipped to evolve their role within digital forensics into more responsibility, such as from analyst to investigator. Using the heatmap illustrated in Figure 3.2 below, the relationships between the multiple elements of the educational roadmap have been laid out in a manner that shows how an individual's competencies, both technical and nontechnical, represent the roles and titles within the digital forensics profession.

Portrayed in Figure 3.2, the following methodology was applied as criteria for representing both the role and title of an individuals as they increase their technical and nontechnical competencies throughout the educational roadmap;

■ The x-axis represents the technical knowledge of an individual starting with introductory skills (left) and progressing into advanced skills (right). Progressing on this axis, as characterized by the increase in technical skills, is depicted by the alphabetic representation of the digital forensic role found in the accompanying legend.
■ The y-axis represents the nontechnical knowledge of an individual starting with introductory skills (bottom) and progressing into advanced skills (top). Progressing on this axis, as characterized by the increase in nontechnical skills, is depicted by the color scheme representing the digital forensic titles.

Digital Forensic Experts

Absent from the heatmap above is the use of the title *expert*. As discussed previously, we understand that the interpretation of an expert is any individual who has been authoritatively recognized for their knowledge and experience in digital forensics. The need to be authoritatively recognized implies that the use of the expert title is then respectively held by individuals who have established themselves in the digital forensic profession and have been granted use of the title by a person or group qualified to do so. In turn, this now begs the question of "Who is qualified to decide whether an expert is really an expert?"

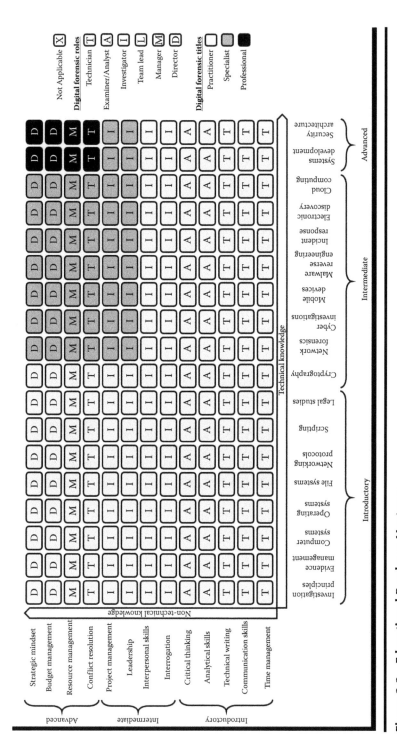

Figure 3.2 Educational Roadmap Heatmap

For the longest time, there was an ongoing debate about whether it makes sense that judges and juries in the legal system are the authoritative bodies qualified to decide when an person is an expert. At the core of this debate is the fact that judges and juries might have limited technical knowledge and may not easily understand the technical issues in question; so how can they be qualified to determine when a witness is an expert?

At the simplest level, this debate can be settled by accepting the consensus of the digital forensic professional community that an individual is qualified to use the title of expert. There are numerous certifying bodies and institutes that the courts look upon to demonstrate that an expert has some type of relevant certification or accreditation (refer to Appendix B: Education and Professional Certifications for a list of digital forensic certifications). Yet, doubt can still arise about holding a credential as a qualifying means of being an expert because the courts are simply placing their trust and reliability in the certifying bodies or institutes to qualify individuals as an expert.

Under U.S. Federal Rules of Evidence, Article VII, Rule 702, any person is qualified as an expert if he or she possesses "knowledge, skill, experience, training, and education" on the subject relating to his or her testimony beyond common experience. However, determining if a person qualifies as an expert in a legal pro-ceeding depends on whether his or her "scientific, technical, or other specialized knowledge will help the trier of fact to understand the evidence or to determine the fact in issue." Therefore, academic degrees and certifications are not necessarily requisite to determine expertise. So how does someone qualify as a digital forensic expert?

Because roles and titles are used quite interchangeably to describe a person in the digital forensic profession, it is challenging to find authoritative reference material that outlines what is required of someone to become a digital forensic expert. In fact, the qualifications and skills required of a digital forensic expert remain an issue because there are no standards by which expertise can be mea-sured. Establishing a set of standards that qualify individuals as a digital forensic expert means creating policies and requirements that addresses expected education and qualifications.

Educational Resources

As discussed previously, there are countless resources available that are designed to educate people about digital forensics from the basics to more advanced topics. The following is a partial list of publications that can be used as learning tools for digital forensics:

Contemporary Digital Forensic Investigations of Cloud and Mobile Applications. Elsevier Science & Technology Books, 2016. ISBN: 9780128053034.
Practical Digital Forensics. Packt Publishing Ltd, 2016. ISBN: 9781785881084.

Cybercrime and Digital Forensics: An Introduction. Routledge, 2015. ISBN: 9781138021303.

Digital Forensics with the AccessData Forensic Toolkit (FTK). McGraw-Hill Osborne Media, 2015. ISBN: 9780071845021.

Hacking Exposed Computer Forensics: Secrets & Solutions, 3rd ed. McGraw-Hill Osborne Media, 2015. ISBN: 9780071817745.

Handbook of Digital Forensics of Multimedia Data and Devices. Wiley-IEEE Press, 2015. ISBN: 9781118640500

Operating System Forensics, 1st ed. Syngress, 2015. ISBN: 9780128019498.

Computer Forensics and Digital Investigation with EnCase Forensic v7. McGraw-Hill Osborne Media, 2014. ISBN: 9780071807913.

Official (ISC)² Guide to the CCFP CBK. CRC Press, 2014. ISBN: 9781482262476.

The Basics of Digital Forensics, 2nd ed. Syngress, 2014. ISBN: 9780128016350.

Windows Forensic Analysis Toolkit: Advanced Analysis Techniques for Windows 8, 4th ed. Syngress, 2014. ISBN: 9780124171572.

Computer Forensics InfoSec Pro Guide. McGraw-Hill Osborne Media, 2013. ASIN: B00BPO7AP8.

Computer Incident Response and Forensics Team Management, 1st ed. Syngress, 2013. ISBN: 9781597499965.

Digital Forensics Processing and Procedures, 1st ed. Syngress, 2013. ISBN: 9781597497428.

Summary

Throughout an organization, there are many different stakeholders involved in the digital forensic program, a program which requires them to have accurate and up-to-date knowledge and skills depending on their role and responsibilities. For those individuals who are directly involved in the organization's digital forensic program, the knowledge and experience required in the digital forensic profession is a continuous process for individuals to increase their education and advance their career.

Glossary

1. **Common body of knowledge (CBK)** is the complete concepts, terms, and activities that make up a professional domain.
2. **Separation of duty** is the concept of having two or more people involved in completing an activity or task as a control to mitigate fraud and error.
3. **Electronically stored information (ESI)** is information created, manipulated, communicated, stored, and best utilized in digital form, requiring the use of computer hardware and software.

Chapter 4

Laws, Standards, and Regulations

Digital forensics is the application of science to law and, subsequently, must adhere to the precedence set forth by the laws, statutes, and rulings of legal systems. Although existing laws and regulations can be used to address most forms of cybercrime, international lawmakers recognized a need to have laws and regulations that deal specifically with technology-related crimes.

Today, most countries and regions have addressed concerns of cybercrime by either amending existing laws or creating new laws to address the challenges of admitting digital evidence in legal proceedings. This chapter describes how international laws and regulations imposed a level of standard for how electronically stored information (ESI)[1] is considered legally admissible as evidence before a trier of fact.[2]

The Role of Technology in Crime

In relation to crime, technology can play multiple roles that can then be used to gather and process evidence. Depending on how much digital evidence is contained within any given type of technology, it may or may not be authorized for seizure and subsequent collection of evidence as part of an investigation. Although, when technology plays a significant role in criminal activity, it is much easier to justify its seizure so evidence can be processed.

Through the years, several authors have tried to develop a standard classification scheme for the roles technology can play in crime. In the 1970s, Donn Parker was one of the first individuals to recognize the potential seriousness of technology-related crimes, which led him to create the following four categories, which have remained relevant today:

1. *Object of crime* applies when technology is affected by the crime (i.e., when a device is stolen or damaged).
2. *Subject of crime* applies when technology is in the environment in which the crime was committed (i.e., system infected by malware).
3. *Tool of crime* applies when technology is used to conduct or plan crime (i.e., illegally forged documents).
4. *Symbol of crime* applies when technology is used to deceive or intimidate (i.e., falsified investment profits).

Distinguishing when technology plays one role or another is important on many levels. For example, knowing when technology is an object or subject is important, because, from the perspective of the practitioner, this demonstrates intent of the perpetrator. Also, when technology is a tool, like a gun or other weapon, this could lead to additional charges or increased punishment. However, although technology as a symbol may seem irrelevant because no actual system is involved in the crime, when categorized under this role, technology is represented as an idea, belief, or any entity that can be useful in understanding motives for committing the crime. As an example, CEOs are a symbol of their organization and as such can become either the victim or target of crime because of what they symbolize.

In 1994 the U.S. Department of Justice (DOJ) developed their own categorization scheme that made a clear distinction between hardware, being physical components, and information, being data and programs that are stored or transmitted. It is important to note that with a single crime there is the potential to fall into one or more of these categories; such as when a system is used as the instrument of crime, it may also contain information as evidence. The categories proposed by the DOJ include:

- *Hardware as contraband or fruits of crime* (i.e., any item that is illegal to possess or was obtained illegally)
- *Hardware as an instrumentality* (i.e., when technology played a role in committing the crime, such as a gun or other weapon)
- *Hardware as evidence* (i.e., scanners with unique characteristics that can be used and linked to the creation of digitized content)
- *Information as contraband or fruits of crime* (i.e., computer programs that can encrypt content to conceal evidence)
- *Information as an instrumentality* (i.e., programs used to break into other systems)
- *Information as evidence* (i.e., digital artifacts revealing a user's activities on a system)

In 2002 the DOJ updated their categorization scheme as part of their publication titled *Searching and Seizing Computers and Obtaining Electronic Evidence in Criminal Investigations.* The most notable difference in the updated categorization was the realization that data and program content is usually the target of the crime not the hardware, but it also noted that even when information is the target it may be required to collect the hardware.

A Brief History of Crime and Technology

Going back more than 50 years, the first criminal activities involving computer systems were mostly a result of physical damage or sabotage. Perhaps the first documented case of crime involving computer systems was in 1968 when a data processing system in Olympia, Washington, was the victim of gunshots. Following this, the next documented occurrence was in 1969 when a fire broke out at a Canadian university resulting in more than $2 million in computer data and property being destroyed. Since the 1960s, technology has evolved at such a rapid pace that crimes involving computers quickly expanded out to include fraud, extortion, data diddling, and impersonation.

Before the 1980s, the legal system commonly dealt with computer crimes using existing laws, which spurred a movement within law-enforcement agencies to begin developing or amending laws to specifically address technology as a component of criminal activity. Most notably, in 1978 the *Florida Computer Crimes Act* was the first computer crime law enacted to address concerns of fraud, intrusions, and unauthorized access.

With technology becoming more widely available through the 1980s and the 1990s, computer-related crimes expanded to take advantage of the opportunities presented by technology advancements. It was during this time that the shadowy underworld of hacker communities began to form, such as the Cult of the Dead Cow (cDc), where collective efforts were made to commit new types of computer-related crimes, such as password theft, propagating worms, and denial of service (DoS) attacks. This spurred international law enforcement agencies to pay attention and quickly respond by developing new laws or amending existing laws. In 1983 Canada was one of the first to respond by amending their *Criminal Code* to address computer-related crimes. Many other countries followed suit by developing and enacting laws, statutes, and rules to further combat computer-related crimes. Examples include the 1984 U.S. Federal Computer Fraud and Abuse Act, the 1989 amendment of the Australian Crimes Act to include offenses relating to computers, and the 1990 British Computer Abuse Act.

Throughout the 2000s, technology started to proliferate from predominantly being use by corporations and agencies to become more of a household commodity. Increased consumerization, coupled by the explosion of the Internet, meant that computer-related crimes could expand further into new attack vectors. One significant event that proved technology advancement played a huge part in new criminal opportunities was made evident on September 11, 2001. When practitioners were conducting their analysis, it was made quite evident that digital evidence of the attacks was recoverable on computer systems across the world. Not only was this a significant finding for the investigation, but it was also an awakening that criminals were in fact using technology to their advantage; much the same way everyday consumers were. In October 2001, the *U.S. Patriot Act* was enacted as an antiterrorism law which gave law enforcement agencies the ability to search for evidence, including business records and financial records, without having a court order.

Beyond the 2000s, technology made a huge leap forward to the point where almost every device had some form of internal storage and, in some manner, is persistently connected to the Internet. Jumping at the opportunities, criminals again capitalized on the pervasive nature of technology and further expanded their portfolio of technology-related crimes, including phishing campaigns, advanced persistent threats (APT), and distributed DOS (DDoS) attacks. Efforts to combat these new attacks against their information systems, the European Parliament of the European Union enacted *Directive 2013/40/EU* to establish "minimum rules concerning the definition of criminal offenses and the relevant sanctions and to improve cooperation between competent authorities."

If history has taught us anything, it is that technology and crime will continue to evolve together. Looking forward to what is coming next, it is a safe bet that opportunities to commit digital or cyber crimes will continue to expand as the digital world advances and society becomes more reliant on technology. Naturally, this means criminals around the world will also be better trained and have more funding at their disposal because of how quickly information will be accessible from anywhere and at any time. Knowing this, there is a growing concern over jurisdiction when it comes to crimes involving technology that span multiple countries and regions. In the future, laws and regulations addressing digital crime must be assessed sooner rather than later and evolve to support a global approach to tackling the issues of crime and technology.

Types of Laws

There are number of ways to categorize the different type of laws. Generally, the four types of law used to group statutes, standards, and precedence are:

- *Civil law*, which represents a wide variety of laws documented in legal code that are available for public consumption
- *Criminal law*, which addresses violations harmful to society and are enforced by legal systems

- *Tort law*, which allows individuals to seek recourse against one another in the event of physical, personal, or financial injury
- *Private law* (e.g., family, commercial, or labor laws), which regulates relationships between an individual and organizations
- *Public law* regulates government agencies and their relationship between citizens, employees, and other government agencies

The legal aspects of technology crimes have many overlapping areas of laws and regulations. While there are commonalities among them, the number of international laws and regulations enacted do vary when it comes to each country's respective statutes, standards, and precedents. Generally, these laws, regulations, and rulings were created with the intention of bridging the gap between risk (i.e., criminal activity) and technology (i.e., fruit or tool). They were also designed to anticipate the potential for dispute and reduce the likelihood of this occurring.

Computer Law

Perhaps the most common type of technology-related law, *computer law* is an ever-evolving area of the legal system that have been driven mostly as a result of increased use of technology to commit crimes. Areas of interest for computer law include legalities such as file sharing, intellectual property, privacy, and electronic signatures, including:

- *United Kingdom (UK) Computer Misuse Act*: Enacted in 1990, this law introduced three criminal offenses relating to computer crimes:
  1. Unauthorized access to computer material
  2. Unauthorized access with intent to commit or facilitate commission of further offences
  3. Unauthorized acts with intent to impair, or with recklessness as to impairing, operation of computer, etc.
- *Australian (AU) Cybercrime Act*: Enacted in 2001, this law introduced three criminal offenses relating to computer crimes:
  (477.1): Unauthorized access, modification or impairment with intent to commit a serious offence
  (477.2): Unauthorized modification of data to cause impairment
  (477.3): Unauthorized impairment of electronic communication
  (478.1): Unauthorized access to, or modification of, restricted data
  (478.2): Unauthorized impairment of data held on a computer disk etc.
  (478.3): Possession or control of data with intent to commit a computer offence
  (478.4): Producing, supplying or obtaining data with intent to commit a computer offence

Information Technology Law

Unbeknownst to some, most activities on the Internet, whether for business or personal use, are governed by law. *Information technology law*, otherwise referred to as *technology law* or *IT law*, are laws that allow legal systems to regulate the collection, storage, and transmission of digital information within the boundaries of their jurisdictions, such as:

- *Payment Card Industry: Data Security Standard (PCI-DSS)*: Originally introduced in 2008, and last revised in 2016, these standards cover both technical and operational system components included in or connected to cardholder data (i.e., credit cards).
- *Sarbanes-Oxley Act (SOX)*: Introduced in 2002, this legislation is mandatory for all organizations as regulation of financial practice and corporate governance.
- *Health Insurance Portability and Accountability Act (HIPAA)*: Passed by the U.S. Congress in 1996, this mandates industry-wide standards for the protection and confidential handling of protected health information to reduce fraud and abuse.
- *General Data Protection Regulation (GDPR)*: Passed by the European Parliament in 2016, this addresses the unified protection of personal data outside of the European Union (EU) with the primary objectives to 1) give control back to citizens and residents over their personal information, and to 2) simplify the regulatory environment for businesses to operate internationally.

Internet or Cyberlaw

Internet law or *cyberlaw* refers to those laws and regulations that govern issues involving the use of the Internet. Claiming that there are laws that can achieve this form of regulation is somewhat of a stretch today because such laws would struggle to keep the international and volatile nature of the Internet in check. While a few international laws and regulations exist, the Internet is one of the most complex landscapes because it is not geographically bound and national laws do not apply globally across all countries and regions. Internet laws include:

- *United States (U.S.) Electronic Communications Privacy Act*: Originally introduced in 1986, this act applies to email, telephone conversations, and data stored electronically to protect communications being made, in transit, and when they are stored on computer systems. This act has since been amended by the Communications Assistance for Law Enforcement Act (CALEA) of 1994, the USA PATRIOT Act (2001), the USA PATRIOT reauthorization acts (2006), and the Foreign Intelligence Surveillance Amendments (FISA) Act (2008).

- *European Union (EU) ePrivacy Act*: Also known as Directive 2002/68/EC, this 2002 act defines rules to ensure the security in the processing of personal data, the notification of personal data breaches, the confidentiality of communications, and bans unsolicited communications where the user has not given consent.
- *Philippine (PH) Cybercrime Prevention Act*: Officially recorded as Republic Act No. 10175 in 2012, this act addresses legal issues concerning online interactions and the Internet, such as cybersquatting, cybersex, identity theft, and illegal access to data.

Federal Rules of Evidence

Law of evidence govern the proof of facts, and the conclusions drawn from these facts, during legal proceedings. Up until the twentieth century, evidence presented during trial was largely the result of laws derived from case law or decisional law. During the twentieth century, work began to arrange these common laws into formal evidence rules. Enacted in 1975, and last amended in 2015, the U.S. Federal Rules of Evidence (FRE) applies to legal proceedings by regulating when, how, and for what purpose evidence can be placed before a trier of fact for consideration.

Issues of relevance and authenticity are commonly put into question about whether, when validated as part of a general acceptance testing program, evidence is justifiable to be presented before a court of law. Within this context, relevancy is not inherently a characteristic of a specific piece of evidence, but instead exists within its relationship with other pieces of evidence that demonstrate proof of fact. For example, FRE 401 states that evidence is deemed relevant if it has "any tendency to make a fact more or less probable than it would be without the evidence" and that "the fact is of consequence in determining the action." Reinforcing this, FRE 901 states that in order "to satisfy the requirement of authenticating or identifying an item of evidence, the proponent must produce evidence sufficient to support a finding that the item is what the proponent claims it is."

Traditionally, legal systems—such as that in the United States—have viewed digital evidence, otherwise referred to as ESI, as being hearsay evidence[3] because there was no scientific technique to demonstrate that the data is factual. This meant that digital evidence being presented before the courts would commonly be dismissed because its authenticity could not be determined beyond a reasonable doubt. However, as digital evidence became more prevalent with the global adoption of technology and its use in criminal activities, exceptions to admissibility began to arise. Under FRE 803(6), an exception to viewing ESI as hearsay evidence exists whereby digital evidence is admissible if it demonstrates "records of regularly conducted activity" as a business record, such as an act, event, condition, opinion, or diagnosis. However, qualifying digital evidence as a business record within this exception requires that ESI is demonstrated as authentic, reliable, and trustworthy. Within FRE 803(6), the requirements for qualifying digital evidence as a business record can be achieve by proving that:

- The record was made at or near the time by—or information was transmitted by—someone with knowledge[4]
- The record was kept in the course of a regularly conducted activity of a business, organization, occupation, or calling, whether or not for profit
- Making the record was a regular practice of that activity
- All these conditions are shown by the testimony of the custodian or another qualified witness, or by a certification that complies with Rule 902(11) or (12) or with a statute permitting certification
- Neither the source of information nor the method or circumstances of preparation indicate a lack of trustworthiness

Supporting the requirements of *FRE 803(6)* for testimony of the custodian or another qualified witness, FRE 902(11) and 902(12) describes the requirements for certifying domestic records of regularly conducted activity as follows:

- *Rule 902(11)*: The original or a copy of a domestic record that meets the requirements of Rule 803(6)(A)–(C), as shown by a certification of the custodian or another qualified person that must be signed in a manner that, if falsely made, would subject the signer to criminal penalty under the laws where the certification was signed. Before the trial or hearing, the proponent must give an adverse party reasonable written notice of the intent to offer the record—and must make the record and certification available for inspection—so that the party has a fair opportunity to challenge them.
- *Rule 902(12)*: The original or a copy of a foreign record that meets the requirements of Rule 803(6)(A)–(C), as shown by a certification of the custodian or another qualified person that must be signed in a manner that, if falsely made, would subject the signer to criminal penalty under the laws where the certification was signed. Before the trial or hearing, the proponent must give an adverse party reasonable written notice of the intent to offer the record—and must make the record and certification available for inspection—so that the party has a fair opportunity to challenge them.

On occasion, situations arise where business records are challenged during trial on issues involving integrity and authenticity to its original. To lessen these contests, *FRE 1002* describes the need to demonstrate the trustworthiness of digital evidence against its original. Guaranteeing that business records meet this ruling, and subsequently can be admitted into a court of law, means that organizations must have a series of safeguards, precautions, and controls in place to maintain integrity and authenticity of their original ESI.

Good Practices for Computer-Based Electronic Evidence

ESI is valuable evidence and subject to the same standards and principles that apply to traditional (physical) evidence where it must be demonstrated, without doubt, that it is in original, exact, and in an unchanged state. Supporting this, the Association of Chief of Police Officers (ACPO) in the United Kingdom (UK) developed the *Good Practices Guide for Computer Based Electronic Evidence* as a means of addressing evidence-handling steps for digital evidence seized during an investigation.

Originally developed for those who work in law enforcement, the publication now supports a much broader international audience, including private-sector investigations, corporations, and government agencies. While it does not provide a comprehensive guide for practitioners to follow when examining evidence, it does outline four overarching principles that should be followed when handling evidence as a way of maintaining authenticity and integrity:

- *Principle #1*: No action taken by law enforcement agencies or their agents should change data held on a computer or storage media, which may subsequently be relied upon in court.
- *Principle #2*: In circumstances where a person finds it necessary to access original data held on a computer or on storage media, that person must be competent to do so and be able to give evidence explaining the relevance and the implications of their actions.
- *Principle #3*: An audit trail or other record of all processes applied to computer-based electronic evidence should be created and preserved. An independent third party should be able to examine those processes and achieve the same result.
- *Principle #4*: The person in charge of the investigation (the case officer) has overall responsibility for ensuring that the law and these principles are adhered to.

While these principles were created to serve as a guide, it is recommended that these principles are consistently applied so that the authenticity and integrity of evidence is always maintained. From the implementation and steady application of these principle toward digital evidence, organizations can effectively demonstrate how they handle evidence and ensure that it will remain legally admissible throughout its lifecycle.

Legal Precedence

Within the legal system, a precedent is any legal case that establishes a rule subsequently used when deciding a similar issue of fact. Within some legal systems, decisions made within the higher courts (i.e., the U.S. Supreme Court) are mandatory and must be followed by lower courts; this is also known as *binding precedent*.

On the opposite end of the spectrum, decisions made in lower-level courts are not binding to the higher courts. However, there are times when the higher courts will adopt these decisions because of their importance; this is known as *persuasive precedent*. Every once in a while, a decision made by the courts will be so significant that it establishes a new legal principle or changes an existing law; this is referred to as a *landmark decision*. Where differing decisions are made by courts at the same level, they should be carefully weighted upon, but they are not mandated to be followed.

Brady Rule: Inculpatory and Exculpatory Evidence

One of the main goals of conducting an investigation is to establish factual conclusions that are based on credible evidence. With the totality of evidence taken into consideration, practitioners may encounter specific findings that need to be assessed further before factual conclusions can be drawn. Of importance, practitioners need to pay special attention when it is clear that either inculpatory (indication of guilt) or exculpatory (indication of innocence) evidence exists.

Inculpatory evidence is any evidence that demonstrates, or tends to show, a person's involvement in an act that establishes an indication of guilt. For example, a person uses their corporate email account to send confidential customer data to their friend, and that act is flagged in security-monitoring technologies; this could be considered as inculpatory evidence.

Exculpatory evidence is any evidence that is favorable to a person that exonerates, or tends to exonerate, their involvement in an act. Following the example above, through the analysis of ESI it was identified that unauthorized access to the person's email was gained to send the confidential customer data through email; this could be considered as exculpatory evidence.

It is important to know that the suppression of exculpatory evidence is a violation of court rules and can lead to implausible facts. In 1963 U.S. court rulings in the matter of *Brady v. Maryland 373 U.S. 83* were a milestone in setting a precedent for disclosing exculpatory evidence. In a statement, John Leo Brady went on record claiming that he was innocent and that his friend committed the crime. However, the State of Maryland intentionally suppressed a written statement from the friend that contained a confession to committing the murder. As result, the *Brady Rule* was created that ruled the suppression of evidence favorable to a person is a violation of due process, and evidence that proves innocence must be disclosed.

Frye v. Daubert Standard: General Acceptance Testing

The advancements and adoption of technology over the past fifty years has allowed for increased capabilities to apply new scientific techniques for gathering, processing, and presenting digital evidence. However, use of these techniques can provide opportunity to challenge the results and raise concern around its effect on the judicial process.

Within the context of criminal law, there is a need for the admissibility of evidence submitted during trial to be scientifically demonstrated as a result of proper validation[5] and verification[6] testing. Traditionally, courts have resolved the need for general-acceptance testing by applying rulings of the matter involving *U.S. v. Frye, 293 F. 1013 (D.C. Cir. 1923)*. During this trial, a lie detector test was used to support the defendant's claim that he was telling the truth when he denied committing murder. However, the court ruled that evidence was inadmissible because the scientific principles upon which the lie detector test was based were not "sufficiently established to have gained general acceptance in the particular field in which it belongs." As a result, the *Frye Standard* (a.k.a., *Frye Test* or *General Acceptance Test*) became the standard by which scientific evidence and the expert opinion of scientific technique is legally admissible only where it has been generally accepted in the relevant scientific community. The Frye Standard remained precedence for many years until it was superseded by the *Daubert Standard*.

The Daubert Standard came about in 1993 as result of a U.S. Supreme Court decision in the matter of *Daubert v. Merrell Dow Pharmaceuticals, 509 U.S. 579*. Through this ruling, it was identified that *Federal Rules of Evidence 702* did not incorporate a general acceptance test for assessing whether the testimony of scientific experts was based on reasoning or scientific methodology that was properly applied to facts. Furthermore, the court outlined that evidence based on innovative or unusual knowledge is only admissible after it has been established as reliable and scientifically valid. To meet the requirements under this ruling, the Daubert Standard was created where specific criteria were established for determining the reliability of scientific techniques as follows:

1. Has the theory or technique in question undergone empirical testing?
2. Has the theory or technique been subjected to peer review and publication?
3. Does the theory or technique have any known or potential error rate?
4. Do standards exist, and are they maintained, for the control of the theory or technique's operation?
5. Has the theory or technique received general acceptance in the relevant scientific community?

Under the Daubert Standard, for ESI to be legally admissible as evidence, documented testing and experimentation must be completed to demonstrate repeatable[7] and reproducible[8] results. Achieving this legal standard means that organizations must ensure that all tools and equipment used to interact with evidence meets the above criteria, as demonstrated through proper validation and verification testing.

Search Warrants

The extent of where potential evidence exists can be found within the boundary of the organization's span of control (internally). However, depending on the scope of an investigation, evidence may also exist outside the boundary of the organization's span of control—such as a personal residence or service provider—where the ability to thoroughly investigate and establish factual conclusions can be a potentially complicated undertaking. Where this occurs, and evidence is required from external parties to support an investigation, organizations will be required to interface with local law enforcement agencies to facilitate evidence-gathering activities.

Generally, a criminal investigation is any event or incident where the unlawful infringement of legal statutes, acts, or codes has occurred and law enforcement has a duty to investigate. In the criminal justice system, crimes (acts that cause harm) are reported by the victim to law enforcement who may investigate. Penalties imposed if found guilty can include imprisonment, fines and forfeitures, probation, community services, or restitution to the victim. Alternatively, a civil investigation is any event or incident where 1) there is a dispute between two or more parties, or 2) there are disciplinary issues within the organization. In the civil justice system, there is no determination of guilt or innocence; rather, there is a determination of whether the offender is liable for harm caused to the victim. Penalties imposed commonly include the victim seeking compensation (typically monetary) for the damages they have suffered. Most notably, perhaps the most significant difference between criminal and civil matters lies within the burden of proof where a criminal matter is "beyond a reasonable doubt," while a civil matter only requires a "preponderance of evidence."

To legally obtain evidence in either a criminal or civil matter requires the execution of a search warrant. The purpose of a search warrant is to permit law enforcement to find and seize as much relevant evidence as possible, for a limited time, by authorizing them to locate, examine, and preserve all evidence relevant to the event or incident. However, obtaining a search warrant requires the authorization from an officer of the law (i.e., a judge) only after the requestor has met specific criteria that satisfies reasonable grounds that demonstrate that there is in fact evidence relevant to the event or incident, including:

■ The "building, receptacle, or place" to be searched
■ The "thing" being sought as evidence

With these requirements, the term *thing* applies only to tangible objects that can be seized; such as computer devices, articles of clothing, motor vehicles, or fingerprints. For the purposes of a search warrant, it is important to note that a computer device is considered a thing and not a *place*, because it is a physical object. Once seized, the computer device can be further analyzed. Figure 4.1 below illustrates the relationship between the elements of a search warrant.

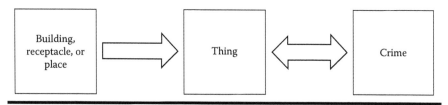

Figure 4.1   **Search warrant element relationships.**

With both civil and criminal matters, there can be instances where evidence is located outside the boundary of the organization's span of control across many different geographies (i.e., countries, regions), or where different jurisdictional laws, standards, or regulations govern both computer-related crimes and access to ESI. It is important that organizations understand the applicability of these different legal and regulatory governance bodies because it can potentially impede or dictate how the investigation will proceed.

Subpoenas

Subpoenas are legal demands for parties who are in possession of ESI or evidence to turn it over or produce it to legal authorities. For example, common types of subpoenas organizations could issue include:

- *Investigative subpoenas,* which commonly originate from governmental investigative bodies, law enforcement authorities, and regulatory authorities. These types of subpoenas are required to be kept confidential and could lead to criminal liability or penalties should the recipient be informed of the existence of a subpoena.
- *Third-party (nonparty) subpoenas,* which commonly request documents and/or a party's deposition in connection with a particular legal matter. Third-party subpoenas are used in a dispute between two or more parties in a legal action.
- *Party subpoenas,* which are commonly served in connection with a legal action where the party has been named in the lawsuit.

It is important to note that a subpoena cannot be ignored, but it can be challenged if the recipient feels it is unfair or invalidly issued. Within an enterprise environment, subpoenas are most likely issued under the rule of civil procedure as applies to pending lawsuits and the discovery of ESI; refer to Chapter 13 titled *"Electronic Discovery and Litigation Support"* for further discussion. Subpoenas are usually issued using letterhead of the issuing court where the case is filed, does include the name of the parties, is addressed by name to the recipient being sought, and does contain specific language with instruction on what is required of the recipient.

Jurisdiction

Jurisdiction is the power, or right, of a legal system (i.e., court, law enforcement) to exercise its authority in deciding over a 1) person, relating to the authority for trying individuals as a defendant; 2) subject matter, relating to authority originating from the country's laws and regulations; or 3) territory, relating to the geographic area where a court has authority to decide. In some cases, depending on the crime committed, concurrent jurisdiction can exist where two different legal systems have simultaneous authority over the same case.

In the simplest of scenarios, a legal matter can be tried in the location (i.e., country) where the crime took place. However, with the ways in which technology, such as the Internet, has an extensive global reach and crimes are committed using this delivery channel spanning several countries, it has become somewhat challenging to determine where to prosecute. In cases when there is contention over where a case should be tried, the jurisdiction of the court needs to be assessed and alternatives considered.

Although modern technology adds an additional layer of complexity to jurisdiction, international courts are becoming more familiar with laws and regulations relating to technology and are making informed decisions about which legal system has jurisdiction.

Summary

From the technology advancements made over the past fifty years, criminals have realized increased opportunities to commit crimes that span across a vast international scale. In response to these technology-related crimes, countries and regions around the world started enacting a series of laws and regulations to deal with the evolving threat landscape.

Glossary

1. **Electronically stored information (ESI)** is information created, manipulated, communicated, stored, and best utilized in digital form, requiring the use of computer hardware and software.
2. **Trier of fact,** or finder of fact, is any person or group of persons in a legal proceeding who determines whether, from presented evidence, something existed or some event occurred.
3. **Hearsay evidence** is secondhand or indirect evidence that is offered by a witness of which they do not have direct knowledge but, rather, their testimony is based on what another person has said to them.
4. **Someone with knowledge** describes any person who has awareness or familiarity gained through experience or learning.

5. **Validation** is the process of evaluating software to determine whether the products of a given development phase satisfy the condition imposed at the start of that phase.
6. **Verification** is the process of evaluating software during or at the end of the development process to determine whether it satisfies specified requirements.
7. **Repeatable** refers to obtaining the same results when using the same method on identical test items in the same laboratory by the same operator using the same equipment within short intervals of time.
8. **Reproducible** refers to obtaining the same results being obtained when using the same method on identical test items in different laboratories with different operators utilizing different equipment.

Chapter 5

Ethics and Professional Conduct

At some point during an investigation, digital forensic practitioners will encounter information that puts them in a difficult position, challenging their ethics and professional conduct. For the most part, these dilemmas can be resolved by following an approach where they recognize, classify, and manage these issues while respecting the boundaries and obligations they have as a professional.

However, differences among individuals, culture, social class, and organizations create challenges in establishing what is ethical and what is not. Abiding to a set of consistent professional ethics and code of conduct relating to digital forensics helps to define the moral principles that provide guidance to avoid potential misconduct.

Importance of Ethics

Whatever the cause of illegal, immoral, or unethical behavior, at the end of the day it is the responsibility of every digital forensic practitioner to do everything in their power to be objective, honest, truthful, and demonstrate due diligence when conducting an investigation. That said, perhaps the best way to illustrate the importance of professional ethics is to explain what it is not. First and foremost, ethics should not be regarded as aspirational, meaning that it should be something applied consistently and not intermittently. Rather, ethics establish a minimum standard of acceptable conduct for all activities performed by all professionals.

Ethics is concerned with the norms of human conduct and follows the same rigors of logical reasoning similar to that of digital forensic science. While some might view ethics as being prescriptive and prohibitive, they have been created to provide professions with reasonable guidance for acting in good faith. Although ethics are not law, conduct outside of these guidelines can lead to harm, liabilities, damages, or other consequences.

Principles of Ethics

Digital forensic practitioners possess specialized and unique knowledge which, if not governed properly, have the potential for misuse. When professionals fail to uphold a minimum level of ethical standards, the resulting impact can lead to potential digital evidence being overlooked or disregarded during an investigation.

Principles of ethical reasoning is an appropriate means of sorting out the good from the bad. Typically, ethics are created as broad and vague guidelines that do not outline every prohibited act to prescribe what proper behavior is.

Personal Ethics

Personal ethics are those values that individuals, or groups of individuals, regard as desirable and are commonly applied to behaviors of people. These are principles that are a reflection of the general expectations of any person without having to formally articulate them. Examples of personal ethics include:

1. Concern and respect for the well-being of others
2. Honesty and the willingness to comply with the law
3. Fairness and the ability not to take undue advantage of others
4. Goodwill and preventing harm to any creature

Primarily, people are motivated to abide by these principles because:

■ Most people want to have a clear conscience and desire to act ethically under normal circumstances
■ It is the nature of people to ensure their actions and behaviors do not cause injury or harm to others
■ Most people are obligated to follow laws and regulations of countries and regions
■ Social and material well-being depends on how one behaves in society

Professional Ethics

A professional is any individual who performs a specific activity, such as digital forensics, within the context of a business environment. Examples of basic ethic principles people are expected to follow in their professional career include:

- Impartiality and objectivity
- Openness and disclosure
- Confidentiality and trust
- Due diligence and duty of care
- Loyalty to professional responsibilities
- Avoidance of potential or apparent conflicts

Computer Ethics

Published in 1992 by the Computer Ethics Institute (CEI), the *Ten Commandments of Computer Ethics*, illustrated in Figure 5.1, was developed to create "a set of standards to guide and instruct people in the ethical use of computers."

Ten Commandments of Computer Ethics:

1. Thou shalt not use a computer to harm other people.
2. Thou shalt not interfere with other people's computer work.
3. Thou shalt not snoop around in other people's computer files.
4. Thou shalt not use a computer to steal.
5. Thou shalt not use a computer to bear false witness.
6. Thou shalt not copy or use proprietary software for which you have not paid.
7. Thou shalt not use other people's computer resources without authorization or proper compensation.
8. Thou shalt not appropriate other people's intellectual output.
9. Thou shalt think about the social consequences of the program you are writing or the system you are designing.
10. Thou shalt always use a computer in ways that ensure consideration and respect for your fellow humans.

Figure 5.1   Ten commandments of computer ethics.

These commandments have been widely quoted and referenced since its original publication as the minimum standards for human conduct when using computer systems.

Business Ethics

Business ethics is the application of the general principles discussed above to behavior within a business environment. Following a minimum standard of ethical business behavior is expected, both by the organization and by the public, to facilitate aspects of business including, but not limited to: improved profitability, nurturing of business relationships, improved employee productivity, and reduction of risk (i.e., strategic,[1] financial,[2] operational,[3] legal,[4] and other[5]).

Organizations need to conduct themselves ethically because they have to exist in a competitive global landscape and demonstrating these values brings credibility. Organizations should act ethically to:

- Protect the interests of themselves, the business community at large, and the public interest
- Meet the expectations of and build trust with stakeholders, shareholders, and investors
- Create an environment whereby employees can act consistently with the organizations values and principles

A *business code of conduct policy* is a management tool for setting out an organization's values, responsibilities, and ethical obligations. This governance document provides the organization with guidance for handling difficult ethical situations relating to business conduct. To be truly effective, the business code of conduct policy needs to be embedded throughout the organization so employees know exactly how it applies to them.

Similar to how organizations have a mission statement, otherwise referred to as a vision statement, aligned to their business goals, it should also develop such statements to promote an ethical culture.

Ethics in Digital Forensics

The majority of education and training available today is focused on the technical aspects of the digital forensic discipline; such as how to examine a hard drive or conduct network traffic analysis. Within the academic curriculum, there is little time spent on the business side of digital forensics, which includes teaching ethics and a code of conduct.

Perhaps the reason for why there is this notable absence in academic curriculum is because the code of ethics that do exist do not encompass the digital forensic community as a whole. While there are professional organizations that have established their own code of ethics, as discussed in the section below, these values and principles are specific to the single entity and are not universally translated to demonstrate the level of competency of a digital forensic practitioner.

Above we discussed personal, professional, computer, and business ethics that can be used to establish a set ethics that can be used in the digital forensic profession. While the following are not structured in the manner of a code of ethics, these values and principles should be consistently applied to digital forensics in terms of how practitioners can conduct themselves in an ethical manner.

Certifications and Professional Organizations

Internationally, there are several professional organizations that have established ethics, or codes of conduct, which certified digital forensics practitioners are expected to adhere by. Even though these ethics put forward by these professional organizations can have a positive effect on the behavior, actions, and judgment of individuals, many organizations do not mandate their employees to become certified. Holding a professional digital forensic certification can be viewed as a deterrence to professional misconduct at the risk of losing the accreditation due to a violation of the code of ethics defined by certifying body.

Ultimately, digital forensic practitioners are held accountable for acting ethically and according to their organization's policies (i.e., business code of conduct policy), their associated professional organizations, and applicable laws where they live and conduct business.

While there might be some professional organizations not specified below, the following are examples of certifying bodies and their respective code of ethics that accredited individuals must adhere.

Digital Forensics Certification Board (DFCB)

The Digital Forensics Certification Board (DFCB) exists to promote public trust and confidence within the digital forensic profession. Specifically, the Digital Forensic Certified Practitioner (DFCP) designation offered by DFCB is a professional certification to enhance the professionalism and distinguish individuals who have a broad comprehension of the common body of knowledge (CBK)[6] within the digital forensic industry (Figure 5.2).

International Association of Computer Investigative Specialists (IACIS)

The International Association of Computer Investigative Specialists (IACIS) is a global nonprofit organization that promotes educational excellence in the digital forensic profession. Specifically, both the Certified Forensic Computer Examiner (CFCE)

Within the DFCB Code of Ethics, it is stated that a certificant shall:

1. Not engage in, or pressure others to engage in, any conduct that is harmful to the profession of digital forensics including, but not limited to, any illegal or unethical activity, any technical misrepresentation or distortion, any scholarly falsification or any material misrepresentation of education, training, credentials, experience, or area of expertise
2. Demonstrate, at all times, commitment, integrity, and professional diligence
3. Avoid any action that could appear to be a conflict of interest
4. Comply with all lawful orders of courts of competent jurisdiction
5. Show no bias with respect to findings or opinions
6. Express no opinion with respect to the guilt or innocence of any party
7. Not disclose or reveal any confidential or privileged information obtained during an engagement without proper authorization or otherwise ordered by a court of competent jurisdiction
8. Examine and consider thoroughly all information (unless specifically limited in scope by court order or other authority) and render opinions and conclusions strictly in accordance with the results and findings obtained using validated and appropriate procedures
9. Report or testify truthfully in all matters and not knowingly make any material misrepresentation of information or otherwise withhold any information that, in so doing, might tend to distort the truth
10. Accept only engagements for which there is a reasonable expectation of completion with professional competence.

Figure 5.2   DFCB Code of Ethics

and Certified Advanced Windows Forensic Examiner (CAWFE) designations offered by IACIS are professional certifications for individuals to demonstrate their knowledge of core competencies and practical skills in the field of digital forensics (Figure 5.3).

International Society of Forensic Computer Examiners (ISFCE)

The International Society of Forensic Computer Examiners (ISFCE) is a nonprofit organization that promotes a community of competent digital forensic practitioners. Specifically, the Certified Computer Examiner (CCE) designation offered by ISFCE is a professional certification that sets a high ethical standard based on

Within the IACIS Code of Ethics, it states that "members must demonstrate and maintain the highest standards of ethical conduct" by:

- Maintaining the highest level of objectivity in all forensic examinations and accurately present the facts involved
- Thoroughly examine and analyze the evidence in a case
- Conduct examinations based upon established, validated principles
- Render opinions having a basis that is demonstratively reasonable
- Not withhold any findings, whether inculpatory or exculpatory, that would cause the facts of a case to be misrepresented or distorted
- Never misrepresent credentials, education, training, and experience or membership status

Figure 5.3   IACIS Code of Ethics.

their knowledge and practical experience within the digital forensic discipline (Figure 5.4).

Principles for Digital Forensics

Currently, there is no universally adopted code of ethics that governs the ethical behavior and conduct of digital forensics as a single community. Perhaps the biggest reason why no such code of ethics exists for the entire digital forensic community is attributed to the challenges that would be faced in establishing one at an international level. Some obstacles that could be faced during this process might include:

- What behavior and conduct would the code of ethics cover?
- What values and principles would the code of ethics address?
- What agency or organization would govern and enforce the code of ethics?
- Whom would the code of ethics apply to? (e.g., just digital forensic practitioners or all individuals involved with digital evidence)

In light of these questions, it might be fair to say that, from the code of ethics illustrated in the section above, there are key values and principles that digital forensic practitioners must ensure their behavior and conduct adheres to. That said, digital forensics is a profession and as such should follow a similar minimum level of values and principles as required for professional ethics, as discussed previously.

Within the ISFCE Code of Ethics, a Certified Computer Examiner (CCE) will, at all times:

- Demonstrate commitment and diligence in performance of assigned duties
- Demonstrate integrity in completing professional assignments
- Maintain the utmost objectivity in all forensic examinations and accurately present findings
- Conduct examinations based on established, validated procedures
- Abide by the highest moral and ethical standards and abide by the Code of Ethics of the ISFCE
- Testify truthfully in all matters before any board, court or proceeding
- Avoid any action that would knowingly present a conflict of interest
- Comply with all legal orders of the courts
- Thoroughly examine all evidence within the scope of the engagement

Within the ISFCE Code of Ethics, a Certified Computer Examiner (CCE) will never:

- Withhold any relevant evidence
- Reveal any confidential matters or knowledge learned in an examination without an order from a court of competent jurisdiction or with the express permission of the client
- Express an opinion on the guilt or innocence of any party
- Engage in any unethical or illegal conduct
- Knowingly undertake an assignment beyond his or her ability
- Misrepresent education, training or credentials
- Show bias or prejudice in findings or examinations
- Exceed authorization in conducting examinations

Figure 5.4 ISFCE Code of Ethics

On this basis, the subject matters to follow should be consistently applied, at all times, by digital forensic practitioners as fundamental values and principles of ethical behavior and conduct.

Impartiality and Objectivity

One of the main goals for conducting an investigation is to establish factual conclusions based on credible evidence. As part of an investigation, there could arise times when the subject is known or familiar with the practitioner. It is the responsibility of the practitioner to maintain the utmost fairness during an investigation to draw conclusions based on factual and credible evidence. This means that practitioners should avoid any action that would appear to be a conflict of interest and otherwise create potential bias in establishing their evidential conclusions.

Openness and Disclosure

Investigations are not "witch hunts" and should be conducted using the utmost fairness and obligation to report factual conclusions based on credible evidence. While analyzing evidence, practitioners may encounter specific findings that need to be assessed further before factual conclusions can be drawn, such as paying special attention to inculpatory (indication of guilt) or exculpatory (indication of innocence) evidence. It is crucial that practitioners take into consideration the totality of all evidence gathered during an investigation before arriving at factual conclusions.

Confidentiality and Trust

The work of a digital forensic practitioner comes with a high level of trust. From time to time, they can come across extremely sensitive and confidential information that needs to be kept confidential and communicated on a need-to-know basis. When these types of information are discovered, human nature tends to kick in, and the desire to disclose details of these occurrences comes about. As a digital forensic practitioner, it is required that evidence is not disclosed or revealed without any proper authorization (e.g., a court order).

Due Diligence and Duty of Care

Legal admissibility of evidence requires practitioners to follow a consistent investigative process model that respects the digital forensic best practices of well-established principles, methodologies, and techniques. Informed decision-making during an investigation must be made in accordance with applicable laws, standards, and regulations to avoid potential consequences. With this in mind, digital forensic professionals must consistently demonstrate their behavior and conduct is done honestly, with prudence, and in compliance with laws and professional norms.

Certifications and Accreditations

Internationally, there are a number of professional organizations that have established certifications and accreditations specific to the digital forensic profession. Predominantly, these certifications are provided by professional organizations with an industry-wide perspective on the digital forensic profession; however, there are a small number of certifications provided by merchants who sell digital forensic products and services.

It is important to keep in mind that while professional certification provides the assurance that an individual meet the required level of knowledge in digital forensics, these accreditations do not provide the in-depth level of education that formal academic programs teach. Refer to Appendix B: Education and Professional Certifications for a list of digital forensic certifications.

Summary

Ethical values and principles are a useful way for sorting out what is considered good and bad behavior and conduct. While there is no code of ethics that universally applies to the digital forensics profession, the morals originating from the combination of personal, professional, computer, and business values and principles can be leveraged to establish a code of ethics to adhere by.

Glossary

1. **Strategic risk** is associated with the organization's core business functions and commonly occur because of business interactions (purchase/sale of goods and services), mergers and acquisitions, or investment relations management.
2. **Financial risk** is associated with the financial structure, stability, and transactions of the organization.
3. **Operational risk** is associated with the organization's business operational and administrative procedures.
4. **Legal risk** is associated with the need to comply with the rules and regulations of the governing bodies.
5. **Other risks** are associated with indirect, nonbusiness factors, such as natural disasters and others as identified based on the subjectivity of the organization.
6. **Common body of knowledge (CBK)** is the complete concepts, terms, and activities that make up a professional domain.

ENHANCING DIGITAL FORENSIC CAPABILITIES

With every day that passes, technology makes significant advancements, organizations place even more reliance on technology, and the threat landscape evolves, presenting new risks. Yet, there are still a percentage of organizations that do not have an appreciation for the risks knocking at their door and the potential financial, operational, reputational, or regulatory impact they introduce to business operations. More so, there are still a percentage of organizations that do not have in-house digital forensic capabilities or know how to manage and handle incidents or misconduct when a threat becomes reality.

Naturally, if an organization does not have in-house capabilities, there are managed-service offerings available that can be contracted to have an external digital forensic team brought in to address a specific incident or investigation. But the reality is, not having an in-house digital forensic team is not justification for an organization to underestimate the importance of enabling digital forensic capabilities.

The execution of digital forensics, from the technical perspective, remains consistent in terms of how the fundamental principles, methodologies, and techniques (discussed throughout the first section) are practiced. However, the execution of digital forensics in terms of implementation and making effective use of the fundamental principles, methodologies, and techniques differs from one organization to the next.

Regardless of whether the digital forensics team is supported in-house or through external managed services, the team's ability to maximize the collection of credible digital evidence depends on whether the organizations recognize the importance for enabling this capability. In this section, we will discuss different strategies for how organizations can enhance their digital forensic capabilities throughout their systems and infrastructure.

Chapter 6

The Business of Digital Forensics

Organizations exist in many different contexts (i.e., size, geography, industry), and within each there are different and unique requirements when it comes to digital forensic capabilities. There is a percentage of organizations that, given their operating model and corporate profile, leverage external managed services to supply a digital forensic team when required. With the remaining percentage of organizations, they have come to a decision that having a digital forensic team in-house is the best strategy for given their operating model and corporate profile. After making this decision, the organization needs to kick-start their long-term digital forensic program by implementing a series of administrative, technical, and physical strategies.

The Role of Digital Forensics in an Enterprise

From the topics covered in the section of this book titled "*Enabling Digital Forensics*," we know that digital forensics is the application of science to law and consists of scientifically proven principles, methodologies, and techniques. While the technical execution of digital forensics within an enterprise environment is similar to the way other organizations and agencies do it, the purpose and roles it serves can be somewhat different. Consider that when law enforcement agencies are performing digital forensics they are doing so in response to criminal activity. True, enterprises also use digital forensics as a reactionary process, but there are many more opportunities to extend the use and application of digital forensics into proactive measures; further discussion about proactive capabilities is found in Chapter 11 titled "*Digital Forensic Readiness*."

Having the opportunity to be both proactive and reactive in their digital forensic capabilities, first and foremost organizations must follow a systematic approach so that their digital forensic capabilities are properly aligned to business and organizational needs. Throughout this chapter are methodologies organizations can use when exploring in-house digital forensic capabilities.

Starting a Digital Forensic Program

What drives an organization to decide it needs in-house digital forensic capabilities? Largely, this need is determined by a combination of both and external factors, such as:

- Countries or regions that have specific laws and regulations that require a process for dealing with incidents leveraging forensic analysis or investigation, such as the Sarbanes Oxley Act (SOX) in the United States
- Regulated industries (i.e., financial, healthcare, insurance) that have specific requirements governing the use, transmission, or storage of information, such as Payment Card Industry–Data Security Standards (PCI-DSS)
- Assisting legal and compliance teams with the discovery of electronically stored information (ESI)[1] for production as evidence
- Facilitating human resources (HR) or employee relations (ER) with evidence supporting employee misconduct or other disciplinary actions (i.e., termination)
- Analysis and correlation of ESI to determine a root cause or the potential of data breaches

Establishing in-house digital forensic capabilities requires following a systematic approach by which implementation is aligned to the organization's needs, with the technical execution aspects following afterward. Below are the steps organizations should follow to answer "who, where, what, when, why, and how" in-house digital forensic capabilities will be implemented.

Step 1: Understand Business Risks

Before implementing digital forensics in an enterprise environment, it is important to take a step back and understand the need for investing time, money, and resources. Doing so requires that organizations understand what their business is (i.e., financial, health, etc.) and the risks that can expose the organization to any form of business impact.

The type of risks that can impact a business is subjective to each organization (i.e., size, geography, industry) and should not be managed as universally equivalent. Risks can be described as any threat event, whether internal (can be controlled within the boundaries of the organization) or external (occur outside the organization and cannot be controlled), that occurs in one of the five major groupings:

- *Strategic risk* is associated with business functions and commonly occur because of:
  - Business interactions where goods and services are purchased and sold, varying supply and demand, adjusting competitive structures, and facilitating the emergence of new and innovative technologies.
  - Transactions resulting in asset relocation from mergers and acquisitions, spin-offs, alliances, or joint ventures.
  - Strategies for investment relations management and communication with stakeholders who have invested in the organization.
- *Financial risk* is associated with the financial structure, stability, and transactions of the organization.
- *Operational risk* is associated with the organization's business operational and administrative procedures.
- *Legal risk* is associated with the need to comply with the rules and regulations of the governing bodies.
- *Other risks* are associated with indirect, nonbusiness factors, such as natural disasters and others as identified based on the subjectivity of the organization.

The approach for how to determine business risk is done by completing a risk assessment as an output of their overall risk management program. Determining the need for investing time, money, and resources into digital forensic capabilities comes from completing both a qualitative and quantitative risk assessment to ensure that a thorough understanding of the potential risks is achieved. Following these assessments, a complete picture of all potential risk can be used to perform a cost-benefit analysis that will ultimately determine whether it is feasible to implement in-house digital forensic capabilities.

At the end of this step, organizations will have answered the question of "why" they need in-house digital forensic capabilities.

Step 2: Outlining Business Scenarios

If a business risk exists and there is a positive return on investment (ROI),[2] then implementing appropriate digital forensic capabilities is beneficial. As stated previously, every organization is unique and has different business profiles that present different requirements for in-house digital forensic capabilities. Enhancing digital forensic capabilities within an enterprise must also take into consideration the influences of the business's operations so that strategies can be developed to adequately manage risk.

Outlined below are multiple business scenarios where digital forensics can be applied to manage business risk. While the applicability of all scenarios might not fit the profile of every organization, it is important that each is illustrated and understood so that they can be considered for relevancy.

- *Reducing the impact of cybercrime*: With information technology (IT) playing an integral role in nearly every business operation, the evolving threat landscape continues to increase risks associated with organizational assets. Using a threat modeling methodology, organizations can create a structured representation of the different ways a threat actor can go about executing attacks and how their tactics, techniques, and procedures can be used to create an impact. The output of this exercise can be put to practical use by implementing appropriate countermeasures that create potential digital evidence.
- *Validating the impact of cybercrime or disputes*: When a security incident occurs, organizations must be prepared to quantify impact. To obtain a complete and accurate view of the cost of an incident, both direct and indirect contributors must be included in the impact assessment. This means incorporating logs generated from different types of controls (e.g., preventive, detective, corrective) or the overhead costs of managing the incident (e.g., people and technology expenses).
- *Producing evidence to support organizational disciplinary issues*: A business code of conduct document promotes a positive work environment that, when signed, strengthens the confidence of employees and stakeholders by establishing an accepted level of professional and ethical workplace behavior. When the guidelines set out in this document have been violated, employees can be subject to disciplinary actions. Where disciplinary actions escalate into a legal problem, organizations must approach the situation fairly and reasonably by gathering and processing credible digital evidence.
- *Demonstrating compliance with regulatory or legal requirements*: Compliance is not a one-size-fits-all process. It is driven by factors such as an organization's industry (e.g., financial services) or the countries where business is conducted (e.g., Canada). Evidence documenting compliance standards are met must be specific to the requirements of both the regulations and laws, and the jurisdiction.
- *Effectively managing the release of court-ordered data*: Regardless of how diligent an organization is, there will always be a time when a dispute ends up before a court of law. With adequate preparation, routine follow-ups, and a thorough understanding of what is considered reasonable in a court of law, organizations can effectively manage this risk by maintaining the admissibility of ESI, such as the requirements described within the U.S. Federal Rules of Evidence. Ensuring compliance with these requirements demands that organizations implement safeguards, precautions, and controls to ensure their ESI is admissible in court and that it is authenticated to its original source.

■ *Supporting contractual and commercial agreements*: From time to time, organizations are faced with disagreements that extend beyond disputes that involve employees. With most of today's business interactions conducted electronically, organizations must ensure they capture and electronically preserve critical metadata about their third-party agreements. This includes details about the terms and conditions or the date the agreement was cosigned. A contract management system can be used to standardize and preserve metadata needed to provide sufficient grounds for supporting a dispute.

In addition to the above scenarios, there are nonforensic scenarios where digital forensic techniques and skills can be used to support other business operations and functions, such as recovering data from old or failed media (i.e., hard drives, floppy disks). Even though these nonforensic scenarios do not have the same requirements to maintain legal admissibility, they can present business risk if there is no other means of performing these functions within the organization.

At the end of this step, organizations will have answered the questions of "where and what" in-house digital forensic capabilities are needed.

Step 3: Establish Governance Framework

An enterprise governance framework involves the administration, management, enforcement, and control of policies, standards, and procedures specific to the discipline. It is designed to provide strategic direction by ensuring the successful completion of organizational goals and objectives from a top-down approach. The concept of a governance framework includes several layers of governance subdisciplines, all of which have relationships with digital forensics.

Illustrated in Figure 6.1 are the relationships between the different governance disciplines implemented throughout the organization, including:

■ *Enterprise governance*, as the top-level governance discipline, is a very broad and an all-inclusive mechanism to ensure the well-being of the entire organization. It is designed to establish relationships between the organization and its shareholders by defining the strategic direction, objectives, and goals.
■ *Information technology (IT) governance* focuses on the use of IT throughout the enterprise to support business operations and functions. It contains a series of documents that are designed to establish how the organization will direct, manage, and control the use of IT resources to support the strategic direction, objectives, and goals.
■ *Information security (IS) governance* manages risks relating to information assets that have been entrusted to the organization. It establishes and maintains control of the environments by which information assets are used, transmitted, and stored.

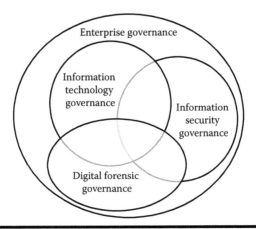

Figure 6.1   Enterprise governance framework.

Given the business risks faced by organizations, it is necessary for all stakeholders throughout the organization to understand the importance of digital forensics and the requirements for utilizing key resources to support its integrated business capabilities. Executive management, with involvement from key stakeholders such as legal, privacy, security, and human resources, work to define a series of documents that describe exactly how the organizations will go about aligning their digital forensic capabilities to address the predefined business risk scenarios.

Governance over digital forensic capabilities is essential within corporate environments looking to enable in-house capabilities. Figure 6.2 illustrates the hierarchy of the governance documentation and the relationships shared between these specific to the direct influence and precedence over others. The implementation of these documents serves as the administrative groundwork for indirectly supporting the subsequent phases where digital evidence is involved. The sections to follow explore these documents individually and provide specifics on the types that contribute to digital forensics.

Policies

As the highest level of governance documentation, policies are created to serve as formalized blueprints describing the organization's overall goals and objectives. These documents are designed to generally address concepts and are not intended to provide an in-depth level of information that would be found in other governance documentation (i.e., standards, procedures).

Before developing a policy, it is necessary to first define the scope and purpose for why it is being created, thus allowing the organization to consider all possibilities and determine what specific policies are required. Ultimately, the types of policy documents that need to be created are subject to each organization and its requirements for digital forensics. Table 6.1 contains a list of common policies that organizations have in place to support their digital forensic capabilities.

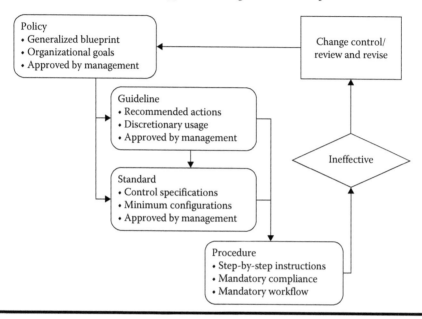

Figure 6.2   Governance documentation hierarchy.

Table 6.1   Common Organizational Policies

Policy	Scope
Acceptable Use	Defines acceptable use of equipment and computing services and the appropriate end-user controls to protect the organization's resources and proprietary information
Business Conduct	Defines the guidelines and expectations of individuals within the organization to demonstrate fair business practices and encourage a culture of openness and trust
Information Security	Defines the organization's commitment to globally manage information security risks effectively and efficiently, and in compliance with applicable regulations wherever it conducts business
Internet and Email	Defines the requirements for proper use of the organization's Internet and electronic mail systems to make users aware of what is considered acceptable and unacceptable use

Guidelines

After policies, guidelines can be developed as recommendations for how the policy blueprints can be effectively implemented. Guidelines are created to provide the organization with a methodology that must be followed, rather than containing specific control or configuration requirements as found in standards (discussed in the following section).

Like policies, the type of guidelines required in each organization is subjective as is its requirements for digital forensics. Table 6.2 contains a list of common guidelines that organizations have in place to support their digital forensic capabilities.

Standards

Next, standards are developed to define the specific requirements for how the policy blueprints and guideline methodologies will be practically implemented. These documents establish the minimum level, or baseline, necessary for the organization to meet the requirements outlined in preceding governance documentation, such as configurations, architectures, or design specifications. A key factor to consider when created standards is that they must be adaptable and dynamic to meet evolving business needs.

Like policies and guidelines, the type of standards required in each organization is subjective and its requirements for digital forensics. Table 6.3 contains a list of common standards that organizations have in place to support their digital forensic capabilities.

Procedures

Deriving from all superseding documentation, the last type of governance document to be created are the procedures that will be used by digital forensic practitioners to follow as they perform their respective job functions.

Table 6.2 Common Organizational Guidelines

Guideline	Scope
Data Loss Prevention	Awareness for end users on how to safeguard organizational data from unintentional or accidental loss or theft
Mobile/ Portable Devices	Recommendations for end users to protect an organization's data stored on mobile and/or portable devices
Passcode Selection	Considerations for end users to select strong passcodes for access into organizational systems
Risk Assessments	Direction for assessors to use documented methodologies and proven techniques for assessing organizational systems

Table 6.3   Common Organizational Standards

Standard	Scope
Backup, Retention, and Recovery	Defines the means and materials required to recover from an undesirable event, timely and reliably, that causes systems and/or data to become unavailable
Email Systems	Define the configurations necessary to minimize business risk and maximize use of email content because of the available and continuity of the supporting infrastructure
Firewall Management	Defines the configurations necessary to ensure the integrity and confidentiality of the organization's systems and/or data, and that it is protected because of the availability and continuity of the supporting infrastructure
Logical Access	Defines the requirements for authenticating and authorizing user's access to mitigate exposure of the organization's systems and data
Malware Detection	Defines the configurations necessary to ensure the attack surface of vulnerable systems is mitigated against known malicious software
Network Security	Defines the requirements for controlling external, remote, and internal access to the organization's systems and data
Platform Configurations	Defines the minimum-security configurations necessary to ensure the organization's system mitigates unauthorized access or unintended exposure of data
Physical Access	Defines the methods used to ensure adequate controls exist to mitigate unauthorized access to the organization's premise

Unlike policy, guideline, and standard documentation, procedures are those documents that have a direct relationship and interactions with the organization's digital forensic capabilities. To better understand the investigative process methodology where procedures are followed to support digital forensic capabilities, refer to Chapter 2 titled "*Investigative Process Methodologies.*"

Enforcing governance over in-house digital forensic capabilities is crucial considering the legal and regulatory implications involved; refer to Chapter 4 titled "*Laws, Standards, and Regulations*" for further discussion about laws and regulations. Not only will having a governance framework instill trust in the organization's digital forensic capabilities, it will also help to:

▪ Clearly define the roles and responsibilities of stakeholders throughout the organization

- Reduce the resources (i.e., time, effort, cost) required to effectively support service delivery and operating models
- Maintain the legal admissibility of digital evidence using consistent; repeatable;[3] reproducible;[4] verified; and validated processes, techniques, and methodologies
- Properly align risk-management strategies that deliver business value

At the end of this step, organizations will have answered the questions of "when, where, and how" their in-house digital forensic capabilities will be needed.

Step 4: Enable Technical Execution

Far too often, figuring out how to achieve a desired outcome comes first, resulting in misaligned, insufficient, or unrelated deliverables. Like the approach followed as part of project management, it is important to clearly understand scope (why, what, when, and where) before proceeding with procurement or implementation. Translating this concept over to digital forensics, before a forensic toolkit can be purchased, the team needs to first understand:

- Why digital forensics is needed
- What role digital forensics has
- When digital forensics is required
- Where digital forensics is used
- How digital forensics is administered

The concept of a "forensic toolkit" is not limited to only those hardware and software technologies that will perform and automate digital forensic tasks, but also includes those physical and administrative components that are needed to support technologies. Within an enterprise environment, there is greater opportunity to develop the forensic toolkit to be more controlled and specific to the organization, as opposed to law enforcement, which will need to have a broader toolkit.

Through this methodology, having completed the previous steps will have already addressed most administrative components that are required as part of a forensic toolkit. Next, organizations need to assess the physical components of their toolkit before they can identify those technical components that are needed.

Forensic Lab Environment

A forensic Lab environment is a secured facility used to process and, depending on the organization, store evidence gathered evidence from a crime scene, security event, or incident. These facilities are built following a similar methodology applied when building a data center where strict security measures are implemented to guarantee contents are protected from unauthorized access and external contamination.

Planning

Foremost, as with any new project, proper planning of the lab environment needs to be done so that, as the project progresses, issues arising later can be reduced, and the project will be successfully completed. This means taking necessary actions to carefully and deliberately set out the scope, schedule, and cost for the forensic lab environment before any work begins on construction.

Within the planning activities, it is important to follow a systematic approach when performing the following sequence of activities:

- Identify and analyze the organization's needs for building a forensic lab environment. Having previously understood the business-risk scenarios for having digital forensic capabilities, along with establishing a governance framework, the work done in this stage should not be exhaustive.
- Assemble a team of individuals who will provide knowledge and support (i.e., management funding approval) in the subsequent activities and tasks. Having previously identified key stakeholders, as discussed in Chapter 3 titled *"Education, Training, and Awareness,"* identifying the project team should not be exhaustive.
- Define the strategy, structure, and schedule by which the remaining activities and tasks will follow. For example, a register of all activities should include a complete list of tasks that need to be completed; accompanied by the individual (or team) who is responsible for completing the task, the allotted timeline for completing the task, and any dependencies that exist between individual tasks so that critical paths to success can be identified.

Designing

Next comes the task of designing the structure and layout of the forensic lab environment. Unfortunately, there is no "cookie cutter" approach that can be universally applied when designing a forensic lab because each environment is subjective to the types of evidence, governance framework, and needs of the organization. Considering the functional requirements of the forensic lab, such as equipment and workspace, organizations should design their lab environment to be adaptable enough so that it supports evolving business needs and continued growth in digital forensic capabilities.

The forensic lab environment must be both physically and logically secured from the organization's general network and office space so that the work being done with digital evidence does not result in contamination, loss, or unauthorized disclosure. Working from the principles and concepts of data centers, the following design elements must be incorporated to guarantee the integrity, authenticity, and admissibility of evidence:

- Construction in a fully enclosed room located in the interior of a building with floor-to-ceiling walls and no windows
- Access doors having internally facing hinges with fire safety windows reinforced with wire mesh
- Walls constructed with permanent materials (i.e., concrete)
- Raised flooring with a fire-suppression system

Building off the physical design considerations, the following are logical design elements that need to be factored when designing a lab environment:

- Principles of least privilege access is applied where only authorized individuals are permitted unattended access.
- Unattended physical access is granted using multifactor authentication mechanisms: including something you know (i.e., passcode), something you have (i.e., smartcard), and something you are (i.e., manager).
- Visitor access must always be logged and escorted.
- Evidence lockers and safes must always remain locked.
- Chain-of-custody logs for tracking evidence ownership must always be tracked.
- Inventory control mechanisms must be implemented to track and maintain complete, accurate, and up-to-date records of all lab equipment (i.e. software, forensic workstations, servers, etc.).
- Governance documents, such as standard operating procedures (SOP) and runbooks,[5] must be readily available to lab personnel (i.e., software currency officials, evidence management professionals).
- A lab manager must be assigned who is responsible for the ongoing maintenance and safeguarding of the lab and its contents (i.e., digital evidence).

In addition to the physical and logical design elements required to secure the lab environment, this stage is when the identification and placement of hardware and software comes into play. When determining what equipment is needed as part of the forensic toolkit, it is important to refer back to the work completed when documenting the business-risk scenarios as the basis for acquiring forensic equipment. Also, it is important to keep in mind that each investigation is unique and, as noted previously, might require specific activities to be conducted either in the field or within the lab environment. Therefore, a variety of different tools and equipment may be required to fulfill a broad scope of potential investigative circumstances.

Selecting the right tools and equipment to properly support digital forensic capabilities requires having a good understanding of the organization's business-risk scenarios, and the technologies used to support their respective business functions. As part of the selection process, it is important that tools and equipment are not blindly purchased without first validating and verifying that they provide the functionality required to gather and process evidence existing throughout the organization.

Digital forensic practitioners must go through proper evaluation and assessment of tools and equipment before purchasing to demonstrate that these technologies will generate repeatable[3] and reproducible[4] results when following their governance documentation to gather and process digital evidence. By completing a proof of concept (POC),[6] the organization will have a level of assurance that the tools and equipment being used to support their digital forensic capabilities are forensically sound[7] and will not introduce doubt into the evidence's integrity.

Whether selecting open-source or commercial off-the-shelf (COTS)[8] technologies for the forensic toolkit, there are many different solutions that can fit within the requirements of the organization's needs. As outlined in the introduction to this book, the focus of topics discussed throughout is not to get into the detailed technical execution of digital forensics. In keeping with this scope, references have been made available in the Resources section at the end of this chapter to lists of forensic tools and equipment. It is important to note that, given how technologies are constantly evolving, the inclusion of a forensic tool or piece of equipment over another does not suggest that these are better or recommended over others that were not included.

Piecing all physical and logical components together, the team must thoroughly document their design plan so they have a complete view of the final lab environment design. With this plan in place, the team should now review what has been identified for inclusion in the lab facility to ensure that it meets the requirements defined by the organization. If there missing components are identified, it is important that the team take time to sort out the design before proceeding to the next step, so that issues arising during construction will be reduced, and the project will be successfully completed.

Construction

Transforming the plan and design into a physical lab environment is the step when organizations will invest most of their resources (i.e., time, effort, money). However, before construction can begin, the team needs to secure management approval of the funding necessary to build the facility. Doing so is done by creating a business case that illustrates the cost-benefit, so that stakeholders have enough details to support their decision making on whether the organization should proceed with implementing the final recommendation. A business-case template has been provided in the Templates section of this book.

With the business case approved and funding available, construction of the lab environment can begin. It is important that the construction work stays within the expected scope, schedule, and cost as outlined in the business case, because any additional funding needed due to delays and issues will require the team to go back to management for approval and explain the unaccounted overage(s). Keeping to the expected scope, schedule, and cost requires having a dedicated individual, such as a project control officer (PCO), to oversee all work being done for the lab. Ultimately, the PCO will be responsible for managing all project resources (i.e., people, funding) to ensure that agreed-upon deliverables meet the requirements within the defined timelines and budget. As a strategy, keeping to the project plan might require that multiple streams of work are done in parallel by different members of the project team to procure and build:

- The physical lab environment, such as walls, floors, and access points (doors)
- The internal workspace equipment, such as desks, evidence lockers, and server racks
- The forensic hardware and software, such as workstations, write-blockers, and storage units

As work is being completed and project milestones are met, it is important to remember that there can be dependencies for how each stream of work can come together for a final deliverable. For example, the physical lab environment must be finished before any equipment or tools can be setup in the facility's workspace, and, in some cases, having workspace equipment needs to come before setting up the forensic hardware and software. However, where there are configuration and setup required before hardware and software can be configured, use of a staging area can help while waiting for equipment to be finalized.

Forensic Workstations

Forensic workstations are a combination of specialized hardware and software technologies that, together, allow for digital evidence to be gathered and processed in a forensically sound manner. In the marketplace, there are several COTS manufacturers of forensic workstations that come prebuilt with the hardware and software required to gather and process digital evidence. References have been made available in the Resources section at the end of this chapter where referrals to lists of forensic tools and equipment can be found. It is important to note that, given how technologies are constantly evolving, the inclusion of a forensic tool or piece of equipment over another does not suggest that these are better or recommended over others that were not included.

If a decision is made to build a custom forensic workstation internally, it is important to note that this has some obvious advantages and disadvantages when compared to the COTS hardware. On one hand, when building a forensic workstation, the forensic team can ensure that they have all the right hardware and software needed to support their needs. However, prebuilt systems come with a level of assurance that all components have been configured and integrated correctly to ensure the integrity, authenticity, and legal admissibility of digital evidence are maintained when being used. Whether a COTS system is acquired preconfigured or custom built, a forensic workstation should include the following components to provide the required digital forensic capabilities:

- Standard operating hardware, such as a central processing unit (CPU), random access memory (RAM), and a primary hard drive. The performance and capacity required of these components is dependent on the forensic team's requirements to support the needs of their organization.
- Add-on hardware components considered optional, subjective to the forensic team's needs, such as:
  - Optical disc bays to read a variety of compact disc (CD) formats (i.e., digital video disc [DVD, Blu-Ray]).
  - Network adaptors to interface with evidence storage networks. Refer to Chapter 10 titled *"Digital Evidence Management"* for discussions on evidence storage networks.
  - Connectors to access a variety of removable devices (i.e., universal serial bus [USB], FireWire).
  - Additional internal or external hard drive bays, verified as write-block enabled, to access a variety of hard drive formats (i.e., integrated drive electronics [IDE], serial advanced technology attachment [SATA], small computer system interface [SCSI], solid state drive [SSD]).
- A primary operating system (OS) that supports the execution of required forensic software. Where needed, additional OS versions can be run using virtual machine (VM) or emulation software applications working from the primary OS.

Before putting the forensic workstation in use, it is important that the forensic team complete thorough testing to verify and validate that the hardware and software components are working as expected and that they do not result in the forensic viability of digital evidence being lost.

Throughout construction, communication is essential to achieving successful project completion. It is important that the PCO track and maintain an up-to-date record of the work being done/completed by scheduling periodic spot checks at critical milestones during the construction.

At the end of this step, organizations will have answered the question of how their in-house digital forensic capabilities will be provided.

Step 5: Define Service Offerings

Implementing digital forensic principles, methodologies, and techniques according to applicable business-risk scenarios requires translating technical components (i.e., tools) of the discipline into a business language that can be clearly and easily understood. Achieving this is done through the creation of an enterprise service catalogue that is designed to align all technical components into the business functions that support the risk scenarios.

A service catalog provides a centralized way to see, find, invoke, and execute digital forensic services from anywhere in the organization. Once implemented, organizations will start seeing the benefits of having a service catalog, because it:

- Positions overall digital forensic capabilities to be run like a business
- Provides a platform for better understanding and communicating the business need for digital forensics
- Helps to market the enterprise awareness and visibility into digital forensics as a means of building stronger business relationships

Most likely, a service catalog already exists within the organization and can be amended to include those services specific to digital forensics. If it has not been created, proper enterprise governance and oversight need to be in place to ensure resources, time, and money are not wasted in creating service catalogs that are not effective. Even though there are no predefined requirements for the specific elements that need to be included in a service catalog, the following are examples of common descriptors that should be used in any service catalog implementation:

- *Service name* should clearly illustrate, in both business and IT terminology, how the service is commonly referred to throughout the organization.
- *Service description* should be written at a very high level, with no more than 2–3 lines, in a nontechnical, business language that is simple and easy to understand.
- *Service family* is the first level of hierarchy for the service that is used to translate services into core business-driven functions, such as *business services.*
- *Service group* is the second level of hierarchy for the service that is used to expand the individual business functions contained within the *service family,* such as *compliance.*
- *Service category* is the third level of hierarchy for the service that is used to specify the individual service functions, such as *corporate investigations.*
- *Service owner* is the person within the organization who provides funding for the service, commonly assigned to the executive management person where the service is offered.
- *Key contacts* of the service are those individuals within the organization who function as the focal points for all communications involving the service, and

are responsible for understanding and supporting the level of service being delivered in line with established service level objectives (SLO).[9]
- *Service costs* provide a quantified representation of the service so the organization understands where funding is allocated across the total cost for ongoing operations of the service. Having identified all contributors to the total service cost, organizations can then implement a chargeback model for performing cost allocations based on the service costs.

At the end of this step, organizations will have answered the question of who provides their in-house digital forensic capabilities.

Maintaining a Digital Forensic Program

Building an in-house digital forensic program is a linear process whereby the many steps previously outlined are performed once. However, once all steps to build the program are completed, there is the matter of ongoing care and feeding to ensure what was built is sustained but also goes through varying levels of continuous improvement.[10]

For a digital forensic program to not just operate at its maximum capability but to also remain at the peak of its capabilities, there must be a systematic approach in place to make intelligent and informed decisions to improving the overall program.

Educational Roadmap

A common question posed to those in the digital forensic discipline is what type of knowledge and training is needed to get into the field, and, subsequently, what kind of education is needed for career advancement. The reality is that there is not one best way to gain digital forensic education, acquire new skills, or keep current on those skills they already have.

Instead of setting out a professional-development plan that digital forensic practitioners should follow, a better strategy is to illustrate the building blocks needed for different types and levels of education a person can gain. Refer to Chapter 3 titled *"Education, Training, and Awareness"* for discussions on the knowledge and experience required in accordance with the scientific principles, methodologies, and techniques of the digital forensic profession.

Forensic Toolkit Maintenance

At this point, the lab environment has been built with all tools and equipment implemented to support the organization's digital forensic capabilities. Ongoing maintenance and upkeep to the lab and equipment are essential in maintaining the required standards for guaranteeing the integrity, authenticity, and legal admissibility of digital evidence. Doing so requires that routine inspections are performed to provide assurance that the lab environment continues to operate within the established level of security controls and operating standard necessary. These reviews should be performed by objective, independent parties who are not directly involved with the digital forensic team to:

- Determine if structural issues are present within the walls, doors, floor, and ceiling
- Inspect all access-control mechanisms to ensure they are not damaged and continue to function as expected
- Review physical access logs for both approved individuals and visitors
- Analyze tracking logs to identify issues with continuity and integrity of evidence

With the advancements in technology, tools, and equipment used within the portfolio of the digital forensic toolkit, these things need to be maintained to ensure they continue to operate at the required level for guaranteeing the integrity, authenticity, and legal admissibility of digital evidence. Within the scope of the ongoing maintenance and support required for the forensic toolkit component, the following activities should be performed regularly:

- Digital forensic workstations must operate at the required security baseline, including:
  - Operating system (OS) patches and updates applied frequently.
  - Security applications, such as antimalware technologies, are updated and scheduled scans of the entire system are enabled.
  - Defragmentation of file systems is executed to improve workstation performance.
    - Using verified data wiping tools to securely remove temporary and cached files or files located in slack or unallocated space.
- Digital forensic software and hardware are upgraded and patched following appropriate validation and verification processes.

Aside from the technology of maintaining the digital forensic toolkit, there is the busi ness side, which cannot be overlooked or forgotten. With all tools and equipment, whether software- or hardware-based, there is ongoing maintenance-support agreements with vendors and manufacturers to ensure that professional services are available when required. Paying the ongoing maintenance support, as a requirement for maintaining the digital forensic toolkit, ensures that organizations have access to upgrades and support resources when or if needed.

Key Performance Indicators (KPI)[11]

Once the digital forensic program is implemented and its services are being used throughout the organization, it should not be left to operate in its current state indefinitely. Relevant KPIs are cornerstones for tracking, measuring, and reporting how the digital forensic program is being delivered and help to make informed decisions about where improvements are needed.

A relevant KPI is significant and attributable to the metric it measures. However, developing relevant KPIs for the digital forensic program can be somewhat of a challenging task, because many of the metrics are focused solely on the execution and operations of the digital forensic program. When developing KPIs, the following can be used as guidelines:

1. Relate measurable metrics to the purpose and priorities.
2. Link organizational goals and objectives to the services offered.
3. They can be used to influence the organization's decision-making process relating to digital forensic capabilities.
4. The use industry best practices and benchmarks for measuring the organization's digital forensic service offerings.
5. They are meaningful and useful to the organization's digital forensic capabilities.

Every organization operates under different contexts (i.e., industry, size) and has unique requirements for implementing in-house digital forensic capabilities, and selecting the most accurate and appropriate KPIs is unique to each organization depending on their business profiles. Before measuring any KPIs, it is important to first calculate the base formulas that will be used universally to multiple KPI measurements, including:

- *Full-time equivalents (FTE)* is calculated as the total number of employees who support the organization's digital forensic investigations service.
- *Work hours (WH)* is the total number of work hours where FTE are dedicated to supporting the organization's digital forensic investigations service. WH is calculated as:

$$Work\ Hours(WH) = (t * hrs)$$

where *hrs* represents the number of hours in a workday and *t* represents the number of days in the evaluation period.

The evaluation period applied to this ratio should be dynamic to allow for measurement adjustments over different reporting periods (i.e., monthly, quarterly, yearly).

- *Overhead time (OT)* is the total number of work hours allocated to noninvestigative functions (i.e., meetings, education, support). The OT ratio is calculated as:

$$Overhead\ Time(OT) = WH - (t * hrs)$$

- *Investigative time (IT)* is the total number of work hours allocated to noninvestigative functions. The IT ratio is calculated as:

$$Investigative\ Time(IT) = WH - OT$$

After inputting the above values into the KPI, the following can be used as an example of a ratio that an organization should consider when measuring the effectiveness of their digital forensic program as it relates to the organization's continuous improvement strategies.

Resource Capacity

The traditional approach to measuring resource capacity is to define and assign tasks, including estimating work effort and availability, on an individual basis. However, modern approaches on resource-capacity management, such as with the Agile perspective, are oriented toward the team as a collective rather than as an individual. This current approach assumes that the different type of work requires different skills and, through the combined experiences and skills of the collective team, the work required to support the organization's digital forensic program can be achieved more effectively than through individual efforts.

Therefore, calculating the *resource capacity* (RC) ratio will be done for the entire team rather than on an individual basis. The RC ratio should include the following factors in its measurement:

- The number of workdays in the period (t)
- The number of team members(FTE)
- The total noninvestigative work hours (OT)
- Planned time off for each team member
- The total investigative work hours, represented as (IT)

The approach to calculating the *RC* ratio is:

1. Multiply the number of workdays(t) in the time by the number of hours per day(hrs). Let's assume a one-week period with five working days and eight hours per day:

$$Work\ Hours\ (WH) = (t * hrs)$$
$$WH = (5 * 8)$$
$$WH = 40$$

2. Subtract the total time allocated for noninvestigative activities and tasks to determine the availability for investigative activities and tasks. Let's assume that collectively the team spends one day per week in meetings:

$$Overhead\ Time\ (OT) = WH - (t * hrs)$$
$$OT = 40 - (4 * 8)$$
$$OT = 40 - 32$$
$$OT = 8$$
$$Investigative\ Time\ (IT) = WH - OT$$
$$IT = 40 - 8$$
$$IT = 32$$

3. To calculate the RC ratio, use three subroutine calculations:
   a. Subtract availability and time off for each team member, then multiple the result by availability to get individual capacity.
   b. Add the individual team member capacities to get the entire team capacity in work hours and divide by eight, the assumed work hours per day value, to get the team's capacity in workdays.
   c. Divide the team's work hour capacity by the total workhours to get the team resources value.

Outlined in Table 6.4 below, the total work hours for team members has been added to the sum of 124.16 work hours, or 15.5 workdays, for the team collectively.

Table 6.4 Resource Availability and Time Off

Team Member			% Availability	Hours Off	Hours
Individual 01			25%		8.00
Individual 02			38%		12.16
Individual 03			75%		24.00
Individual 04			75%		24.00
Individual 05			75%		24.00
Individual 06			50%	16.00	8.00
Individual 07			75%		24.00
Team Member Days Available	15.5	**Team Resources**	3.10	**Team Hours**	124.16

Challenges and Strategies

Implementing a digital forensic program into an enterprise environment comes with challenges. There is no prescriptive way that outlines exactly how enterprise digital forensic programs must be implemented, because every organization is unique and has its own requirements for digital forensic capabilities. Below are questions organizations need to answer before they can successfully implement their digital forensic program.

Team Placement

There is no right answer for where within any or every enterprise an in-house digital forensic service should hierarchically report under. In some instances, for example, digital forensics could report in the information technology (IT), information security (IS), risk management, legal, or even compliance divisions. Going a step further, there is a question of whether digital forensic capabilities should be centralized to a single department or should it be distributed among different regions and business lines.

The placement of digital forensics in the enterprise goes back to the size and the business-risk scenarios outlined previously. Small- and medium-sized business (SMB) environments might decide to centralize their digital forensic capabilities, given that their operations are limited in size and geographic diversity. However, large organizations may decide that it is more effective to have multiple teams in respective department to facilitate a specific business risk, such as to support the legal team with electronic discovery (eDiscovery) collections or within the incident response (IR) team to facilitate incident recovery tasks.

With a distributed approach, there will be varying degrees of responsibilities and involvement of a digital forensic practitioner depending on the scope of their role, such as leader, consultant, or advisor. While the team and functions have been decentralized, it is important that the organization establish a direct-reporting relationship for the team into a common department where digital forensic governance, management, and strategies are defined and are communicated outward. This approach will ensure that even though the organization has distributed its capabilities, all teams will follow consistent principles, methodologies, and techniques when supporting digital forensics capabilities throughout the enterprise.

Industry Regulation

Different laws, standards, and regulations govern the operations of organizations conducting business in different industries. Depending on the regulations applicable to the organization's business, there might be a requirement to have specific digital forensic capabilities support throughout the enterprise. Refer to Chapter 4 titled *"Laws, Standards, and Regulations"* for further discussion on laws, standards, and regulations.

For example, regulatory development such as the Sarbanes-Oxley (SOX) Act of 2002 requires organizations to develop and implement a series of plans and processes that specifically address how the organization handles fraud incidents using digital forensics. Additionally, the Payment Card Industry (PCI) – Data Security Standards (PCI-DSS) has established the PCI Forensic Investigator (PFI) certification that identify organizations or other entities who are complying with all regulatory requirements for conducting investigations relating to the compromise of cardholder data.

The regulations applicable to any specific organization are subjective to their industry and must be known to ensure that digital forensic capabilities can be adapted accordingly. As outlined in the beginning of this chapter, regulatory compliance is not one-size-fits-all. As a business risk scenario supported by digital forensics, demonstrating compliance with regulatory requirements requires the production of factual evidence documenting that standards have been met.

Political Influences

Political jurisdictions can vary between countries and region around the world. Generally, the laws established through these countries and regions where created to bridge the gap between risk (i.e. criminal activity) and technology (i.e. fruit or tool) within the scope of the jurisdictions perspective on digital crime and subsequent access, transmission, and storage of ESI as digital evidence.

Where organizations have a presence in multiple countries and regions, their investigations are increasingly becoming international in nature. Where digital evidence needs to be gathered and processed from multiple countries and regions, a decision must be made as to how respective data-protection laws allow for these activities to occur. For example, the European Union Data Protection Directive 95/46/EC outlines the requirements to protect individuals with regards to the processing of personal data specific to data transmission across borders.

Most often, organizations who leave these political considerations until it is too late find themselves in a situation where quick decisions are made resulting in laws being circumvented or disregarded. However, political influences do not have to impede the organization's ability to conduct international investigations if the right approach is taken and many of the political considerations are addressed early on when establishing the governance framework.

Summary

Enabling digital forensics in an enterprise environment requires a systematic approach that is designed to answer "who, where, what, when, why, and how" in-house digital forensic capabilities will be successfully implemented and continuously improved. While the technical execution of digital forensics within an enterprise environment carries much of the same resemblances to other organizations and agencies, the purpose and roles it serves are unique. Before digital forensics can be readily enabled in an enterprise environment, it is important to understand the role and function it serves to the organizations business.

Resources

21 Popular Computer Forensics Tools, InfoSec Institute. http://resources.infosecinstitute.com/computer-forensics-tools/.

Digital Forensic Tools and Equipment Tools, ForensicsWiki. http://www.forensicswiki.org/wiki/Tools.

Forensic Hardware, Digital Intelligence. https://www.digitalintelligence.com/cart/ComputerForensicsProducts/Forensic-Workstations-p1.html.

Forensic Workstations, Forensic Computers. http://www.forensiccomputers.com/workstations/forensic-workstations.html.

Free Computer Forensic Tools, Forensic Control. https://forensiccontrol.com/resources/free-software/.

List of Digital Forensics Tools, Wikipedia. http://en.wikipedia.org/wiki/List_of_digital_forensics_tools.

OpenSource Tools, Digital Forensic Association. http://www.digitalforensicsassociation.org/opensource-tools/.

Talino Forensic Workstation, InSig2. http://www.insig2.eu/talino-forensic-workstation-31.

Glossary

1. **Electronically stored information (ESI)** is information created, manipulated, communicated, stored, and best utilized in digital form, requiring the use of computer hardware and software.
2. **Return on investment (ROI)** is the benefit to the investor resulting from an investment of some resource.
3. **Repeatable** refers to obtaining the same results when using the same method on identical test items in the same laboratory by the same operator using the same equipment within short intervals of time.
4. **Reproducible** refers to obtaining the same results being obtained when using the same method on identical test items in different laboratories with different operators utilizing different equipment.
5. **Runbooks,** both electronic and physical, are a compilation of routine procedures and operations used as a reference.
6. **Proof of concept (POC)** is a process by which a certain concept, theory, method, or idea has its feasibility demonstrated or its principle proven.
7. **Forensically sound** qualifies and, in some cases, justifies the use of a particular forensic technology or methodology.

8. **Commercial off-the-shelf (COTS)** describes items that are available for purchase through the commercial marketplace, including, but not limited to, software or hardware products, installation services, and training services.
9. **Service level objectives (SLO)** are specific quantitative characteristics used to measure service delivery in terms of availability, throughput, frequency, response time, or quality.
10. **Continuous improvement** is a condition by which any subject matter can achieve and sustain success.
11. **Key Performance Indicator (KPI)** is a quantifiable measurement used to evaluate the success in meeting objectives for performance.

Chapter 7

Controlling Mobile Devices

Due to significant technology advancements made over the past decades, business has transformed into a much more dynamic and mobile workforce. Since its inception, the world of mobile technologies has evolved quickly where new devices, operating systems, and threats are emerging every day. Within the context of an organization's digital forensics capabilities, mobile devices present a unique challenge because of how quickly these technologies are changing and the shifting of traditional digital forensic concepts, such as establishing a perimeter around systems and data. This leads to the inherent challenge of maintaining best practices for mobile device usage while continuing to enable digital forensic capabilities.

Brief History of Mobile Devices

Mobile devices were introduced in the early 1970s when the world's first mobile phone, a Motorola, allowed for thirty minutes of talk time and took around ten hours to charge. Given the times, these mobile phones only provided simple telephony features and did not support the multipurpose smartphone device features currently available in today's market.

In 1983 the first commercial mobile phone was released, but these phones were not necessarily designed with end users in mind because the primary audience was organizations who could afford them. Beginning in the 1990s, the design and portability of mobile phones drew the attention of direct consumers, and, by the late 1990s, these devices became commonplace. Yet, mobile phones were still limited to simple telephony features and did not offer much to the digital forensic community in terms of gathering or processing digital evidence. Early efforts to examine mobile devices involved analyzing content directly via the display screen and photographing important content found there.

In 1999 the first Blackberry handset was released, providing consumers with more features than simple telephony, such as email and messaging. This device was a major technology breakthrough that laid the foundation for many other mobile devices through the early 2000s. Now, not only could these mobile devices be used to make telephone calls, but they could contain email, web browsing information, location data, contacts, and text messaging records. It was during this time that organizations started paying attention to the mobile device market and started leveraging these technologies to give their employees the flexibility to shift between personal and work use from anywhere at any time.

With mobile devices crossing between business and personal use, smartphones were used as part of criminal activities, and the digital forensic community recognized the potential for digital evidence to exist in these technologies. However, as the number of mobile devices increased, it was quickly discovered that gathering and processing digital evidence from these devices could not be met using existing methodologies and techniques. At first, like the early days of computer forensics, digital forensic practitioners used the common system administration tools, such as synchronization tools, to gather and process electronically stored information (ESI).[1] Following suit with computer forensics, commercial solutions started emerging, which allowed digital forensic practitioners to consistently apply the same methodologies and techniques toward gathering and processing digital evidence from mobile devices.

A major step forward came in 2007 when the Apple iPhone was released, which proved to be a momentous evolution in changing the face of the mobile device marketplace forever. Not only did this device provide consumers with smartphone features, but the expanded capability to install and use application of all sorts meant that ESI could exist beyond the commonly known cellphone evidence sources, such as phone logs, email messages, and instant messaging records. When organizations came to the realization that their data was being accessed and stored on mobile devices they had little to no control of, this is when manufacturers and vendors capitalized on the opportunity and a mobile device management (MDM) solution was brought to market.

Since the revolution of 2007, other manufacturers have released their own version of mobile devices that also provided organizations with the challenges of controlling how, when, why, with whom, and under what circumstance their data can—and cannot—be used on mobile devices.

Persistent Threats and Challenges

In today's world of technology, mobile devices (including smartphones and tablets) make up much of the marketplace. When these mobile devices are intended for business use, whether they are personally or corporate owned, organizations need to adopt a series of best practices to secure its people, systems, and data.

Before mobile devices, organizations applied traditional information security best practices and methodologies by defining their network perimeter and then designing their intranets and systems accordingly. Today, however, organizations must accept the reality that it is now common for mobile devices to allow multiple simultaneous connections to different types of networks, hence eroding the logical network perimeter and introducing a certain unknown hostility that was previously controlled and managed.

At the same time, mobile devices have allowed for business to transform into a much more mobile and dynamic workplace where employees can work anywhere at any time. However, with a mobile workforce, it is quite common that mobile devices, both personal and corporate owned, are being used to conduct business transactions and store corporate data. Staying ahead of the curve in an ever-evolving landscape, the digital forensic community is constantly faced with challenges of gathering and processing evidence from all sorts of changing technology.

Loss

Mobile devices, for the most part, are small compared to traditional computer systems making them more prone to being lost. The probability of this happening is good given how easily it is for these small devices to accidentally slide out of a pocket or unintentionally be left somewhere.

When this happens, these devices are like landmines until they have been properly wiped or deactivated to mitigate the opportunity for other persons to access applications and data on the device. Most manufacturers and vendors provide capabilities to locate and deactivate their mobile devices; but this is essentially a race to the finish line in terms of who gets access to the device first. Within an enterprise environment, there are third-party solutions available that allow for remote management of mobile devices discussed later in this chapter.

Theft

Mobile devices have significant appeal because of their popularity among consumers and the potential resale value they have. Understandably, there are dishonest and immoral people who would not think twice about getting their hands on your device and using it to commit crimes if you turn your head for a minute or happen to misplace it.

Smartphones are like landmines in the hands of the wrong person(s), and it is a race to have the device wiped or deactivated to mitigate the potential for unauthorized access to the device and its content. As stated previously, most manufacturers and vendors provide capabilities to locate and deactivate their mobile devices, and there are third-party solutions available to organizations.

Replacement

Mobile devices are periodically upgraded because newer technologies are released with new features and capabilities, which comes with a certain appeal. When this happens, there can be times when standard operating procedures (SOP) are not followed, resulting in the old mobile devices not being wiped or deactivated. Much like being lost or stolen, until the potential for unauthorized access to the organization's data and applications on the device has been mitigated, old smartphones in the wrong hands can lead to data loss or exposure.

Local Storage

Some time ago, technology advancements saw an explosion in storage capacity for traditional computer systems, something which has naturally progressed into mobile devices. The expanded storage on these devices presents a growing possibility for confidential or sensitive data to be persistent beyond the control an organization commonly employs. An organization's capability to manage their data when a device is in use,[2] in transit,[3] or at rest[4] is essential to mitigate data loss or exposure when these devices have been lost, stolen, or are replaced.

Cloud Storage

As quickly as technology advances, there is a limit to which local storage capacity is available within mobile devices. Alternatively, manufacturers and vendors have turned to cloud computing as a means of storing data because of the ways in which cloud environments can quickly increase and accommodate growing volumes of information. Unsurprisingly, this creates increased concerns about data security when it is beyond the scope of an organization's control.

Encryption

When it comes to mobile devices, perhaps the biggest wish of any digital forensic practitioner is that they encounter devices with no passcodes.[5] However, following the National Security Agency (NSA) breach in 2013, mobile device manufacturers and vendors implemented stronger and more stringent encryption standards that rendered most passcode bypass techniques obsolete, and the use of digital forensic technologies to gather and process digital evidence more difficult.

Within an enterprise environment, there are third-party solutions available that allow for remote management of mobile devices, as discussed later in this chapter. These solutions allow organizations to remotely reset the device passcode to allow digital forensic practitioner access to gather and process digital evidence. However, it is important to note that by performing a remote passcode change, potential evidence on the mobile device could be modified, deleted, or lost, and a remote passcode change should be done with caution and performed only by knowledgeable individuals with direct supervision of a digital forensic practitioner.

Burner Phones

The term *burner* refers to a cheap mobile device that is used for a short time, or for a specific purpose, then disposed of. For the most part, the data ports on these devices are disabled, and they do not come with application programming interface (API)[6] support, both of which are required to gather and process digital evidence.

Burner phones extremely troublesome for the digital forensic community because there is almost no potential for accessing the content on these devices. The only option that exists is using advanced techniques, such as:

- *Joint Test Action Group (JTAG) analysis* is the common name given to the technique of connecting to the standard test access port (TAP) on a mobile device and instructing the processor to transfer raw data. Using this technique requires both a high level of knowledge and training as well as specialized equipment, which makes it somewhat of a difficult and time-consuming technique to gather and process digital evidence from mobile devices. This technique was later standardized as the Institute of Electrical and Electronics Engineers (IEEE) 1149.1 Standard Test Access Port and Boundary-Scan Architecture.
- *Chip-off analysis* involves physically removing the flash memory chip(s) from a mobile device and gathering raw data using specialized equipment. While this technique allows digital forensic practitioners to gather a complete physical image of a mobile device, it is destructive and can render the device inoperable. Much like the JTAG technique above, chip-off analysis also requires a high level of knowledge and training, which also makes it a difficult and time-consuming technique.

Refer to Chapter 10 titled *"Digital Evidence Management"* for further discussion about data-centric security.

Refer to Chapter 8 titled *"Cloud Computing Enablement"* for further details about enabling digital forensic capabilities within cloud computing environments.

Mobile Device Governance

Implementing technology to secure mobile devices, as a precursor to enabling digital forensic capabilities, is only one piece of an organization's broader strategy to governing use of these technologies. Before digital forensic capabilities can be realized, there needs to be approved documentation that establishes the requirements for using mobile devices to securely access corporate networks and data, as well as what is considered acceptable and unacceptable conduct. Combined with the documentation created as through the organization's overall enterprise governance framework, standard operating procedures (SOP) are fundamental for performing digital forensics on mobile devices.

Within the enterprise governance framework, there needs to be a series of documents that specifically address mobile device use and access with respect to the organization's networks, systems, and data. These documents provide the organization with a foundation for planning the eventual implementation of mobile device management capabilities and guidelines for user behavior and conduct, as well as serving as a driver for enabling digital forensic capabilities.

Detailed discussion about digital forensics processes, procedures, and how an organization's Enterprise Governance Framework complements digital forensics, can be found in Chapter 6 titled *"The Business of Digital Forensics."*

Business Code of Conduct Policy

As discussed in Chapter 6 titled *"The Business of Digital Forensics,"* policies are the highest level of governance documents that establish formalized blueprints to address specific topics or subject areas. When it comes to mobile devices, while they can be owned personally or by the corporation, the reality is that they are being used to conduct business on behalf of the organization, and there is an expectation in terms of how employees conduct themselves when using the devices.

The first document to be created does not direct fall within the scope of mobile devices but has significant influence on how they are drafted. A code of conduct is a management tool for setting out an organization's values, responsibilities, and ethical obligations. This governance document provides the organization with guidance for handling difficult situations relating to unacceptable business conduct. To be truly effective, the code of conduct needs to be embedded throughout the organization, so employees know how it applies to them.

(Un)Acceptable Activity

As part of the code of conduct, organizations need to define what they deem as acceptable and unacceptable conduct within their business environment. Communicating these expectations needs to be done in clear and concise language, so that there is no opportunity for confusion or perceived gray areas that allow unacceptable conduct to persist.

Acceptable conduct is any action, behavior, or communication that is within the defined boundaries as outlined in the governance documentation. As an example, the use of corporately owned and managed encryption solutions for the transmission of customer information is considered within the boundaries of acceptable activity.

Alternatively, unacceptable conduct is any action, behavior, or communication that is explicitly prohibited because it falls outside the defined boundaries as outlined in the governance documentation. Using personal email accounts to conduct business transactions where confidential or sensitive data is being transmitted is an example.

Acceptable Use Policy (AUP)

As mobile devices continue to become more prominent as the technology of choice for an ever-growing mobile workforce, it is authorized (and unauthorized) use to conduct business continues to expand. Following the same approach of establishing governance for compliance purposes, best practices call for the same establishment and enforcement of formalized policies to minimize business risk and maximize compliance.

Not considering size, geographic location, or industry, all organizations need to enforce an acceptable use policy (AUP) that governs the use of mobile devices to conduct business on their behalf. Regardless of whether a mobile device is personally or corporate owned, it is being used to access and store the organization's data, and, as such, must comply with the requirements set forth in the AUP.

If there are no rules in place, employees will not have a clear understanding of what the organization deems acceptable, which could result in activities such as transmitting confidential customer data that violates specific laws or regulations. Given the potential risk that exists for both acceptable and unacceptable use of mobile devices, it is essential that organizations formally establish and enforce an AUP that defines how, when, why, with whom, and under what circumstance employees can—and cannot—use mobile devices for business purposes.

User Acknowledgment and Agreement

As a supplement to the AUP and as part of the onboarding process before employees are permitted to use mobile devices for business purposes, a user acknowledgment and agreement must be signed by all employees using mobile devices for business purposes.

The purpose of such documents is to set forth the terms and conditions by which organizations make available to their employees information technology (IT) resources that have been deemed authorized. These IT resources may include software, networks, email services, and data storage capabilities accessible using mobile devices that have met the required security and configuration standards. It is important that employees understand that their use of mobile devices for business purposes is a privilege, not a right, and that their signing of a user acknowledgement and agreement makes them responsible for their actions. The following are examples of terms and conditions found in these agreements:

- Abide by all organizational policies, standards, and guidelines relating to IT
- Agree to have mobile device security and configurations settings pushed to this mobile device(s)

- Make appropriate backups of personal information to mitigate loss of information should the device be lost, stolen, or replaced
- Do not make backups of any data belonging to the organization onto any storage medium that has not been authorized for use
- Allow the organization to wipe the device at their discretion for the purposes of securing data belonging to the organization
- Report a lost or stolen device immediately to the organization's IT support helpdesk

Also, it must be clearly defined that failure for employees to follow these terms and conditions will be handled with a disciplinary action, such as:

- Suspension, blocking, or restriction of access to the organization's IT resources
- Financial liability for costs incurred due to data breach, loss, or illegal disclosure

Enterprise Management Strategies

Even if a mobile device is personally owned, the organization's data is still being accessed and potentially stored on it. The reality is that many organizations still struggle to define how, when, why, with whom, and under what circumstance mobile devices access their data. Also, there are some organizations who are not adequately equipped to ensure that, when an incident happens, they have the capabilities to gather and process digital evidence.

Organizations providing their employees with the flexibility of conducting business using mobile devices must have strategies in place to manage the expectations of the employees in terms of usage, not only the device and business content. Developing and implementing a mobile device management strategy is a separate topic that requires organizations to have a strong understanding of the administrative, technical, and physical requirements that make it successful. The intention of this section is not to provide readers with a comprehensive guide that they can take away and implement a mobile device management strategy; rather this chapter is designed to provide readers with the components of mobile device management that should be known to digital forensic practitioners.

At the end of this chapter, Resources have been provided for readers who are interested in learning more about mobile device management strategies.

Security and Configuration Standards

As discussed in Chapter 6 titled "*The Business of Digital Forensics,*" standards are used as the drivers for policies by defining a baseline by which it is necessary to meet applicable policy requirements. When it comes to mobile devices, these standards can be used to establish a minimum level of configuration or specification that must be met to meet the boundaries of acceptable action, behavior, and communication when using mobile devices.

Illustrated in Table 7.1, examples of recommended safeguards and controls for mobile devices, both personally and corporate owned, that can help organizations establish a baseline of security and configuration standards.

Table 7.1 Safeguards and Controls for Mobile Devices

Required Controls (Minimum Level)	Recommended Controls
Mobile Device Management (MDM) Third-party solutions that enforce configuration and security policies. Refer to the following section for additional information.	**Mobile Application Management (MAM)** Third-party solutions that control the installation and execution of applications. Refer to the following section for additional information.
Encryption Implemented to maintain confidentiality of data at rest, in transit, and in use. Commonly enforced through third-party MDM solutions.	**Data Loss Prevention (DLP)** Monitors, filters, and protects the loss or exposure of data at rest, in transit, and in use. Availability of these solutions are dependent on supported capabilities on different types of devices.
Virtual Private Networking (VPN) Establish secure communication channels for transmitting data. This is commonly applied on an application-by-application basis through third-party MDM solutions.	**Network Access Control (NAC)** Permits only trusted and authorized device to gain access to networks, systems, applications, and data. Availability of these solutions are dependent on supported capabilities on different types of devices.
Authentication Enforcement of acceptable passcodes to mitigate unauthorized access. This is commonly enforced through third-party MDM solutions.	**Multi-Factor Authentication (MFA)** Use of two or more types of authentication mechanisms (i.e., passcode, biometric, token) to access devices.
Anti-Malware Restrict known malicious applications from being installed or executed. Availability of these solutions are dependent on supported capabilities on different types of devices.	**Application Whitelisting** Permit known trusted and authorized applications to be installed or executed. Some mobile device manufacturers and vendor natively provide this capability. Otherwise, availability of these solutions is dependent on supported capabilities on different types of devices.

(Continued)

Table 7.1 Safeguards and Controls for Mobile Devices (*Continued*)

Required Controls (Minimum Level)	Recommended Controls
Remote Wipe Permits remote wiping or resetting of devices to mitigate data loss or exposure if the device has been lost, stolen, or replaced. Commonly enforced through third-party MDM solutions.	**Compliance Monitoring** Supervising usage trends, device configurations, and the user's overall compliance with the organization's governance framework. This information can be used to facilitate investigative capabilities. Refer to the following section for additional information.
Audit Logs Provides information to facilitate investigative capabilities. Refer to the following section for additional information.	**Web Browsing** Filtering Internet browsing activity through dynamic content analysis. Use of a proxy server is commonly enforced through third-party MDM solutions.

Device Management Methodologies

Technology has become so engrained in both our personal lives and business environments that organizations have started to take the desires of their employees into account when deciding how to handle provisioning of mobile devices.

Generally, there are four main approaches when it comes to organizations deciding to what level of freedom their employees can have when using mobile devices for business purposes: corporate-owned business only (COBO), corporate-owned personally enabled (COPE), bring your own device (BYOD), and choose your own device (CYOD). However, each of these deployment models comes with its own benefits and drawbacks with respect to enabling digital forensic capabilities.

Corporate-Owned Business Only (COBO)

One of the traditional method of mobile device deployment, COBO is where organizations choose and pay for the device then apply their most restrictive security policies. Essentially, mobile devices provisioned following COBO are limited to business use only and do not permit any personal use. To the digital forensic community, COBO is the preferred model because it eliminates the potential for interactions between personal and business activities, thus, reducing the scope of digital evidence to sources under control by the organization.

Corporate-Owned Personally Enabled (COPE)

With COPE, employees are still supplied with a mobile device, chosen and paid for by the organization, but can use these devices for personal activities. Under this model, organizations control how much freedom employees have in terms of what actions, behaviors, and communications they can perform. With COPE, this means digital forensic practitioners have a broader scope of potential digital evidence at their disposal—in comparison to COBO—as well as increased concerns over privacy over what visibility they have into the employee's personally enabled components.

Bring Your Own Device (BYOD)

Under the BYOD model, employees are granted full responsibility for choosing and supporting the mobile device they use, because it is their personal device. While this model is most popular among small-medium businesses, largely because of the cost savings that it comes with, more enterprising environments are exploring it as an option because it reduces the technology overhead and expenditures associated with lost, stolen, or replaced devices. Even though BYOD is considered a way of pleasing employees, because they get to use their device of choice, it can become a disaster because of the extent to which there is no control over security, reliability, or compatibility with the organization. In terms of digital forensics, BYOD further complicates gathering and processing potential digital evidence because the organization does not own the device and is not legally entitled to seize it—without the involvement of law enforcement—to facilitate investigations.

Choose Your Own Device (CYOD)

CYOD provides organizations with a solution in terms of getting the best of both COPE and BYOD. With this model, employees are offered a suite of technology choices but the organization retains control over security, reliability, and durability. This means that organizations maintain a list of preapproved mobile devices and do not have to deal with the variability, yet allow employees to have some degree of flexibility and privacy. For digital forensic practitioners, depending on the restrictions enforced by the organization, there is potential for flexibility in allowing personally enabled components to be available and potential access to a broad scope of digital evidence—along with complications over privacy.

Device Management Capabilities

Even if a mobile device is personally owned, it is still the organization's data that is being accessed and stored on it, and with that comes the need to have in place a series of controls to properly manage data access and use. Once the organization has implemented their required administrative controls, as discussed previously, resources can now be turned toward realizing these controls through appropriate technology capabilities. However, when it comes time to select the right technology solution, organizations are again faced with the questions of how, when, why, with whom, and under what circumstances do they require mobile devices to be managed.

Within the marketplace, there are a wide range of commercial off-the-shelf (COTS)[7] solutions that cater to the varying needs of mobile device management capabilities. On one side of the coin, organizations might decide to put all their eggs in one basket[8] by selecting a single COTS solution that provides multiple capabilities. In going this direction, organizations should consider:

- Common look and feel
- Higher level of integration
- Centralized management and interface exchanges
- Lower total cost of ownership[9] (TCO)
- Limited offerings of fully integrated solutions

Alternatively, a decision might be made to select the best-of-breed[10] COTS solutions to meet specific mobile device management capabilities. In deciding to go this direction with technologies, organizations should consider:

- Increased customization to fit business requirements
- Minimal compromises made on technology components
- Acquisition of solutions that are best suited to your organization
- Compatibility between different vendors can be troublesome
- Assurance of cross-vendor support for the overall system

To make an educated decision about what technical capabilities are needed to enforce the administrative governance controls, it is good to understand what the different types of mobile device management solution must offer.

Mobile Device Management (MDM)

Mobile device management (MDM), sometimes referred to as mobile security management (MSM), is a software-based solution designed to manage a mobile device, or a segregated part of it, by enforcing security and configuration policies. Generally, MDM solutions do not provide organizations with more security to mobile devices or corporate data, but the main advantage is the device-level control.

With MDM solutions, organizations can determine what amount of control they want to enforce on mobile devices, keeping in mind that control is always placed on the whole device and not against users or applications. However, where deployment models like BYOD are used, there may be instances where users are reluctant to surrender their personal devices to this level of control. The following list are categories within MDM solutions where setting and configuration policies can be applied at the mobile device level:

- *Security settings* are made to improve device-level security that help to mitigate unauthorized access (i.e., passcodes specifications).
- *Encryption settings* are made to require the use of encryption standards to mitigate exposure or loss of data when in use, in transit, or at rest.
- *Malware settings* are made to restrict known malicious applications from being installed or executed. Availability of these solutions are dependent on supported capabilities on different types of devices (i.e., Android, iOS, macOS, Windows).
- *System settings* are made to control specific features available throughout the operating system (i.e., screen capture, user account control).
- *Cloud settings* are made to restrict the use and transmission of data within a cloud computing environment.
- *Email settings* are made to control the transmission and use of email-based resources.
- *Application settings* are made to enforce the feature availability of native system applications (i.e., web browser, application store).
- *Device capability settings* are made to enforce the feature availability of device-level components (i.e., camera, Bluetooth).

It is important to note that the MDM policy categories outlined above have been provided as examples of setting and configuration groups available using third-party solutions. Also, depending on the MDM solution selected, these policy categories can vary in how they are made available for use.

Mobile Application Management (MAM)

Mobile application management (MAM) is a software-based solution designed to provide, secure, and manage the access and actions of mobile applications rather than the device. While MAM solutions can be bundled together as a complementary capability to MDM solutions, they are used where organizations are exploring a more flexible, relaxed approach to mobile device management.

With MAM solutions focused on applications, they are predominantly used to scan mobile devices and track installed applications to detect any unapproved (or unauthorized) applications, and subsequently notifying users of policy violations. Typically, an approach to mitigating installation of rogue applications is done by supplying users with a corporate application store where organizations can create, secure, and deliver approved applications that permit access into their networks and resources.

MAM solutions provide organizations with a way of getting a handle on which applications are being installed and run on the mobile devices that use and access their corporate networks and resources. However, MAM solutions do not provide the same level of security offered through MDM solutions, with which organizations can lock down or limit features/capabilities of mobile devices.

Mobile Content Management (MCM)

Mobile content management (MCM) is a software-based solution designed to securely grant and manage the use and access of data through the enforcement of multifactor authentication, authorization, and access controls, such as usernames, passcodes, internet protocol (IP) addresses, and tokens.

MCM solutions focus on securing corporate data without placing restrictions on the mobile device or applications. These solutions differ from MDM and MAM where a specific single application is delivered to mobile devices that functions as a container to securely grant and manage use and access of data. While MCM solutions are perhaps the least intrusive form of mobile device management capabilities, because they do not impose any device or application restrictions, they follow a data-centric security model that enforces high levels of protection to the organization's data.

Refer to Chapter 10 titled *"Digital Evidence Management"* for further discussion about data-centric security.

Mobile Device Process Methodology

Ever since mobile devices became commonplace, the digital forensic community has seen an increasing demand to gather and process digital evidence from these devices, which has presented numerous challenges. With the proliferation of mobile devices as technologies designed for consumers and businesses alike, the potential for digital evidence evolved leading to the formal specialization of mobile device forensics as a subdiscipline of digital forensics.

No longer do mobile devices only contain data relating to traditional telephony functions, such as contacts, call history, and text messages. The reality is that ever since these technologies became smart devices with functionality like computer systems, they have contained much more potential for digital evidence that needs to be gathered and collected during an investigation, such as photographs, calendar entries, email, and web browsing history. And, while these devices use a variety of potential evidence repositories (i.e., internal, removable, and online), it is essential that digital forensic principles and techniques are applied as a foundation toward building a consistent methodology for enabling mobile device forensics.

Gathering and processing digital evidence from mobile devices can differ depending on the manufacturer and the retail vendors/service providers. With these potential variations, it is understandable that there is not a well-established methodology by which mobile device forensics is performed. However, with the intricacy involved in performing mobile device forensics, it is necessary for organizations to implement guidelines and processes by which their digital forensic practitioner can gather and process potential digital evidence.

Illustrated in Figure 7.1, the high-level digital forensic process model, discussed previously in Chapter 2 titled *"Investigative Process Methodologies,"* will be applied to the activities and tasks involved in conducting mobile device forensics. It is important to note that while this book does cover the fundamental principles, methodologies, and techniques of digital forensics, it largely focuses on outlining how the people, processes, and technology areas are used to defend the enterprise through integrating digital forensic capabilities with key business functions. This book is not designed to provide readers with the technical knowledge about digital forensics, including the hands-on and how-to aspects of the discipline, such as how to forensically acquire technology devices.

Phase 1: Preparation

As outlined in Chapter 2 titled *"Investigative Process Methodologies,"* the activities and tasks performed in this first phase are essential in successfully executing all subsequent phases of the investigative workflow. Outside of an enterprise environment, an argument could be made that many of the investigative activities and tasks performed are done after a mobile device has been seized. This is primarily attributed to how, given the different manufacturers and vendors available in the market today, preparation involves specific research into technologies, as well as the techniques and tools required to gather and process evidence. However, within an enterprise environment, there is greater opportunity to be proactive in preparation of investigative activities and tasks because the organization has control over which types of mobile devices are approved for use within their environment.

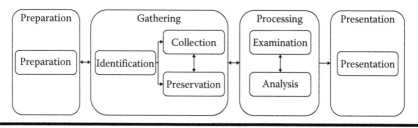

Figure 7.1　High-level digital forensic process model.

Processes and Procedures

With mobile device forensics being a subdiscipline of digital forensics, the existing baseline of standards, guidelines, and techniques discussed in Chapter 6 titled *"The Business of Digital Forensics"* become the foundation for creating new documentation specific to mobile devices.

Digital forensic standard operating procedures (SOP) still apply to mobile device forensics when gathering and processing digital evidence. However, given that mobile devices differ in that they use cellular technology, there is a need to develop specific SOPs so that digital forensic practitioners know how to handle them. These considerations to gathering and processing digital evidence from mobile devices will be discussed further in Phase 2.

Education, Training, and Awareness

Like digital forensics, an individual's role with respect to mobile forensics determines the level of knowledge they are provided. Detailed discussion about the different levels of education, training, and awareness an organization should require of their people in support of digital forensics can be found in Chapter 3 titled *"Education, Training, and Awareness."*

General Awareness

As the lowest type of education, this is a generalized level of training and awareness that is intended to provide people with foundational knowledge without getting too specialized into mobile device forensics. Leveraging the education and training that has already been put in place for digital forensics, this education provides people with the competencies they need about organizational policies, standards, and guidelines so that they indirectly contribute, through some form of behavior or action, to the organization's digital forensic program.

Examples of topics and subjects that should be included as part of a mobile device forensic awareness program include, but is not limited to, the following:

- ◼ Business code of conduct
- ◼ Mobile device acceptable use policy
- ◼ Data protection and privacy

Basic Training

Essentially, the difference between this training and the previous awareness is that the knowledge gained here is intended to teach people the skills necessary to directly support the organization's digital forensic program in terms of how, where, and to what extent mobile device are used for business purposes.

Information communicated at this level is more detailed than the previous type of education because it must provide people with the knowledge required to support a specific role or function, such as administering the MDM solution.

For example, as part of basic mobile device forensic training, information about audit logging and retention should be covered. This topic relates to recording events and preserving them, as per the organizational governance framework, to facilitate digital forensic investigations.

Formal Education

A working and practical knowledge of mobile device forensics requires people to first and foremost have the skills and competencies necessary to ensure that all digital forensic principles, methodologies, and techniques are understood. Once the fundamental knowledge is gained, practitioners can then start pursuing a specialization into mobile device forensics.

However, unlike digital forensic education programs, the availability of curriculum dedicated entirely toward mobile devices is limited. Most commonly, mobile device forensics is taught as a specific course in higher/postsecondary institutes or as a professional education module led by an industry-recognized training institute.

Refer to Appendix B: Education and Professional Certifications for a list of higher/postsecondary institutes that offer formal education programs.

Technology and Toolsets

Within the dedicated lab environment, organizations will need to acquire specific software and hardware to support their mobile device forensic capabilities. However, the extent to which an organization invests in their toolkit is subjective to their environment and the degree to which they want to gather and process digital evidence from these mobile devices.

Considerations for technologies and tools to gathering and processing digital evidence from mobile devices will be discussed in Phase 2, where it is applicable to the investigative workflow.

Phase 2: Gathering

As discussed in Chapter 2 titled *"Investigative Process Methodologies,"* the second phase of the investigative workflow consists of the activities and tasks involved in the identification, collection, and preservation of digital evidence. The same requirement for establishing the meaningfulness, relevancy, and legal admissibility of digital evidence applies for mobile devices. However, given the use of cellular hardware with this technology, there are additional activities and tasks that need to be performed.

Identification

Regardless of the evidence that has been identified, both physical and logical, digital forensic practitioners must follow consistent and repeatable processes to secure, document, and search their crime scene. Sample templates that can be used to secure, document, and search crime scenes have been provided in the Templates section of this book.

As a best practice, when an inactive mobile device is encountered at a crime scene, meaning that it is powered off, it is important that it is left powered off and seized following documented SOPs. Also, all associated cables and media must also be seized with the mobile device, such as subscriber identity module (SIM) cards and secure digital (SD) cards.

Alternatively, when encountered with a mobile device at a crime scene that is active, meaning that it is still powered on, it is important to take the necessary steps to isolate the device from other devices and technologies to mitigate the potential for digital evidence to be contaminated. As a best practice, digital forensic practitioners can use the following three basic methods for isolating mobile devices that are active:

- *Place the device in airplane mode.*[11] This method requires interaction with the mobile device's keyboard, which poses potential risk whereby if the individual is not familiar with the device, or the device has been preconfigured with a logic bomb,[12] this can result in potential contamination of loss of digital evidence. It is important to note that with some devices, enabling airplane mode does not disable all cellular communications (i.e., global positioning system [GPS] data).
- *Turn the device off.* This method may also require interaction with the mobile device's keyboard and can activate authentication mechanisms (i.e., passcodes) to gain access later. In addition to the similar risk posed to digital evidence, this method also introduces complications and delays when it comes to acquiring and processing evidence from the mobile device.
- *Keep the device on.* This method does not require interaction with the mobile device but does need to consider the need for prolonged battery life. With this method, mobile devices are placed in a Faraday bag to reduce cellular and wireless communications. It is important to note that Faraday bags do not completely eliminate the potential for cellular and wireless communications. Also, if the Faraday bag is not properly sealed, mobile devices may unknowingly be allowed to access cellular or wireless networks. Several techniques exist to support this method and can be found in the Resource section at the end of this chapter.

Collection and Preservation

Where activities and tasks differ is when it comes time to collection and preservation of digital evidence from a mobile device. Similar traditional computer systems, the order of volatility, as discussed in Chapter 2 titled *"Investigative Process Methodologies,"* applies to mobile devices because they also contain both volatile and nonvolatile data. Therefore, it is important that gathering volatile evidence from mobile devices follows the same methodology as traditional computer systems.

Memory configurations for mobile devices has evolved significantly over time where, within today's smartphones, there can be three different types of memory storage used:

- *NAND* flash memory is nonvolatile and offers higher storage capacity, but is less stable and only allows for sequential access to data. Types of data located in NAND memory include, but are not limited to:
  - PIM data
  - Multimedia (video, audio, images)
    - User files
- *NOR* flash memory is nonvolatile and has faster read times, but slower write times than NAND, that is nearly immune to data corruption. Types of data located in NOR memory include, but are not limited to:
  - Operating system (OS) code
  - Kernel and device drivers
  - OS and user application execution instructions
- *Random access memory (RAM)* is volatile and typically used to temporarily store program execution data. Types of data located in RAM include, but are not limited to:
  - OS and user credentials (username and passcodes)
  - OS and application configuration files

Where possible, mobile devices that support data-at-rest[4] encryption capabilities should be triaged at the crime scene, as volatile data may no longer exist if the screen is locked or power is lost. Depending on the context of the investigation, it may be required to conduct an on-site triage to collect and preserve volatile data. When determining whether to conduct on-site triage, organizations should consider the following benefits to the overall investigation:

- Work being performed in a digital forensic lab may be reduced because potential evidence sources can be ruled out beforehand
- Investigative activities and tasks can be focused or prioritized based on the immediate results of findings
- Existing resources, including people and technologies, can be enhanced by intelligence gained from the results
- Use of triage tools are typically designed to require less knowledge and experience as compared to in-depth analysis tools
- Triage tools typically are more affordable as compared to in-depth analysis tools

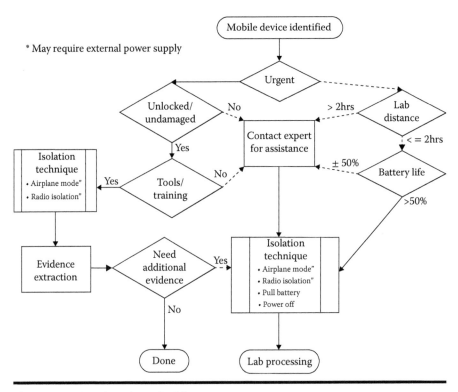

Figure 7.2   On-site triage decision tree.

As a best practice, organizations should develop a scoring mechanism that can be used to decide whether on-site triage is required. Illustrated in Figure 7.2 is a decision tree that can be used by organizations as a guide when deciding whether on-site triage is required. The following list describes the decision points contained within the decision tree:

- *Urgent*: Do the circumstances warrant on-site triage and extraction of evidence?
- *Unlocked or undamaged*: Is the device in an unlocked and functional state for evidence to be extracted?
- *Battery life*: Does the device show more than 50% battery life remaining?
- *Lab distance*: Can the device be transported to the forensic lab in less than two hours?
- *Tools*: Does the forensic toolkit support on-site triage and extraction of evidence?
- *Training*: Are trained individuals available to conduct on-site triage and extraction of evidence?
- *Need additional evidence*: After on-site triage is completed and assessed, is additional evidence required?

Where the path taken through the decision tree results in on-site triage, forensic acquisition of the mobile device is the most common technique performed. Performing an acquisition during on-site triage does have advantages, including avoiding the potential loss of volatile data. However, unlike a lab environment, performing acquisitions during on-site triage may be challenging to find a controlled environment by which the work can be completed. Tools used to perform forensic acquisitions of mobile devices will be discussed in Phase 3 of the investigative workflow.

Phase 3: Processing

Within this third phase, activities performed include the examination and analysis of evidence for relevancy. Throughout this phase, maintaining the authenticity and integrity of evidence is essential to guaranteeing a forensically sound and legally admissible investigation. For the most part, tools and equipment used to support this phase of the investigative workflow provide automated capabilities to validate and verify the one-way cryptographic hash algorithm created when the digital evidence was seized, allowing practitioners to prove beyond doubt that their interactions did not impact the integrity and authenticity of evidence.

The selection of an appropriate tool for examining and analyzing mobile devices depends on several factors: the goal(s) of the investigation, the type of mobile device in question, and resource knowledge and availability. Ultimately, there is no single tool available to retrieve all data from every make and model of mobile device because of the difference in the way digital evidence needs to be extracted from each technology. The following set of criteria can be used as guidance when deciding which tool is best suited:

- *Usability*: the presentation of data in a format that is easy for users to navigate and understand
- *Comprehensive*: the presentation of all available data, so factual conclusions can be drawn
- *Deterministic*: the output of data from the tool is reproducible when provided identical instructions and input data
- *Accuracy*: the quality of outputted data from the tool has been verified
- *Verifiable*: ensuring the accuracy of outputted data through presentation of results
- *Tested*: determination if data contained within mobile devices remains authentic and is accurately reported by the tool

Leveraging the above criteria to identify tools, consideration now needs to be given to the potential digital evidence sources that exist within mobile devices. The data present on any mobile device depends not only its features and capabilities, but also on the cellular (voice and data) services used by the device. Primarily, evidence sources from mobile devices are extracted from: contact data, call data, text messaging, multimedia, application-related logs, and OS information. The following list are examples of other data sources where digital evidence can be extracted from mobile devices:

- SIM data objects:
  - Service provider name (SPN)
  - Integrated circuit card identifier (ICCID)
  - Location information (LOCI)
  - Short message service (SMS)
  - General packet radio service (GPRS)
- Internal memory data objects:
  - International mobile equipment identifier (IMEI)
  - Personal information management (PIM) data (i.e., address book, calendar entries, to-do list, memos)
  - Call logs
  - SMS text messages
- Electronic mail
- Web browsing information
- Unstructured documents (i.e., word processing)
- Multimedia content (i.e., photographs, videos, graphics)

It is important to remember that with every mobile device there are different features, capabilities, applications, etc., available, which determine the potential of digital evidence existing. Having completed preliminary work to prepare for mobile device examination, consideration should be given to prioritize the order in which tools will be used to process digital evidence. In doing so, digital forensic practitioners will benefit by applying a consistent and repeatable methodology to their investigative techniques.

Phase 4: Presentation

As discussed in Chapter 2 titled *"Investigative Process Methodologies,"* documentation is a critical element of every investigation that needs to start at the beginning of an investigation and be carried on to the end. In this last phase of the investigative workflow, the final investigative report will be created to communicate factual conclusions by demonstrating the processes, techniques, tools, equipment, and interactions used to maintain the authenticity, reliability, and trustworthiness of digital evidence. Some things to consider when writing a final investigative report include:

- Structure and layout should flow naturally and logically.
- Content should be clear and concise to accurately demonstrate a chronology of events.

- Use of jargon, slang, and technical terminology should be avoided, and, where used, a glossary should be included to define terms in a natural language.
- Where acronyms and abbreviations are used, they must be written out in full on the first use.
- Because final reports are written after the fact, being after an investigation, content should be communicated in the past tense, but content can change tense where conclusions or recommendations are being made.
- Format the final report not only for distribution within the organization, but also with the mindset that it may be used as testimony in a court of law.

A template for creating written formal reports has been provided as a reference in the Templates section of this book.

Legal Considerations

Establishing a clear and detailed governance framework of policies, standards, and other materials, in writing, is the best approach in making certain that the organization is abiding by applicable laws and regulations when it comes to controlling, monitoring, and accessing mobile devices. With this governance in place, it is equally important that employees have read and fully understand what is expected of them when it comes to use of mobile devices to access the organization's information. Achieving both items helps protect organizations from lawsuits when disputes arise.

However, in some jurisdictions and industries, there are laws and regulations that govern which types of personal information can be read and accessed on mobile devices. Although these laws and regulations address the matter of what access and control organizations must impose to protect their confidential and sensitive information, these laws and regulations do not address what access and control organizations should not have. This can be viewed as somewhat of a gray area in the sense that there is no definitive governance framework in place, and it is usually based on the determination of what is believed to be reasonable.

When implementing a mobile device management strategy that involves mobile devices owned and managed by the organizations (i.e., COBO, COPE, CYOD), the potential gray area is limited because the employer and employees both have a clear understanding of the ownership and business/personal use rights. However, when mobile devices are owned by the employee (i.e., BYOD) yet managed by the organization, the potential gray area increases due to differing interpretations of what is considered reasonable in terms of personal privacy. Understandably, BYOD is becoming a top strategy of many organizations because of the financial and operational benefits it provides. However, BYOD gets complicated when digital evidence from a mobile device (belonging to the employee) needs to be gathered and processed for an investigation. Generally, the organization does not legally own the mobile device and can't seize it as they would for any other technology considered their property (i.e., laptop, desktop). In this case, the organization must request permission to access any information that falls outside of the scope of business-enabled data, which in some instances could require the involvement of law enforcement.

Establishing a governance framework that contains clear and concise language that is easy to understand and readily accessible to all parties (employer and employees) is extremely important. Not only does this help organizations secure and manage their data regardless of the selected mobile device management strategy, it also guarantees the employees consent and cooperation when an incident involving their personal technologies occurs.

Further discussion about laws, standards, and regulations can be referenced in Chapter 4 titled *"Laws, Standards, and Regulations."*

Summary

Mobile devices became commonplace in the late-1990s, leading to their proliferation as technologies that coexist within both our personal and business lives. As business continues to transform into a more dynamic and mobile workforce, the appropriate use of mobile devices to conduct business needs to be clearly articulated and controlled to mitigate any potential data security risks. However, when an incident involving mobile devices occurs, it is important that organizations have adopted their investigative process methodology to support the work of digital forensic practitioners.

Resources

It is important to note that while the resources included below may not be complete, inclusion of a specific resource does not suggest it is better or recommended over other resources that were not included in this section.

Choo, Kim-Kwang Raymond; Dehghantanha, Ali. *Contemporary Digital Forensic Investigations of Cloud and Mobile Applications.* Syngress Press, 2016.
Doherty, Eamon P. *Digital Forensics for Handheld Devices.* CRC Press, 2016.
Ho, Anthony T.S., Li, Shujun. *Handbook of Digital Forensics of Multimedia Data and Devices.* John Wiley & Sons, 2016.
Martin, Andrew. *Mobile Device Forensics.* SANS Institute, 2009. https://www.sans.org/reading-room/whitepapers/forensics/mobile-device-forensics-32888.
National Institute of Standards and Technology (NIST) Special Publication 800–101 Revision 1. *Guidelines on Mobile Device Forensics.* http://nvlpubs.nist.gov/nistpubs/SpecialPublications/NIST.SP.800–101r1.pdf.
NIST Special Publication 800–124 Revision 1. *Guidelines for Managing the Security of Mobile Devices in the Enterprise.*
http://nvlpubs.nist.gov/nistpubs/SpecialPublications/NIST.SP.800–124r1.pdf.

Glossary

1. **Electronically stored information (ESI)** is information created, manipulated, communicated, stored, and best utilized in digital form, requiring the use of computer hardware and software.
2. **Data in use** applies to data that is actively stored in a nonpersistent state, such as memory, for consumption or presentation.
3. **Data in transit** is the flow of information over any type of public or private network environment.
4. **Data at rest** refers to the protection of inactive data that is physically stored in any digital form (i.e., database, enterprise data warehouse, tapes, hard drives, etc.)
5. **Passcode** is a string of characters used to authenticate into information technology resources, including lowercase and uppercase letters, numbers, and symbols.
6. **Application programming interface (API)** is a set of computer programming subroutines, definitions, protocols, and tools for building application software.
7. **Commercial off the shelf (COTS)** describes items that are available for purchase through the commercial marketplace, including, but not limited to, software or hardware products, installation services, and training services.
8. **Eggs in one basket** is a term used to describe the increased risk of losing an investment because of concentrating all resources into a single item.
9. **Total cost of ownership (TCO)** is a financial estimate to determine the direct and indirect expenses and benefits of an investment.
10. **Best of breed** is a term used to describe the solution that generates the most value by providing the greatest functionality for a specific niche or subject area.
11. **Airplane node** is a setting that prevents mobile devices from sending and receiving cellular and wireless communications.
12. **Logic bomb** is a set of instructions that have been secretly incorporated into a system or application so that when a condition is satisfied, the instruction will be carried out.

Chapter 8

Cloud Computing Enablement

Through the combination of several major technology concepts, cloud computing has evolved over several decades to become the next generation of computing models. As cloud computing continues to mature, providing organizations with an inexpensive means of deploying computing resources, it is driving a fundamental change in the ways technology is becoming a common layer of service-oriented architectures. Cloud computing presents a unique challenge to an organization's digital forensics capabilities because of the dynamic nature in which information exists and a shift to less control for organizations over physical infrastructure assets. This leads to the inherent challenge of maintaining best practices for cloud computing while continuing to enable digital forensic capabilities.

Brief History of Cloud Computing

When thinking of cloud computing, we often think of historical milestones when ideas and solutions started to arise throughout the twenty-first century. However, cloud computing is not a new concept. The reality is that the concepts that eventual led to cloud computing have existed for several decades, building out an infrastructure path that eventually led to formalizing computing models.

Dating back to the 1950s, the fundamental concepts of cloud computing emerged with the introduction of mainframe systems. When organizations started to prioritize the efficiency of their large-scale computing resources, where multiple users could simultaneously access central computer systems using terminals, the gradual evolution toward cloud computing began. Because technology was costly to buy and maintain at the time, providing shared access to a single resource was the economical solution that made sense for organizations who used them.

Move forward to the 1970s, the concept of virtual machines (VM) emerged, where it was possible to execute one or more operating systems (OS) simultaneously inside one physical piece of hardware. This technology advancement was an important catalyst in taking shared computing to the next level, and in further evolving communication and information sharing capabilities.

During the 1990s, the World Wide Web exploded onto the scene allowing for Internet-based computing to really take off. Before the Internet, telecommunication providers could only offer single and dedicated point-to-point connections. Now, the concept of virtual private network connections was introduced, which, instead of building out physical infrastructure for each connection, organizations could now leverage shared access using the same physical infrastructures. In this time, cloud computing was in its infancy where it was enabling the electronic business (eBusiness), such as online shopping, streaming content, and managing bank accounts.

Following the dot-com explosion in the early 2000s, several organizations played key roles in the further development of cloud computing services where the availability of high-capacity networks and low-cost computing resource was introduced, together with pervasive adoption of virtualization and service-oriented architectures. In this time, cloud computing was maturing to where it was now providing expanded information technology (IT) as service capabilities, such as virtualized environments for storage and computing capacity.

Today, most attention on cloud-based services is within the enterprises who are focused on using it as an alternative for sourcing technology resources and capacity. As cloud computing evolves into its next level of maturity, the concept of "everything as a service" will enable most enterprise infrastructure and applications to be sourced through on-demand service models.

What is Cloud Computing?

The origin of the term *cloud* stems back to the telecommunications world where networks and the Internet were commonly visualized on diagrams depicted as clouds. Generally, the use of clouds in these diagrams was to signify areas where information was moving and being processed without persons needing to know what was happening. This philosophy is still central to cloud computing today where the customer requests for and receives information and services without knowing where it resides or how it is transmitted.

Generally, cloud computing is a model for enabling convenient and on-demand delivery of computing resources (i.e., systems, storage, applications) over a network (i.e., Internet) that can be rapidly provisioned and released with minimal effort or interaction. From all advancements made throughout history, the major technology concepts that ultimately explains the evolution and creation of cloud computing are:

- *Grid computing* to solve large problems using parallel computing systems
- *Utility computing* to offer computing resources as a metered service

- *Software as a service (SaaS)* to allow for network-based subscriptions to applications
- *Cloud computing* to provide anywhere and anytime access to computing resources that are delivered dynamically as a service

Characteristics

Within all cloud computing infrastructures, there are five essential characteristics:

- *Rapid elasticity*: With cloud computing, it is challenging for cloud service providers (CSP) to anticipate usage volumes or demands. Therefore, cloud capabilities need to provide dynamic scalability, in some cases automatically, to rapidly meet the customer's computing resourcing demands.
- *On-demand self-service*: The ability to utilize a self-service model that consumers can automatically provision and release computing resources, such as systems or storage, as needed without requiring human interaction with the CSP.
- *Broad network access*: In a society that is always connected from anywhere, cloud computing services need to be available over networks through standard interfaces that promote use by a wide variety of platforms (i.e. mobile devices, laptops).
- *Measured service*: Cloud systems have metering capabilities that have a level of abstraction appropriate to the type of service (i.e., bandwidth, storage, users), so that resources can be monitored, controlled, and report transparently.
- *Resource pooling*: Providing cloud computing under a multitenant model, both physical and virtual resources are dynamically assigned and reassigned based on demand, without consumers having control or knowledge over where resource are located (i.e., country, datacenter).

Service Models

Within all cloud computing infrastructures, there are three distinct service models as follows:

- *Software as a service (SaaS)*: Consumers can use the provider's applications running within the cloud infrastructure. These applications are commonly accessible from a variety of client devices (i.e., web browser, program interface). Consumers do not manage or control the underlying cloud infrastructure (i.e., network, systems, storage, applications), except where user-specific application configurations are permitted.
- *Platform as a service (PaaS)*: Consumers are provided with capabilities to deploy, onto the cloud infrastructure, any applications they have created or acquired using the programming tools (i.e., languages, libraries, services) supported by the CSP. Consumers do not manage or control the underlying

cloud infrastructure (i.e., network, systems, storage), but have control over deployed applications and the user-specific configurations.

- *Infrastructure as a service (IaaS)*: Consumers are provided with capabilities to provide and release computing resources (i.e., processing, storage, networks) where OS and applications can be used. Consumers do not manage or control the underlying cloud infrastructure (i.e., network, systems), but have control over the operating systems, applications, storage, and select network components (i.e., host-based firewalls).

Delivery Models

Within all cloud-computing infrastructures, there are four types of deployment models:

- *Private cloud*: This model is provisioned exclusively for use by a single organization. It may exist either on or off the organization's premises where it can be owned, managed, and operated by the organizations or by the CSP.
- *Community cloud*: This model is provisioned for use by a specific community of consumers that have a shared interest (i.e., security requirements, compliance needs). It may exist either on or off the organizations premise's where it can be owned, managed, and operated by the organizations or by the CSP.
- *Public cloud*: This model is provisioned for open use by the public. It exists exclusively within the CSP premises and can be owned, managed, and operated by either the CSP or another entity (i.e., organization, academic institution, managed service provider [MSP]).
- *Hybrid cloud*: This model is provisioned as any combination of two or more other cloud models (i.e., private, community, public) bound together by technologies that enable data and application portability (i.e., load balancing).

Isolation Models

Within all cloud computing infrastructures, there two types of isolation models as follows:

- *Dedicated*: Where infrastructure is reserved and isolated for specific users or customers
- *Multitenant*: Where infrastructure is shared among several groups of users or customers

Illustrated in Figure 8.1, each of the three delivery models previously discussed are shown to be complimentary building blocks to the others and form the basis for which cloud computing environments are created.

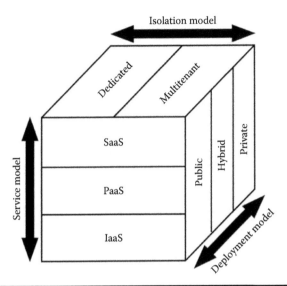

Figure 8.1   Cloud computing model dimensions.

Persistent Threats and Challenges

Cloud computing has revolutionized the ways in which an organization's electronically stored information (ESI)[1] is stored, processed, and transmitted. From the information security perspective, corporate information being stored in these services are, for the most part, beyond the boundaries of their control and are increasingly vulnerable because the controls may (or may not) meet their security requirements (i.e., encryption, data residency, logical access). With the transition from using traditional approaches of standalone technologies, organizations are faced with many challenges in determining how their digital forensic capabilities extend into the various types of cloud computing environments.

Largely, there are numerous challenges facing the digital forensic community when it comes to gathering and processing evidence in cloud computing environments. These—broadly categorized as technical, legal, or organizational—challenges can impede or ultimately prevent conducting digital forensics. While cloud computing possesses similarities to its predecessor technologies, the introduction of this new operating model presents significant challenges with digital forensics.

Outlined in the following sections, challenges within cloud computing environments cannot be solved solely based on technology, law, or organizational principles. Rather, overcoming these difficulties requires approaching the combined principles—technological, legal, and organizational—to develop mitigation strategies based on people, process, and technology.

Mobility

The proliferation of mobile devices as business tools has created a shift in terms of where and how an organization's data can be stored. For example, confidential information can be configured to synchronize across multiple devices or other cloud-based services, further aggravating the issue of where an organization's data is located and increasing the possibility of the information being compromised, lost, or stolen.

Hyperscaling

Hyperscale environments are distributed computing infrastructures where the volume of data and demand for certain types of processing can increase exponentially and still be accommodated quickly in a cost-effective manner. Virtual resources used are extremely short-lived and can also use container orchestrations, discussed in the section below, to the tune of thousands of instances. They are often associated with cloud computing because it helps organizations become more efficient, use less power, and respond quickly to their own customer's needs. The nonpersistent and volatile nature of ESI within these environments can leave little, if any, digital evidence for gathering and processing.

Containerization

For a long time, a traditional means of deploying applications was as much a science as it was a systematic process. Similarly, the use of a container to deploy applications allows organizations to standardize the computing environment and take away the need to specify the underlying operating system and hardware. As the use of containers continued to grow, there was a need to better manage the extraction of containers much in the same function as that of a data center with traditional computing systems. The reality is that many of the existing digital forensic tools and processes are not aware of or capable of analyzing containers; which requires alternatives to be explored.

First Responders

Responding to security incidents where systems are not owned by the organization, such as when cloud-based services are managed by a CSP, there is reliance on others to perform initial triage of systems. The reality is that most organizations are often faced with concerns of confidence, competence, and trustworthiness that the expectations of incident first responders will be upheld. While contractual service level objectives (SLO)[4] and service level agreements (SLA)[5] can be defined to ensure CSPs respond accordingly, a joint incident response plan needs to be developed with the CSPs to outline how to manage different types of security incidents.

Evidence Gathering and Processing

With cloud-based systems managed by CSPs, organizations do not have direct access to the technologies to gather and process evidence following traditional methodologies and techniques. As a result, collection and preservation of cloud-based evidence that is relevant to a specific organization's investigation can be challenging, with factors such as multitenancy, distributed resourcing (cross-borders), or volatile data persistent. Furthermore, organizations may encounter issues where correlation and reconstruction of events is not easily achieved because artifacts exist within multiple CSPs or across several virtual images.

Cloud Computing Governance

Implementing technology to secure cloud computing as a precursor to enabling digital forensic capabilities is only one piece of an organization's broader strategy to govern use and access of these technologies. Before digital forensic capabilities can be realized, there needs to be documentation approved that establishes the requirements for using cloud-based services to secure data storage and access, as well as what is considered acceptable and unacceptable conduct. Combined with the documentation created through the organization's information security governance framework, standard operating procedures (SOP) are the backbone for performing digital forensics within cloud computing environments. Within the information security governance framework, there needs to be a series of documents that specifically address use of and access to cloud computing with respect to the organization's data. These documents provide the organization with a foundation for planning the eventual enablement of cloud computing capabilities, as well as guidelines for user behavior and conduct. They can also serve as a driver for enabling digital forensic capabilities.

Further discussion about digital forensics processes, procedures, and how an organization's information security governance framework complements digital forensics, can be found in Chapter 6 titled *"The Business of Digital Forensic."*

Business Code of Conduct Policy

As discussed in Chapter 6 titled *"The Business of Digital Forensic,"* policies are the highest level of governance documents that establish a formalized blueprint to address topics. When it comes to cloud computing, organizations need to be explicit on the appropriate business use of these services so that employees have a clear understanding of expectations for their conduct.

The first document to be created does not directly fall within the scope of cloud computing but has significant influence on how they are drafted. A business code of conduct is a management tool for setting out an organization's values, responsibilities, and ethical obligations. This governance document provides the organization with guidance for handling unacceptable business conduct. To be truly effective, the business code of conduct needs to be embedded throughout the organization so employees know how it applies to them.

(Un)Acceptable Activity

As part of the business code of conduct, organizations must define what they consider to be acceptable and unacceptable conduct within the scope of their business environment. Communicating these expectations needs to be done in a clear manner so that there is no opportunity for confusion or gray areas that allow for certain types of conduct to persist.

Generally, acceptable conduct is any action, behavior, or communication that is within the defined boundaries as outlined in the governance documentation. As an example, the use of corporately owned and managed encryption solutions for the transmission of customer information is considered within the boundaries of acceptable activity.

Alternatively, unacceptable conduct is any action, behavior, or communication that is explicitly prohibited because it falls outside the defined boundaries as outlined in the governance documentation. As an example, using personal email accounts to conduct business transactions where confidential or sensitive data is being transmitted would be considered unacceptable behavior.

Acceptable Use Policy (AUP)

As cloud-based services continue to become widespread and more readily adopted by organizations, its authorized and unauthorized use to conduct business also continues to expand. With the increasing compliance and risk management challenges that come with cloud computing environments, best practices of establishing enterprise governance for compliance purposes and enforcement of formalized policies is required.

Not considering size, geographic location, or industry, all organizations need to enforce an acceptable use policy (AUP) that governs the use of cloud computing environments to conduct business on their behalf. Regardless of whether cloud-based services are being used for personal or business purposes, it can be used to store organizational data and, as such, must comply with the requirements set forth in the AUP.

If there is no organizational governance in place, employees will not have a clear understanding of what the organization deems acceptable, which could result in activities such as storing confidential customer data in a location that violates laws or regulations. Given the potential risk that exists for both acceptable and unacceptable use of cloud computing environments, it is essential that organizations formally establish and enforce an AUP that defines how, when, why, with whom, and under what circumstance employees can and cannot use cloud-based services.

User Acknowledgment and Agreement

As a supplementary to the AUP and during the onboarding process before employees are permitted to use cloud-based services for business purposes, they must sign an agreement that acknowledges their responsibilities for using cloud-based services.

Generally, the purpose of these documents is to define the terms and conditions by which organizations make available to their employees IT resources that they deem authorized. These IT resources may include (but are not limited to) software, networks, services, and storage capabilities provisioned as part of cloud-based services that have met the organization's required security and configuration standards. It is important that employees understand their use of cloud computing for business purposes is a privilege, not a right, and that their acknowledgment makes them responsible for their actions. The following are examples of term and conditions found in these documents:

- Abide by all organizational policies, standards, and guidelines relating to cloud computing resources
- Subscribe to only those cloud-based services approved by the organization
- Agree to use only enterprise accounts to access cloud-based services; no personal accounts will be used
- Define the classification of information permitted to be created, transmitted, and stored in cloud computing environments
- Utilize approved IT resources to access, create, and transmit data within cloud-based services

Also, it must be clearly defined that failure for employees to follow these terms and conditions will be handled as a disciplinary action result, such as:

- Suspension, blocking access, or restricting access to the organization's IT resources
- Financial liability for costs incurred due to data breach, loss, or illegal disclosure

Enterprise Management Strategies

For many years, the cloud played a more simplistic role as simply a code word for the mishmash of remotely connected networks and devices beyond an organization's span of control. However, as business use of the Internet grew so did the use of the term *cloud*, and it evolved into a symbol of something more substantial and specific. With cloud now being used to represent the interactions between an end user and a specific service provided over the Internet, cloud computing continues to present new business challenges and opportunities.

An important factor of enabling cloud capabilities is to ensure that the building blocks for allowing business to securely use cloud-based services is established. This is not to say that solely understanding the architectural and technical models that make up cloud computing is sufficient, but that there needs to be a holistic approach whereby complimentary administrative, technical, and physical controls are given equal treatment as part of the enterprise cloud management strategy.

Developing enterprise strategies for cloud computing is subjective to the business profile and use cases of each organization, and it should be done following a risk-based methodology so that informational assets are not unknowingly or accidentally exposed to unauthorized parties. The extent to which these strategies should be developed to enable cloud computing is, however, beyond the scope of this book and will not be covered in details. Alternatively, two significant components of enabling cloud computing within an enterprise, as pertains to enhancing digital forensic capabilities, have been illustrated in the sections below.

Security and Configuration Standards

For the most part, security controls found within cloud computing environments are no different than those found within any traditional IT environment. However, there is a difference in the reference models that cloud computing employs, which may present slightly different risks to the organization that traditional IT environments do not.

With cloud computing environments, the scope of security responsibilities of both the CSP and the consumer differ based on the service model. Understanding the difference in how security controls are deployed between cloud service models is critical for organizations to manage their business risk of using cloud computing environments. For example:

- In SaaS environments, the scope of security controls—such as SLO, privacy, and compliance—are negotiated as part of the terms and conditions outlined in formal contractual agreements.
- In IaaS environments, CSPs are responsible for implementing security controls to the underlying infrastructure and abstraction layers,[6] while the consumer is responsible for the remainder of the stack (i.e., OS, applications, etc.).
- In PaaS environments, securing the platform is the responsibility of the CSP while securing applications (either developed or purchased) belongs to the consumer.

Reference Architectures

With the differences in methods, services, and responsibilities for securing the different deployment models, organizations are faced with significant challenges in properly assessing their risk and identifying the necessary level of security controls to protect their data.

Security reference architectures (SRA) are used to provide a comprehensive and formal model that serves to overlay security within cloud infrastructures. Using an SRA to secure cloud-based services lays out a risk-based approach for organizations to determine CSP responsibilities for implementing specific controls throughout a cloud ecosystem. Generally, the SRA framework provides a high-level summary to:

- Identify the core security components that can be implemented in a cloud ecosystem
- Provide the core set of security components, based on deployment and service model, that are within the responsibility of the CSP
- Define the formal architecture that add security-centric layers to cloud computing environments

Illustrated in Figure 8.2, there are multiple layers of interactions found throughout enterprise technology stacks where security controls can be deployed and implemented. As modern technologies such as mobile devices, virtualization, and cloud computing continue to proliferate as tools for conducting business, organizations are increasingly faced with the need to expose their business records and applications beyond the borders of their traditional network perimeter.

Addressing security requirements in cloud computing environments should follow the traditional risk-based approach that focuses on agnostic controls that

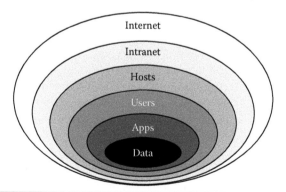

Figure 8.2 Security control layers.

can be applied to most systems or software development methodologies to reduce their attack surface. Alternatively, instead of managing the security of cloud-based solutions through specific technology components, organizations should manage their attack surfaces using security control families based on the type of cloud models deployed. Examples of security control families relevant to cloud computing environments include, but are not limited to:

- Access controls
- Awareness and training
- Audit and accountability
- Security assessment and authorization
- Configuration management
- Identification and authentication
- Incident response
- Media protection
- Physical and environmental protection
- Risk assessment
- System and information integrity

With cloud computing environments built based on a standardized multitier architecture, security control families should be implemented based on the security concerns found throughout each layer. Generally, there are four (4) technology solution domains within cloud-based solution that describe security concerns and can be used to map security control families appropriately:

- *Presentation services* are the interface between end users and the cloud-based solution. The requirements for security controls within this domain will vary by the type of cloud service model provided (i.e., PaaS, Iaas, SaaS) and the interface with the user (i.e., mobile device, website, etc.). Examples of security control families within this domain include, but are not limited to, access controls and identification/authentication.
- *Application services* are the rules and processes, behind the presentation services, that interact and manipulate information on behalf of end users. The requirements for security controls within this domain is to ensure that the development processes used to build services within this tier maintain the integrity of information. Examples of security control families within this domain include, but are not limited to, configuration management and system/information integrity.
- *Information services* prioritize, simplify, and manage the risk associated with the storage of information. The requirements for security controls within this domain are to properly manage the extraction, transformation, normalization, and loading of information within the technology solution.

Examples of security control families within this domain include, but are not limited to, risk assessment and system/information integrity.

■ *Infrastructure services* provide the core technology capabilities required to support the higher-level tiers of a cloud-based solution architecture. The requirements for security controls within this domain are to provide physical security capabilities that match the risk characteristics found throughout the higher-level cloud technology solution domains. Examples of security control families within this domain include, but are not limited to, media protection and physical/environmental protection.

Providing a detailed mapping of security control families to the cloud technology solution domain is beyond the scope of this book. Alternatively, the following security reference architectures can be used as guidance for securing cloud computing environments and have also been provided in the Resources section at the end of this chapter:

■ *NIST Cloud Computing SRA* contains detailed guidance for organizations to adopt best practices and security requirements for cloud service contracts, SLOs, SLAs, and deployment of cloud computing environments.
■ *Trusted Cloud Initiative (TRI) SRI* provides a comprehensive approach to securing identity-aware cloud ecosystems that combines the best-of-breed architecture models (i.e., Information Technology Infrastructure Library [ITIL])

Contractual Agreements

When data is transferred to a cloud-based services, the responsibility for protecting and securing the data against loss, damage, or misuse commonly remains the responsibility of the data custodian, meaning the organization. In deployments where the organization relies on a CSP to host or process its data, it is essential (and in most cases legally required) that a written legal agreement is signed to ensure the obligations of all parties involved in the cloud-based service offerings will fulfill their responsibilities.

The cornerstone of enabling cloud computing within any enterprise is having a master service agreement (MSA) in place to function as the legal framework to which all parties will operate under throughout the course of their relationship. This MSA must contain clauses whereby due diligence (before execution) is defined and continuous audits (during execution) are performed. Other terms and conditions an MSA should include, but not limited to the:

■ Objective for having the MSA in place
■ Duration for which the MSA will govern the relationship
■ Reason(s) for which termination of the contract can occur, and the subsequent consequences for all parties involved

- Structure and system of governance that will be applied—such as monitoring the service (i.e., SLO, SLA) or the rights and responsibilities of all parties involved
- Requirements for supplying, managing, and reporting administrative, technical, and (where feasible) physical security control implementations

Entering a legal agreement with another party should not be done blindly. Organizations need to demonstrate due diligence in assessing their business practices, needs, and restrictions so that they have a clear and concise understanding of the what is required of them—such as from a compliance standpoint—or what (legal) barriers they may encounter. In some cases, due diligence on the CSP may be necessary to determine whether the provider is fully capable of fulfilling its continued obligations outlined in the contract agreement.

Most commonly, a formal and complex contract agreement, tailored to meet specific requirements, is negotiated between an organization and the CSP. However, where CSPs provide organizations with a click-wrap agreement,[7] careful assessment of risk against benefits needs to be completed to ensure that the provisions of this contract meet the needs and obligations of all parties throughout its lifecycle. If a contractual agreement is entered into where needs and obligations cannot be addressed, organizations must consider alternatives and not willingly accept the faults of the potential relationship, such as seeking out a CSP who is willing to enter a mutually agreeable contract relationship.

Data-Centric Security

Traditionally, enterprise defenses followed a methodology where a perimeter around the corporate network was established, and internal resources were secured from external threats. This approach was very static in nature because technology required network connection to access corporate resources, which was easier to secure and manage. However, given the ever-increasing mobility and dynamic nature of the modern workforce that can be connected anywhere at any time, the traditionally static approach to securing corporate resources does not necessarily work as intended.

In today's business landscape, securing corporate resources needs to focus primarily on data so that, when an incident happens, there are digital artifacts that can be used to investigate. Supporting this methodology, a data-centric security model is an approach that focuses on data and information rather than networks, servers, or applications. Assessing the requirements for providing data-centric security means having a good understanding of the data and the context by which it is used throughout the organization.

Refer to Chapter 10 titled "*Digital Evidence Management*" for further discussion about data-centric security.

Cloud Computing Process Methodology

Generally, cloud forensics is a cross discipline of cloud computing and digital forensics. Gathering and processing digital evidence from cloud environments differs from the traditional approaches of digital forensics where organizations do not (in cases) own the infrastructural components. Understanding that cloud computing is based on the requirement for broad network access, cloud forensics is therefore a subset of and adaptation of network forensics principles, methodologies, and techniques. However, with the potential limitations in conducting cloud computing forensics, it is necessary for organizations to implement guidelines and processes by which their digital forensic practitioner can gather and process potential digital evidence.

Illustrated in Figure 8.3, the high-level digital forensic process model, discussed previously in Chapter 2 titled *"Investigative Process Methodologies,"* will be applied to the activities and tasks involved in conducting cloud forensics. It is important to note that while this book does cover the fundamental principles, methodologies, and techniques of digital forensics, it largely focuses on outlining how the people, processes, and technologies are used to defend the enterprise through integrating digital forensic capabilities with key business functions. This book is not designed to provide readers with the technical knowledge about digital forensics, including the hands-on and how-to aspects of the discipline, such as how to forensically acquire technology devices.

Phase 1: Preparation

As discussed in Chapter 2 titled *"Investigative Process Methodologies,"* the activities and tasks performed in this first phase are essential in successfully executing all subsequent phases of the investigative workflow. Outside of a corporate environment, an argument could be made that many of the activities and tasks performed here are done after an incident involving a cloud environment has occurred. This is primarily attributed to how, given that law enforcement agencies are not party to the relationships between organizations and CSPs, involvement requires their engagement to assist in gathering and processing evidence. However, within an enterprise environment, there are greater opportunities to be proactive in preparation activities and tasks because the organization has total control over which CSPs they work with and the type of data that will be used or stored within cloud environments.

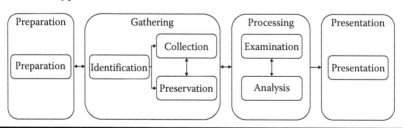

Figure 8.3 High-level digital forensic process model.

Processes and Procedures

With cloud forensics being a subdiscipline of network forensics, which is a subdiscipline of digital forensics, the existing baseline of standards, guidelines, and techniques discussed in Chapter 6 titled "*The Business of Digital Forensic*" become the foundation for documentation specific to cloud forensics.

For the most part, the SOP created for digital forensics still apply to cloud forensics when processing digital evidence. However, given that cloud infrastructure may not be owned by the organization, there is a need to develop specific SOPs so that digital forensic practitioners know how to engage CSP to facilitate gathering evidence when or if required. Considerations for gathering and processing digital evidence from cloud environments will be discussed further in the phase below where it is applicable to the investigative workflow.

Unlike how organizations are predominantly responsible for ensuring their internal resources are educated and experienced to support in-house digital forensic capabilities, with cloud-based services there is a requirement to ensure that CSP resources also have the required skills and knowledge to support cloud forensic capabilities.

Education, Training, and Awareness

Like digital forensics, depending on an individual's role with respect to cloud forensics determines the level of knowledge they are provided. Detailed discussion about the different levels of education, training, and awareness an organization should require of their people in support of digital forensics can be found in Chapter 3 titled "*Education, Training, and Awareness.*"

General Awareness

As the lowest type of education, this is a generalized level of training and awareness that is designed to provide people with foundational knowledge without getting too deep into cloud computing or cloud forensics. Leveraging the education and training that has already been put in place for digital forensics, this education provides people with the competencies they need about organizational policies, standards, and guidelines so that they indirectly contribute, through some form of behavior or action, to the organization's digital forensic program.

Examples of topics and subjects that should be included as part of a mobile device forensic awareness program include, but are not limited to, the following:

- Business code of conduct
- Cloud computing acceptable use policy
- Data protection and privacy

Basic Training

Essentially, the difference between this training and the previous awareness is that the knowledge gained here is intended to teach people the skills necessary to directly support the organization's digital forensic program as relates to how, where, and to what extent cloud devices are used for business purposes.

Information communicated at this level is more detailed than the previous type of education, because it must provide people with the knowledge required to support a specific role or function, such as managing cloud computing ecosystems.

For example, as part of basic mobile device forensic training information about audit logging and retention should be covered. This topic relates to recording events and preserving them, as per the organizational governance framework, to facilitate digital forensic investigations.

Formal Education

A working and practical knowledge of cloud forensics requires people to first and foremost have the skills and competencies necessary to ensure that all network forensics—as a subdiscipline of digital forensic principles, methodologies, and techniques—is understood. Once the fundamental knowledge is gained, practitioners can pursue knowledge of cloud computing and work toward a specialization in cloud forensics.

However, unlike digital forensic education programs, the availability of curriculum dedicated entirely toward cloud computing environments is still limited. Most commonly, cloud forensics is taught as a specific course in either higher or postsecondary institutes, or as a professional education module led by an industry-recognized training institute.

Refer to Appendix B: Education and Professional Certifications for a list of higher/postsecondary institutes that offer formal education programs.

Technology and Toolsets

Within the dedicated forensic lab environment, discussed in Chapter 6 titled "*The Business of Digital Forensic*," organizations will need to acquire specific software and hardware to support their cloud forensic capabilities. However, the extent to which an organization invests in their toolkit is subjective to their environment and the degree to which they need to gather and process digital evidence from cloud environments.

Considerations for technologies and tools for gathering and processing digital evidence from cloud environments will be discussed further in Phase 2, where it is applicable to the investigative workflow. As a subset of network forensics, tools and techniques used for cloud forensics will include a suite of network monitoring and collection utilities that allow digital forensic practitioners to replay and analyze traffic patterns. It is important that all tools used can process large datasets, given the potential volume of traffic on any given network segment, and subsequently pinpoint, with accuracy, where each piece of information was derived from. Further discussion about digital forensic tools and technologies can be found in Chapter 6 titled "*The Business of Digital Forensics.*"

Phase 2: Gathering

In Chapter 2 titled "*Investigative Process Methodologies,*" we discussed how this second phase of the investigative workflow consists of the activities and tasks involved in the identification, collection, and preservation of digital evidence. The same requirement for establishing the meaningfulness, relevancy, and legal admissibility of digital evidence applies for cloud computing. However, given the predominant use of virtualization for cloud-based services and that an investigation might also involve multiple entities (the organization and the CSP), there are additional activities and tasks that need to be performed for cloud forensics.

Identification

Largely, the activities and tasks performed here are no different than those discussed in Chapter 2 titled "*Investigative Process Methodologies.*" Regardless of the evidence that has been identified, both physical and logical, digital forensic practitioners must follow consistent and repeatable methodologies and techniques to secure, document, and search a crime scene. Sample templates that can be used to secure, document, and search crime scenes have been provided in the Templates section of this book.

Where cloud environments have been identified as relevant to an investigation, and there is some component of the cloud-based service being provided by a CSP, the scope of an investigation widens significantly to include identification of evidence located in sources that are indirectly owned and managed by the organization. Further complicating the scope of an investigation, although organizations have a contractual agreement in place with their direct CSP, most cloud applications often have dependencies on other CSPs that need to be considered. For example, the dependencies in a chain of business-to-business (B2B) or business-to-client (B2C) relationships can prove to be dynamic and introduce a level of complexity in the ability to establish a thorough and complete chain of evidence between all parties involved in the cloud-based service offering(s). Refer to Chapter 10 titled "*Digital Evidence Management*" for further discussion about the chain of evidence.

Where any combination of CSPs have been identified, the importance of policies and SLAs are a requirement to facilitate the communication and collaboration in forensic activities during an incident or investigation. To establish cloud forensic capabilities that ensure digital evidence will maintain legally admissible, each CSP must be equipped with educated and experienced resources (people) to assist in all forensic activities.

Because of the dynamic and distributed nature of cloud computing environments, in addition to the number of potential resources connected to the cloud, identifying all sources of evidence can be a significant undertaking. Establishing where potential digital evidence exists involves working through the order of Volatility, discussed in Chapter 2 titled *"Investigative Process Methodologies,"* subjective to the technology infrastructure involved in the incident or investigation. Without a documented architecture that illustrates the interconnectivity between technologies, systems, and the cloud environment, potential data sources could be missed leading to inconclusive facts based on the evidence identified.

Collection and Preservation

Generally, there are six layers of cloud environments where techniques used to gather digital evidence will differ, as illustrated in Table 8.1. Working down through the cloud layers, there comes a different level of trust in that the information within is secure and trustworthy. Ultimately, this means that if there are concerns about the integrity of information at any layer, the courts can render a legal decision not to admit the evidence. As a strategy for addressing these issues, digital forensic practitioners should follow scientifically proven and documented techniques to verify and validate the integrity and authenticity of evidence.

Depending on the nature of the investigation, organizations need to determine which layer of evidence outlined in Table 8.1 needs to be collected and preserved. Ultimately, making this assessment involves two key decision criteria: first, the organization's technical capability to forensically gather evidence at that layer,

Table 8.1 Cloud Layers of Trust

Cloud Layer	Acquisition Technique	Trust Level
(6) Applications/Data	Subjective to applications/data	Guest OS, Hypervisor, Host OS, Hardware, Network
(5) Guest OS	Digital Forensic Tools	Guest OS, Hypervisor, Host OS, Hardware, Network
(4) Virtualization	Introspection	Hypervisor, Host OS, Hardware, Network
(3) Host OS	Access to Virtual Disk	Host OS, Hardware, Network
(2) Physical Hardware	Access to Physical Disk	Hardware, Network
(1) Network	Network Forensic Tools	Network

and second, the level of trust in the data at that layer. Where cloud environments are located within the organization's boundaries of control, technical probability and level of trust will be relatively higher because network forensic tools and techniques can be used to gather evidence from known and managed infrastructures.

However, when there is no physical infrastructure present within the enterprise, a digital forensic practitioner needs to turn to their suite of enterprise security controls to gather network traffic data relevant to the incident or investigation. Doing so requires that a well-defined SOP be in place to gather the maximum amount of evidence possible, while causing minimal impact to the business, that maintains both forensic viability and legal admissibility. Chain of custody must be strictly enforced to guarantee there is no potential for the integrity or authenticity of this data to be questioned.

When gathering evidence that is located beyond the organization's network perimeter, contractual agreements with CSPs are factored in to gather evidence. Where CSPs are involved with service offerings, access to evidence might be limited because organizations might have little to no control over the physical infrastructure involved in the incident or investigation. For the most part, many CSPs do not provide customers with options or the interfaces necessary to gather evidence from these cloud environments, leaving organizations faced with no option but to collect evidence at a high level of abstraction. Given that most cloud ecosystems are implemented using virtualization technologies, the most common form of evidence gathered from cloud environments is in the form of an object or container, such as virtual hard drive images.

Phase 3: Processing

As a result of the network forensic activities, there will most likely be various datasets from the different network forensic tools that can prove to be valuable in answering questions of "who, where, what, when, why, how." As disparate pieces of evidence, processing network logs can be cumbersome and challenging because, on their own, these datasets do not provide a complete representation of all events. Aggregating all evidence into one large dataset will allow for improved correlation and chronological sequencing to be established so that relevant and meaningful evidence is not lost, skipped, or misunderstood. Doing so allows for evidence to be methodically searched so redundant and unrelated information can be removed, and that the results of examining and analyzing the large volume of information will lead to fact-based conclusions.

Beyond analyzing the network forensic datasets, the tools and equipment used to process virtual hard drive images are the same as those used for traditional digital forensics, with the exception that there will most likely only be logical evidence, nothing physical (i.e., a hard drive). At this stage of the investigation, the traditional methodologies and techniques used to analyze and examine digital evidence should follow the SOPs to ensure consistent and repeatable processes are being followed to establish the fact-based conclusions.

Phase 4: Presentation

As discussed in Chapter 2 titled *"Investigative Process Methodologies,"* documentation is a critical element of every investigation that needs to start at the beginning of an investigation and be carried on throughout. In this last phase of the investigative workflow, the final investigative report will be created to communicate factual conclusions by demonstrating the processes, techniques, tools, equipment, and interactions used to maintain the authenticity, reliability, and trustworthiness of digital evidence. Some things to consider when writing a final investigative report include:

- The structure and layout should flow naturally and logically
- Content should be clear and concise to accurately demonstrate a chronology of events
- Use of jargon, slang, and technical terminology should be avoided. Where used, a glossary should be included to define terms in common language.
- Where acronyms and abbreviations are used, they must be written out in full expression on the first use.
- Because final reports are written after the fact, being after an investigation, content should be communicated in the past tense but can change tense where conclusions or recommendations are being made.
- Format a final report not only for distribution within the organization, but also with the mindset that it may be used as testimony in a court of law.

A template for creating written formal reports has been provided as a reference in the Templates section of this book.

Legal Considerations

The growth of cloud computing has heightened concerns of who has custody over data and where it is located. Before making a strategic decision to move business operations into a cloud computing environment, it is important to answer the question: "What data residency concerns do I need to address?" In many countries, there are strict laws and regulations around data residency that prescribe the extent to which data can be stored in other geographical locations.

With this increased utilization in cloud environments, CSPs are opening facilities across multiple regions and countries where several laws and regulations govern the use, transmission, and storage of different types of information. For example, the General Data Protection Regulation (GDPR) of the European Union (EU), also known as EU Directive 95/46/EC, was issued to strengthen and unify data protection requirements by giving EU citizens back control of their personal data. Likewise, the Personal Information Protection and Electronic Documents Act (PIPEDA) sets out the rules for how private-sector organizations collect, use, and disclose personal information—of customers and employees—as part of their business activities.

Organizations are constantly faced with concerns of data residency and the ways in which the geographically distributed infrastructures may violate laws and regulations. Where a legal or regulatory violation of data residency has occurred, whether done intentionally or accidentally, the consequences organizations can face include, but are not limited to:

- Financial penalties as a result of legal or regulatory fines, compensation to victims, or the cost of remedying the violation
- Legal ramifications of lawsuits by those whose data was in violation, or law enforcement and governing agencies
- Operational impact due to loss of reputation, customer (client) base, or right to conduct business in certain geographical regions

The reality is that, if the data can be accessed, and you demonstrate control over it, the local jurisdictions will most likely demand that the data is produced as evidence even if it is stored in another jurisdiction. As a means of mitigating this, and guaranteeing that data is secure in cloud environments, organizations are implementing data-at-rest[2] encryption following a bring your own key[3] (also referred to as bring your own encryption) approach. Further discussion about laws, standards, and regulations can be referenced in Chapter 4 titled *"Laws, Standards, and Regulations."*

Summary

Cloud computing introduces a unique set of challenges to the digital forensic community because of the shift away from traditional technology architectures; where organizations now have less control over the physical infrastructure assets. As a subset of network forensics, and ultimately of digital forensics, organizations must address these concerns head on by understanding and identifying how (and where) their digital forensic capabilities must adapt to support cloud-based service offerings.

Resources

Cloud Security Alliance. Quick Guide to the Reference Architecture: Trusted Cloud Initiative. https://cloudsecurityalliance.org/wp-content/uploads/2011/10/TCI_Whitepaper.pdf.

Cloud Security Alliance. Security Guidance for Critical Areas of Focus in Cloud Computing V3.0. https://downloads.cloudsecurityalliance.org/assets/research/security-guidance/csaguide.v3.0.pdf.

NIST Cloud Computing Security Working Group—Information Technology Laboratory. NIST Cloud Computing Security Reference Architecture. http://collaborate.nist.gov/twiki-cloud-computing/pub/CloudComputing/CloudSecurity/NIST_Security_Reference_Architecture_2013.05.15_v1.0.pdf.

Glossary

1. **Electronically stored information (ESI)** is information created, manipulated, communicated, stored, and best utilized in digital form, requiring the use of computer hardware and software.
2. **Data-at-rest** refers to the protection of inactive data that is physically stored in any digital form (i.e., database, enterprise data warehouse, tapes, hard drives, etc.).
3. **Bring your own key** is a security model that allows customers to use and manage their own encryption keys to protect data hosted in business applications.
4. **Service-level objectives (SLO)** are specific quantitative characteristics used to measure service delivery in terms of availability, throughput, frequency, response time, or quality.
5. **Service-level agreements (SLA)** are official commitments between parties that define the level of service expected by the customer from the provider.
6. **Abstraction layers** are ways of hiding implementation details of a set of functionalities to facilitate interoperability and platform independence.
7. **Click-wrap agreement** is a type of nonnegotiable contractual agreement where consumers must agree to the terms and conditions set forth before using the product or service.

Chapter 9

Combatting Antiforensics

Nowadays, criminals are familiar with the techniques and methods by which digital forensic practitioners gather digital evidence. Because of this, intruders and attackers are routinely trying to evade detection by using countermeasures intended to impede the investigative process, often resulting in no evidence being identified. For the most part, enterprise environments have implemented multiple layers of administrative, physical, and technical security controls designed to protect the organization's assets (i.e., people, information) from intruders or attackers. Intended to deter, detect, deny, or delay malicious activity from occurring, these security controls also contribute toward mitigating the potential of antiforensics being used and enabling digital forensic capabilities.

What Are Antiforensics?

There is a broad interpretation from throughout the digital forensic community as to what antiforensics truly are. Much like the name suggests, antiforensics consist of a combination of specific methods and techniques that are used to render digital evidence difficult or impossible to obtain. As an analogy to describe antiforensics, consider Newton's third law of motion, which formally states that "for every action, there is an equal and opposite reaction." Following the concept of Newton's law, if digital forensics is the application of science to law, then antiforensics is the equal and opposite reaction, being the application of science to crime.

However, to date there is still no formal definition for antiforensics, and, without one, there can be no formal agreement as to what they are. While not having unanimous agreement from the forensic community, several attempts have been made to define antiforensics based on personal experiences to characterize the terminologies used for describing the techniques used, which are explored further in the following section.

Traditional Techniques

The concept of antiforensics dates as far back as the 1960s when computer crimes first started to become prevalent (i.e., data diddling); refer to Chapter 4 titled *"Laws, Standards, and Regulations"* for further details on the history of computer crime. Over the decades, the practice of antiforensics has become much more prevalent because of the evolution of information technology and the misuse of software that was originally designed with good intentions, such as the use of certificates to ensure confidentiality of information (Figure 9.1).

Naturally, the growth coupled with continuous evolution has brought about a suite of sophisticated tools that combine a variety of different antiforensics techniques. For the most part, these tools provide simplified and user-friendly interfaces so that even the nontechnical user can use them to aid in their modus operandi[1] of evading detection.

While antiforensics are commonly used on information systems (i.e., laptops, servers, etc.), it is much more than about technology. The reality is antiforensics are an approach to criminal activity that makes it difficult or impossible to identify, gather, and process digital evidence that is required to establish factual conclusions. Contained in the sections below are antiforensic subdomains where techniques are

In 2015–16, Apple Inc. received and objected to (or challenged) at least 11 court orders compelling them to use their existing capabilities to assist in extracting data from locked iPhones seized as part of criminal investigations.

Most notably, and of relevance to antiforensics, is the high-profile case between the Federal Bureau of Investigation (FBI) and Apple Inc. in February 2016. Following the shooting in December 2015 in San Bernardino, California, the FBI seized an iPhone 5C belonging to the attacker. However, the iPhone was locked with a four-digit passcode, which hindered the FBI's ability to gain access and acquire the device's data.

The FBI requested Apple Inc. to create and electronically sign new software that would enable them to bypass the device's security controls and unlock the phone. Apple Inc. declined to create the software, and a court hearing was scheduled to compel them to assist. Eventually, a zero-day exploit was identified which allowed the FBI to bypass the device's security controls and gain access to the iPhone.

In this case, while the use of cryptography was intended to prevent unauthorized access to the device, it was used as an antiforensic technique to conceal evidence, making the work of investigators more difficult, time-consuming, and expensive.

Figure 9.1 Apple vs FBI.

applied to conceal information and make the job of a digital forensic practitioner more challenging.

It is important to note that this section is not intended to be a comprehensive illustration of every different antiforensic techniques and methods used. Rather, the sections below are intended to provide a high-level overview so there is an understanding of the different antiforensic techniques and methods.

Data Hiding

A common antiforensic technique is to hide data from plain sight. At one end of the spectrum, data hiding does not require the use of specialized tools to conceal information and can be performed by individuals with little technical knowledge. However, as data hiding techniques become more sophisticated and we move toward the other end of the spectrum, we find more advanced methods that require some form of specialized tools and varying degree of technical knowledge being used to hide data.

File Manipulation

Perhaps the most basic form of data hiding is achieved by making changes to data attributes. The following are examples of file manipulation techniques that can be used independently or in any combination with other antiforensic techniques:

- Appending or renaming file extensions to disguise file types and association with default software. For example, renaming a file extension (from .doc to .dll) so that it will not be associated with installed word processing software and is not visibly recognizable as in its original data format.
- Storing files in nonstandard directory paths that are commonly associated with system-generated data, and not user-created data. For example, storing word processing documents in filesystem directory locations that are known to be used by the host operating system (OS), such as in C:\Windows\ system32 in Microsoft Windows.
- Modifying file and directory attributes so that they are not visibly displayed in the filesystem. For example, new technology file system (NTFS) natively allows users to access the properties of files and the directory where manual configurations can be made to hide the file and directory from being visibly listed by the filesystem.

File System Manipulation

Another type of data-hiding technique is achieved by making changes to the ways in which the file system interacts and manages its hosted data. Below are examples of file system manipulation techniques can be used independently or in any combination with other antiforensic techniques.

- *Alternate data streams (ADS)*[2] allow users to split (or fork) information into alternate data attributes of existing files without affecting the existing file size or change its functionality, ultimately rendering the forked data hidden from the common file system. For example, using the native command line utility in Windows (cmd.exe), information can be written to a text file's ADS using the statement "echo hidden > new.txt:hidden. txt." Subsequently, the hidden content can be accessed through the native command line utility using the statement "notepad new.txt:hidden.txt"; whereas using the statement "notepad new.txt" will result in no data being visible. Additional information about ADS can be referenced on the Microsoft TechNet website provided in the Resources section at the end of this chapter.
- *Slack space*[3] can be used to store data in the unused and remaining space that is not being occupied by a given file or by the filesystem. For example, an NTFS filesystem allocates a size of 4 kilobytes (KB) to store data in a single cluster. If a file being stored is only 3KB in size, there is 1KB remaining in the cluster known as slack space. Using specialized tools, data can be stored in the slack space making it otherwise inaccessible and hidden to the native file system.
- *Timestamps* are a sequence of characters, commonly date and time values, used to identify when a certain event occurred within a fraction of a second. However, it is important to note that the use of timestamps across different filesystems will vary in the ways they are recorded. For example, within the NTFS filesystem, timestamps are stored inside the Master File Table (MFT)[4]; whereas in File Allocation Table (FAT) filesystems timestamps are recorded within each directory entry. Regardless of the filesystem being used, recording of timestamps is susceptible to antiforensics techniques in several ways. First, if the OS time configurations are changed to an incorrect value, then all timestamps recorded afterward will be inaccurate making the use of timeline analysis techniques more challenging. Secondly, there are specialized tools that can be used to change timestamps values by setting them to fake entries, such as back to the when epoch time[5] first began. Lastly, the consistent use of all timestamps (created, written, modified, access) across different filesystems varies in the type of date/time event being captured, and, in some instances, whether a specific timestamp is being recorded.

Hard Disk Manipulation

Another layer of data hiding that can be performed is done below the software level on the hardware of the information system. The following are examples of hard disk manipulation techniques that can be used independently or in any combination with other antiforensic techniques:

■ When an OS partition is created on a hard disk, it has boundaries by which the underlying filesystem can operate within. Typically, these boundaries start at the absolute first sector of the hard disk and extend to occupy a defined portion of hard disk depending on the space required. For example, if a hard disk provides for 1 terabyte (TB) of total storage capacity, the OS would occupy available space less the total size available, perhaps 900 gigabytes (GB). In this case, between the end of the OS partition and last sector of the hard disk is a portion of the hard disk that is left unused. For all intended purposes, this unused space of the hard disk is empty and essentially hidden from users, the host OS, or even the basic input/ output system (BIOS). With specialized tools, antiforensic techniques can be used to take advantage of the potential to hide information in this unused space.

■ Within many hard disks available in the marketplace today, there are two hidden areas that were originally intended for good but, as a result of their potential for misuse, have fueled the expansion of antiforensics.
  – The *host protected area (HPA)* is a hidden area found on many hard disks today. The HPA was originally designed to store information, such as hard disk utilities, diagnostic tools, and boot sector code, in such a way that, much like unused hard disk space, neither users, the host OS, or the BIOS can gain access to read or modify it. When this hidden area was discovered and the realization was made that data can be hidden here, specialized tools were developed allowing antiforensic techniques to take advantage of its potential.
  – The *device configuration overlay (DCO)* is a hidden area that was originally designed as a way for system vendors to purchase hard disks from different manufacturers and configure them to have the desired characteristics, such as size and the number of sectors. Like the HPA, when the potential for hiding data in this area was realized, specialized tools were developed allowing antiforensic techniques to take advantage of its potential.

With the potential for antiforensic techniques to capitalize on the existence of either the HPA or DCO, most digital forensic tools and technologies today provide support for identification and gathering evidence in these areas.

Encryption

The use of encryption is one of the quickest antiforensic techniques used to render information inaccessible. Because there is such a variety of encryption techniques that can be used, it is important to understand the common forms to better prepare digital forensic practitioners for what they may encounter during an investigation:

- *Filesystem encryption*, sometimes referred to as file and folder encryption, occurs when individual files or directories on a filesystem are encrypted.
- *Application encryption* is the process by which all data generated or modified by individual applications is encrypted before it is written to storage medium.
- *Disk encryption*, sometimes referred to as full disk encryption, is a technology that protects information by encrypting every bit of a physical storage devices.
- *Network encryption* is a process that applies cryptographic service at the network-layer of the open system interconnection (OSI) model.[6]

Use of these different forms of encryption has been made available as a feature in most antiforensic tools as well as standard features in all hostile and intrusive software applications found in today's threat landscape. The following are examples of encryption being used independently or in any combination with other antiforensic techniques:

- *Bit-shifting* is an operation that allows for the binary value of data to be moved by a determined number of places either to the left or the right. Most commonly, the bit order[7] used is where the zeroth bit, also known as the least significant bit (LSB), is the first bit read in a byte in the normal bit direction of data. With specialized tools, the bit order of any given file can be changed resulting in the contents becoming scrambled and unreadable. To access the data in its original format, the number of bit order changes must be known and similar tools needed to restore the data to its original bit order. When used as an antiforensic technique, bit shifting is quite effective because, not only does it make obscure data unreadable, but it is also nearly impossible to detect.
- *Network tunneling* is a mechanism used to encapsulate the communication and transmission of information by creating point-to-point interfaces between systems. A common implementation of tunneling within an enterprise environment is to establish secure connections with the organization over untrusted network environments through virtual private network (VPN) technologies. While the implementation of network tunneling was intended to provide organizations with a means of securing their information while in transit, it is also commonly used as a means of concealing data so it cannot be detected by any security controls. Where this is the case, it is nearly impossible to detect through traffic analysis, because the content is unreadable as it is transmitted between systems.

■ *Certificate-based encryption* is a system where certificate authorities use identity-based (i.e., user name, system name) cryptography to produce a certificate for both implicit (encryption) and explicit (signatures) purposes. For example, just like a passport is used to identify individuals, a digital certificate is an electronic passport that provides identifying information that can be used to securely exchange information. Otherwise known as public key infrastructure (PKI), certificates are relatively resistant to forgery and are most often used to verify identify because they are issued by official and trusted agencies, such as the organization themselves for internal certificate use. Although there is an authoritative entity involved in the issuance of certificates, there is nothing preventing cybercriminals from having a certificate issued with the intention of concealing information. Although, once detected and the certificate has been revoked along with the authority, it will no longer function.

Steganography

Perhaps the most advanced antiforensic technique used to hide data is by using steganography. Essentially, steganography is the practice of concealing information, such as text or entire files, within other data objects using three main methods:

1. *Substitution* uses the LSB approach where the last bit in a byte is replaced with the bits of the secret message. Using this method will result in a carrier file that has been changed to be so insignificant that it will be least detectable.
2. *Injection* inserts the secret message directly into the carrier file. For example, a secret message could be injected into the lossy or lossless space found within certain image files.
3. *Creation* takes a secret message and uses it to generate a file from scratch. For example, the following message encodes the secret message "antiforensics" into an innocent-looking email message where the recipient would use specialized tools to decode it and receive the secret message.

The main advantage of using steganography is that the secret messages does not arise suspicion because it is relying on human perception to be detected. For example, if an email message is encrypted and then sent, it is still intercepted during transmission by systems that assume there is something sensitive in the email. However, if a secret message is injected into an image carrier file, unless the intercepting parties know the secret message exists, they will not assume there is anything sensitive. This makes steganography the ultimate antiforensic technique.

Virtual Systems

With the advancements made over the years, technologies now exist that allow for computer systems to be emulated in a nonpersistent and dynamic condition. These virtual systems, requiring the use of any combination in specialized hardware and software, function like a physical computer system does where there is a host OS installed with an array of applications. To the host computer system, virtual systems are typically stored within a container that reside in a single file on the host system and resources, such as random access memory (RAM), are allocated as defined through the specialized hardware and software. Quite often, virtual systems are considered disposable simply because of how quickly they can be deleted to avoid detection or recovery of artifacts. However, it is important to remember that even though the virtual container holding the OS and data might be deleted to conceal activities, there are potential artifacts recoverable as result of using system resources (RAM).

Nested Volumes

Within most OS, there is support for up to 24 different volumes, each of which are assigned a drive letter from C to Z, with A and B traditionally being reserved for floppy disks. Volumes are managed and assigned using native tools commonly installed as part of the host OS. However, specialized tools exist that allow for logical volumes to be created and assigned independent to the OS that, like virtual systems, are typically stored within a container that resides in a single file on the host system. Using specialized tools, these containers can be mounted as a logical volume allowing for seamless data interactions with the OS. When the container is unmounted, the volume becomes inaccessible to the host OS, and any information stored within the container cannot be accessed. Going a step further, these specialized tools also allow for the volume container to be encrypted, such as with a password, requiring users to have knowledge to access data, making this an excellent technique for hiding data.

Memory Injection

Memory injection is a technique used to load executable code into the host system's memory space, or into the memory space of another process, without having any artifacts created or left on the host filesystem. For example, injected code could be used to alter or augment calls to system functions (i.e., keyboard) or read contents of password fields that are otherwise inaccessible on the filesystem. This technique has significant implications to gathering and processing evidence during an investigation because there are no recoverable artifacts on the host filesystem that can be used as evidence. Alternatively, digital forensic practitioners will need to leverage their tools and technologies to acquire the contents of RAM prior to the host system being shut down and any potential evidence is lost. Refer to Chapter 2 titled "*Investigative Process Methodologies*" for further discussion on gathering nonpersistent evidence following the order of volatility.

Artifact Wiping

When a file is deleted, it does not permanently erase the information from the hard disk, even if the trash or recycle bin is subsequently emptied. The reality is that the data still resides in the unallocated space of the filesystem until it is overwritten by new data. Another common form of antiforensic technique is to deliberately destroy data that could otherwise be used as evidence. With all artifact wiping techniques, there is a need to use any number of tools designed specifically to completely and thoroughly destroy data. Because there is such a variety of artifact-wiping techniques that can be used, it is important to understand the common forms to better prepare digital forensic practitioners for what they may encounter:

- *File wiping* destroys all electronic data associated specific files, folders, or software applications so that the information cannot be recovered using digital forensic tools and techniques.
- *Disk wiping* destroys all electronic data residing on all sectors of physical storage media, such as hard disks and universal serial bus (USB) devices, in accordance with industry standards and government regulations, such as the Payment Card Industry Data Security Standards (PCI-DSS) or Sarbanes-Oxley Act (SOX).
- *Degaussing* is the process rendering electronic storage media unusable by neutralizing, decreasing, or eliminating the magnetic field of data stored.

Use of these different forms of artifact wiping has been made available as a feature in most antiforensic tools as well as through standalone freeware software application readily available on the Internet today. Below are examples of where artifact wiping is used independently or in combination with other antiforensic techniques:

- *Registry cleaners*: Within the Microsoft Windows OS, there is a hierarchical database that is used to store low-level settings both for the OS and applications. Known as the "registry," it is intended to hold information to improve overall application experience but can also provide artifacts useful during an investigation. Registry cleaner software is designed to locate those hives within the registry where artifacts can be used as evidence and permanently delete them so they cannot be recovered.
- *Internet cache*: Most Internet browsers maintain local copies of content recently accessed to improve the overall user experience while browsing the Internet. This cached content, including such content as graphical images and Hypertext Markup Language (HTML) webpages, is commonly stored

in specific folders within the respective user's personal directory on the file system. Given the volumes of evidence that can be retrieved from an Internet cache, file-wiping tools have been created to permanently delete this information so it is not recoverable.

■ *Thumbnails*: The majority of consumer-based OS provide a user-friendly feature whereby when a folder is accessed and the files being stored are actively listed, small thumbnails of all images are rendered to provide a preview to users without having to open the image. These thumbnail renderings are subsequently stored in a cache to improve overall user experience, so all previews of the image to follow are presented quickly. This thumbnail cache, hidden from normal user visibility, remains within the respective folders and does not purge contained thumbnails even after the image has been deleted. With the potential for evidence to be retrieved from these thumbnail caches, wiping tools exist to permanently delete this information so it is not recoverable.

■ *Metadata*[8]: Specific file types have an additional layer of information that contains additional information about its usage. For example, some word processing files retain information about the user who last saved it, when it was last printed, and when it was originally created (in addition to the file system timestamps). This metadata is persistent within each file in the sense that it is retained for the lifecycle of that data object, regardless of where it is accessed, transmitted, or stored. Understanding that this metadata can be used as evidence during an investigation, antiforensic tools provide scrubbing functionality to overwrite the information with incorrect values, such as purging the fields completely.

Trail Obfuscation

When crimes are committed, either in the physical or digital realms, perpetrators can take precautions to ensure that their true identities cannot be traced back as a result of their actions and the tools they used. Typically, in the digital realm, perpetrators will use a combination of antiforensic techniques, such artifact wiping or data hiding, to disorient and divert investigators from "fingerprinting" them. The following are examples where specific obfuscation techniques can be used independently or in any combination with other antiforensic techniques:

■ *Proxy servers* are widely used by organizations for many different purposes; such as controlling employee access to the Internet or accelerating service requests by caching content. At the same time, "bad guys" are also making use of proxy server because of the way in which these technologies hide their true origin and identity when conducting attacks. There are many ways in which origin and identity can be hidden from the use of proxy servers, such as onion routing.[9]

Attacks Against Forensics

Traditionally, antiforensic techniques have focused on hiding, altering, or destroying data that would otherwise be meaningful and relevant evidence for an investigation. Recently, there has been a shift to antiforensic techniques focusing on attacking the tools and technologies used during an investigation, which has the potential to be the most devastating antiforensic technique used.

For example, through hash and file signature analysis, a group of hostile and intrusive software applications are identified and need to be analyzed further in sandbox[10] environment. Under normal circumstances, the target application should execute as expected allowing for interactions with the host OS to be observed. However, specialized tools such as program packers, sometimes referred to as "software packers" or "runtime packers," are used to compress executable files into a form of encrypted self-extracting archive. With some packers, the authors can complicate any means of detection by having the packed executable understand the conditions by which it is being called (i.e., virtual system, antimalware scanning) and responding differently, such as not unpacking or unpacking only specific portions.

For the most part, several antimalware technologies can detect where a packer has been used; but in most cases, packers are a very effective antiforensic technique to hide tools from being reverse engineered or detected. Regardless, this form of anti-reverse engineering needs to be considered as more and more cybercriminals are using packers to obfuscate their code and deflect attempts made to extract evidence.

Detection Methods

Inevitably, a time will come when digital forensic practitioners encounter digital evidence that has been rendered inaccessible due to antiforensic techniques. The application of antiforensic tools, techniques, and methods are becoming increasingly difficult obstacles for the digital forensic community to overcome. Although, depending on the type of antiforensic technique used, such as overwriting data, the ability to detect the presence or use of antiforensics is not always straightforward. Given that most users of these techniques have little to moderate technology knowledge, their attempts to conceal information is often ineffective or obvious because there is a greater chance they missed something.

Contained in the sections below are examples of methods that either 1) enterprise security controls can be implemented to mitigate the use of antiforensics, or 2) digital forensic practitioners can use to determine if antiforensic techniques were used.

Antimalware Technologies

The term malware has evolved over time where it is now used to describe a broad variety of hostile and intrusive software applications that exist in the modern threat landscape; including but not limited to: viruses, Trojans, worms, adware, bots, spyware, keyloggers, ransomware, and rootkits. Forms of software applications that fall under the umbrella of malware can include (but are not limited to) executable code, active content (i.e., JavaScript), and other scripting programs.

Traditionally, mitigating malware involves implementing blacklisting[11] technology (i.e., antivirus solutions) to detect and mitigate known hostile and intrusive software from executing on host systems. However, current antivirus solutions suffer from a low detection rate, due to the rate at which new malware is being released, and thus are suffering from reduced effectiveness to protect information systems and assets from malicious attacks. Alternatively, rather than continuing to mitigate hostile and intrusive software applications (i.e., antiforensic tools) using the traditional blacklisting approach, which relies on knowing what is "bad," another option is to leverage a whitelisting[12] approach, which is based on knowing what is "good."

Because both blacklisting and whitelisting approaches can be implemented to detect and identify hostile and intrusive software, using different approaches, the term antimalware is used to describe the functionality they provide. Although the effectiveness in using blacklisting technologies is somewhat declining, that is not to say taking a whitelisting approach to detecting hostile or intrusive software applications (i.e., antiforensic tools) is not necessarily the means to an end. Why? Well the reality is that even tough whitelisting might reduce overhead on networks and systems for the continuous updating of blacklist signatures, it is not easily manageable on dynamic systems where there is a constant influx of changes being made; such as end-user systems. This is not to say that whitelisting does not work with end-user systems, just that it requires more machine learning and fine tuning to ensure users still have the flexibility to perform their job functions while continuing to be protected against hostile and intrusive software applications.

Hash Analysis

Currently, the most common means of generating a digital fingerprint in digital forensics is to use a one-way cryptographic hash algorithm, such as the Message Digest Algorithm family (i.e., MD5, MD6)[13] or the Secure Hashing Algorithm family (i.e., SHA-1, SHA-2, SHA-3).[14] The near uniqueness of these cryptographic algorithms makes them an important technique for documenting the authenticity and integrity of digital evidence. While the potential for hash collisions exists, the use of the Message Digest Algorithm family or Secure Hashing Algorithm family remains an acceptable way of demonstrating the authenticity and integrity of digital evidence (Figure 9.2).

In 2004–05, experts identified that the MD5 and SHA-1 algorithms contained flaws where two unique inputs, having distinctively different properties and characteristics, would result in the same computational hash value being outputted.

Dubbed a "hash collision," this meant that the same computational hash value could be engineered in a way that multiple pieces of digital evidence could return the same hash value. Naturally, this raised concerns in the digital forensic community about the impact it will have on the legal admissibility of digital evidence.

In 2009, during the matter of United States v. Joseph Schmidt III, the court ruled that the chance of a hash collision is not significant and is not an issue. Specifically, a digital fingerprint of a file still produces a unique digital algorithm that uniquely identified that file. This ruling meant that the integrity of digital evidence that was done using either the MD5 or SHA-1 algorithms can be relied upon as legally admissible.

Figure 9.2 Hash collision ruling.

Generally, hash analysis works by computing the one-way cryptographic hash algorithm for a specific data object, such as a text file, and performing a comparison against a repository of hash values of known data objects. However, given the number of different files that exist today, it is unrealistic to start from the ground up and build an in-house hash set repository of known data objects. Alternatively, there are two best practices organizations can use to support hash analysis:

1. Creating hash sets of known-good data objects using the organization's base OS image, also referred to as a "gold image," for computer systems found throughout the enterprise. Once created, the challenge with maintaining this hash repository is sustaining the continuous changes being made to the base image, such as OS patches and new approved software installations. Keeping one step ahead to ensure there is visibility into when changes will be made to the base image requires integrating this process with the software currency processes or leveraging other hash repositories for continuous updates.

2. As a way of increasing efficiencies while processing digital evidence, it is crucial that digital forensic practitioners reduce their data volumes so they can identify relevant and meaningful information. One method of achieving this is by sorting out all known data objects using a repository of hash values. The National Software Reference Library (NSRL) maintains multiple repositories of hash values for known data objects that is readily available in digital forensic tools and technologies (where supported). Using these NSRL hash

repository, hash analysis can be performed to identify known-good files, such as those files that come installed with OS patches, or known-bad files, such as antiforensic tools. The NSRL website is listed in the Resource section at the end of this chapter.

File Signature Analysis

Within any information system, there are several different file types that exist. Many of these file types have been standardized and possess a unique signature, or header, that precedes their data stream to denote the file type. When a standardized header is present, compatible applications installed in the host OS can recognize files by their signature. In addition to having a unique header, many files also possess a unique file extension, such as .doc, that is directly associated with the standardized file signature.

Generally, the concept of file signature analysis is to identify the header of a file, if one is present, and compare that value to the extension currently assigned to the file. Using a file type database of known file signatures and extensions, the result of this analysis identifies whether the signature and extension match the known and standardized file signatures, or whether they are mismatched.

Most commonly, file signature analysis is used to identify where file manipulation techniques have been used to hide data by changing basic attributes associated with the data. For the most part, file signature analysis is not readily available as an enterprise solution for detecting antiforensics. Alternatively, file signature analysis capabilities are commonly integrated into a large majority of digital forensic tools and technologies available in the marketplace.

Integrity Monitoring

Integrity monitoring solutions, also referred to as either host or file integrity monitoring, are used to detect unauthorized changes being made to, and within, a file system. Typically, integrity monitoring is deployed as an early warning indicator of potentially malicious activity and the presence of unwanted or unauthorized applications in a network environment.

The foundation of integrity monitoring is to establish what the known-good operating conditions of an information system are. This known-good baseline preserves a snapshot of the system in its approved, known and normal operating state. Creating this snapshot is done using any combination of attributes that can be used as part of continuous verification and validation, such as:

- Permissions and entitlements
- Data content of files

- Metadata attributes, such as file size or timestamps
- Cryptographic values, such as the message digest or secure hashing algorithm families

Using the snapshot as the baseline, integrity monitoring continuously watches all changes to, and within, a system (i.e., registry, files, directories). If subsequent scans detect that a monitored object's attribute has changed, an event is generated and, depending on the policy, action is taken, such as generating an incident ticket for security to investigate, in order to remediate the change by reverting the file system back to the known-good snapshot.

Strategic Countermeasures

Traditional approaches to defending the enterprise involved implementing signature-based technologies, also known as blacklisting, to identify and mitigate specific threats to information systems and assets. However, in the modern threat landscape, it is no longer feasible to continue playing the cat-and-mouse game when cybercriminals have invested significant efforts in understanding the weaknesses, strengths, and even how these technologies handle different attack patterns. As the effectiveness of signature-based technologies declines, creating greater opportunity for cyberattacks, our strategies need to turn toward implementing agnostic security controls that reduce the organization's overall attack surface (Figure 9.3).

During World War II, the German military developed the Enigma machines which functioned as sophisticated enciphering mechanisms to send messages securely. With the help of Polish mathematicians, the algorithm used in the Enigma machine was broken, and communications could be read in clear text.

Although Polish mathematicians figured out how to decipher the Enigma messages, the German military increased the security of their communications by changing the enciphering algorithms daily, making the task of understanding the coded messages extremely difficult.

Eventually in 1939, an English mathematician named Alan Turing took on a full-time role as head of the Hut 8 team, which carried out top-secret work to decipher the Germany military codes used in the Enigma machine.

Figure 9.3   Enigma machine.

The best approach to reducing the potential for antiforensic techniques to be applied is to eliminate the opportunity for them to be used. Following the methodology of implementing agnostic strategies to reduce attack surfaces, rather than specific threats and risks, the sections below are examples of countermeasures that organizations can implement to mitigate antiforensic techniques. Largely, the countermeasures used by organizations to mitigate antiforensics are found within the combination of strategic administrative, technical, and physical (cyber and information) security controls.

While the strategies illustrated below are a high-level representation of strategic countermeasures that can be implemented to mitigate the risk of antiforensics, they are discussed in further detail in Chapter 14 titled *"Information Security and Cybersecurity."*

Positive Security Approach

Traditional approaches of managing information security through checklists, rules, and compliance cannot keep up with the modern threat landscape or increasing volumes of cyber-related threats and attacks. Alternatively, by following a positive security approach or risk-based methodology, organizations can reduce their overall attack surface by implementing agnostic solutions that employ deny by default security controls.

Defense-in-Depth Approach

Traditionally, security controls are deployed and implemented throughout the enterprise following an overall defense-in-depth strategy. As the enterprise workforce becomes increasingly mobile, and access to information assets and system is done by unmanaged devices (i.e., mobile devices), organizations need to deploy re-evaluate the placement of their layered security controls to be more data-centric to ensure adequate protection of information assets and systems. Refer to Chapter 10 titled *"Digital Evidence Management"* for further discussion about data-centric security.

Summary

The use of antiforensic techniques can result in devastating effects to an investigation and the potential for gathering and processing relevant and meaningful evidence. Combatting these techniques requires organizations to implement layered strategic and risk-based countermeasures that provide for an agnostic method of detecting antiforensics throughout the enterprise.

Resources

Alternate Data Streams in NTFS; Microsoft TechNet. https://blogs.technet.microsoft .com/askcore/2013/03/24/alternate-data-streams-in-ntfs/.

Australian Signal Directorate; Strategies to Mitigate Cyber Security Incidents.
http://www.asd.gov.au/infosec/top-mitigations/mitigations-2017-table.htm.
National Software Reference Library (NSRL); National Institute of Standards and
Technology (NIST).
http://www.nsrl.nist.gov/

Glossary

1. **Modus operandi** is a distinct pattern, way, or method of doing something, or operating, that indicates or suggests the work of a specific subject.
2. **Alternate data streams (ADS)** are attributes only found on the NTFS file system that contain metadata for locating a specific file by author or title.
3. **Slack space** is the area between the end of a stored file and the end of the allocated file cluster on storage media.
4. **Master file table (MFT)** is a database in which information about all files and directories within an NTFS filesystem volume are stored.
5. **Epoch time,** also known as Unix time or POSIX time, is a system used to describe instants in time, defined by the number of elapsed second, since 00:00:00 Coordinated Universal Time (UTC), 01 January 1970, not including leap seconds.
6. **Open system interconnection (OSI) model** is a conceptual reference model that characterizes and standardizes to understand how telecommunications or computing systems communicate over networks.
7. **Bit order** is the direction in which bits are represented in a byte of memory.
8. **Metadata** is data about data that is used to describe how and when and by whom a particular set of information was collected and how the data is formatted.
9. **Onion routing** is a technique used to anonymize network communication by encapsulating messages in layers of encryption.
10. **Sandbox** technologies are security mechanisms to isolate the execution of unverified, untested, and untrusted software applications or code.
11. **Blacklisting** is an access control mechanism that permits all access (read, write) to objects and execution of functions except those that are explicitly defined.
12. **Whitelisting** is an access control mechanism that denies all access (read, write) to objects and execution of functions except those that are explicitly defined.
13. **Message Digest Algorithm family** is a suite of one-way cryptographic hashing algorithms that are used to verify data integrity through the creation of a unique digital fingerprint of differing length based on version used.
14. **Secure Hashing Algorithm family** is a suite of one-way cryptographic hashing algorithms that are used to verify data integrity through the creation of a unique digital fingerprint of differing length based on version used.

Chapter 10

Digital Evidence Management

Whether the evidence is physical or digital, at the center of every investigation is the need to gather and process such evidence to establish fact-based conclusions. The methodologies and approaches used to gather, process, and handle evidence ultimately affects the meaningfulness, relevancy, and admissibility of electronically stored information (ESI)[1] as digital evidence. Like the CIA Triad (confidentiality, integrity, and availability) that applies to the basic principles for security controls, the APT Triad (administrative, physical, and technical) is used to describe critical areas of controls to guarantee evidence is properly managed.

Types of Digital Evidence

Historically, the legal system has viewed evidence, in the form of ESI, as hearsay evidence[2] because there were no scientific techniques to ascertain that the data is factual. This meant that digital evidence being presented before the courts would commonly be dismissed because its authenticity and integrity could not be determined beyond a reasonable doubt. However, as digital evidence became more prevalent with the global adoption of technology and its use in criminal activities, exceptions to admissibility began to arise. For example, under the Federal Rules of Evidence 803(6), an exception to viewing ESI as hearsay evidence exists whereby digital evidence is admissible if it demonstrates "records of regularly conducted activity" as a business record, such as an act, event, condition, opinion, or diagnosis.

However, to qualify digital evidence as a business record within this exception requires that ESI is demonstrated as authentic, reliable, and trustworthy.

Criteria for what type of data constitutes an admissible business record falls within the following categories:

- *Technology-generated data*, or background evidence, is any ESI that has been created and is being maintained because of programmatic processes or algorithms (e.g., log files). These records fall within the rules of hearsay exception on the basis that the data is proven to be authentic because of properly functioning programmatic processes or algorithms.
- *Technology-stored data* is any ESI that has been created and is being maintained because of user input and interactions (e.g., word productivity document). These records fall within the rules of hearsay exception on the basis that the individual creating the data is reliable, trustworthy, and has not altered the data in any way.

Building off these evidence categories, the following groupings can also be applied to provide another perspective on types of evidence:

- *Background evidence* is any ESI that has been created as part of normal business operations that are used to establish facts and conclusions during an investigation. Examples of this type of evidence include, but are not limited to:
  - Network devices, such as routers, switches, or firewalls
  - Authentication records, such as directory services or physical access systems
  - Data management solutions, such as backups, archives, or classification engines
  - Audit information, such as system, application, or security logs
- *Foreground evidence* is any ESI that has been created as a result of objects (human, application, or system), interactions, or activities that directly support an investigation or identify perpetrators. Examples of this type of evidence include, but are not limited to:
  - Real-time monitoring systems, such as intrusion prevention systems (IPS), packet sniffers, or antimalware technologies
  - Application software, such as file integrity monitoring (FIM) and data loss prevention (DLP)
  - Business process systems, such as fraud monitoring
  - Address books, calendar entries, to-do list, memos
  - Electronic communication channels, such as email, text, chat, instant messaging, or web browsing history

With both technology-generated and technology-stored data, it is important to keep in mind that historically the legal system viewed all digital artifacts as hearsay evidence and would not admit them as evidence. However, given how technology evolved to become so pervasive, the courts amended their ruling where exceptions can be made given the authenticity and trustworthiness of the digital evidence being presented.

Further discussion on legal and regulatory precedence relating to digital evidence can be found in Chapter 4 titled *"Laws, Standards, and Regulations."*

Common Sources of Digital Evidence

Traditionally, digital evidence was primarily gathered from computer systems, such as desktops, laptops, and servers. However, the reality now is that digital evidence exists in the form of structured[3] and unstructured[4] ESI across many different technologies. This includes traditional computer systems, such as networks, removable devices (i.e., universal serial bus [USB]); mobile devices; and cloud computing environments.

With the widespread use of technology in business operations, every organization will have ESI that is considered potential digital evidence generated across many different sources. Because of this, careful consideration needs to be given when identifying data sources of potential digital evidence. While the examples below are by no means exhaustive or a complete representation of where digital evidence can be identified, the following data sources should be included as sources of relevant and meaningful ESI to be used as digital evidence.

NOTE: While this book does cover the fundamental principles, methodologies, and techniques of digital forensics, it largely focuses on outlining how the people, process, and technology areas are used to defend the enterprise through integrating digital forensic capabilities with key business functions. This book is not designed to provide readers with the technical knowledge about digital forensics, including the hands-on and how-to aspects of the discipline such as how to forensically acquire technology devices.

Log Files

As a form of background evidence, log files are typically generated from the operation of many different systems and applications. When used as evidence, these logs can be a valuable source of information to correlate and reconstruct events . For example, different types of technology-generated logs that can exist within an enterprise environment include, but are not limited to:

- *Access* logs contain records of authentication, authorization, and admittance by systems and users into systems and information assets.
- *Audit* logs contain records of a specific operations, procedures, or activities associated with interactions and communications between systems and users.

- *Error* logs contain records of faults, unexpected events, or abnormal behaviors that occur during normal system operations.
- *External* logs contain records of interactions and communications between Scotiabank and external systems or users.
- *Infrastructure* logs contain records of specific operations, procedures, or activities associated with operational systems and services.
- *Transactional* logs contain records associated with the interaction with and transmission of information assets between systems and users.
- *Security* logs contain records of events associated with continuous security monitoring of systems and users.

Depending on the type of log file, there will be different data attributes available that can be logged as part of a single event record. However, across all log types there are common data attributes that should be recorded, including, but not limited to:

- *Unique identifier* is a distinctive value representing a single event record (e.g., A1728C27F0)
- *Log timestamp* is the full date and time of when the event was recorded in the log file, including relevant time-zone information if not in coordinated universal time (UTC).
- *Event timestamp* is the full date and time of when the event occurred including relevant time-zone information if not in UTC.
- *Event type* is ranking the event specific to the type of record entry created.
- *Event priority* is ranking the event specific to its potential impact.
- *Event category* is ranking the event specific to the type of interaction and communication occurring between systems and users.
- *Event message* is additional detailed information about the event not contained within any other attribute field of the event record.
- *Account name* is the full name of the account associated with the event.
- *Source IP address* is the IP address where the event originated.

Computer Systems

Perhaps the oldest technology where digital evidence existed is traditional computing systems such as servers, workstations, and laptops. For decades, their form factors[8] were predominantly used to support both personal and business users where many formats of digital evidence can exist in some variation, including both technology-generated (background) or technology-stored (foreground) ESI.

Within computer systems, there are many different digital artifacts created, some unbeknownst to users, that can be used as digital evidence. For example, the following are digital artifacts that can be gathered from computer systems as background evidence:

- Random access memory (RAM) containing information such as username and passwords, running processes, and network connections
- Event log files maintaining records of security, system, or access events
- Temporary files such as caches (i.e., browsing history), dump files, or paging/swap files
- Registry hives and keys containing artifacts associated with applications and the host operating system (OS)

In addition to the background evidence artifacts, computer systems have also incorporated and support a wide variety of third-party software applications that allow users to create, interact, and store many different types of ESI. For example, the following are digital artifacts that can be gathered from computer systems as foreground evidence:

- Configuration and application-specific files (i.e., data outputs, runtime instructions)
- Malicious code or applications (i.e., root kits, backdoors)
- Unstructured documents (i.e., word-processing files)

With all digital evidence on computer systems, it is important to consider the order of volatility when deciding which digital evidence needs to be gathered, as discussed in Chapter 2 titled "*Investigative Process Methodologies.*" Understanding that there are several different OS used with traditional computer systems, the types of digital artifacts that can exist will be inherent to each and may not be present in all instances.

Infrastructure Devices

From the point where network communications were introduced, the potential sources of digital evidence have expanded beyond stand-alone computer systems. In today's technology world, most notably within an enterprise environment, infrastructure devices (i.e., routers, firewalls, proxies, etc.) are actively monitoring and capturing all communications and actions passing through its backplane.[5] The events captured and recorded by these technologies, as technology-generated data, are an excellent source of background evidence that can be used to correlate and corroborate the movement of an attack through the organization. Further discussion about network forensics can be found in Chapter 12 titled "*Incident Management and Response.*"

In line with the statements made in the preceding section, it is important to remember that legal admissibility of technology-generated data requires that authenticity and trustworthiness of the digital evidence is demonstrable.

Further discussion on legal and regulatory precedence relating to digital evidence can be found in Chapter 4 titled "*Laws, Standards, and Regulations.*"

Virtual Systems

Virtualization has become an extremely attractive option to operate both computer systems and infrastructure devices because they are a cost-effective means of quickly provisioning technology resources. For the most part, the systems hosted in these virtual environments will produce similar digital artifacts as found in traditional computer systems with physical hardware. However, within these rapidly elastic virtual environments exists a networking backplane of system communications that do travel beyond the physical host system where virtualization is being run.

Because of how this internal backplane operates, all indicators that an attack is moving between virtualized systems are not going to be available—in typical technology-generated log files—because of the way in which virtualization works. Where this type of internal communication exists, digital forensic practitioners need to remember that the network communications between virtualized systems can only be observed using network forensic tools and techniques directly on the physical host system.

As illustrated in Figure 10.1, virtualized systems have an underlying host environment (hardware and software) where digital evidence can be generated and collected. When a virtual system is involved in an incident or discovered during an investigation, it is important that all data objects associated with the virtual systems are gathered from both host and guest systems, such as:

■ Virtual machine images containing a guest operating system, file system, and data objects

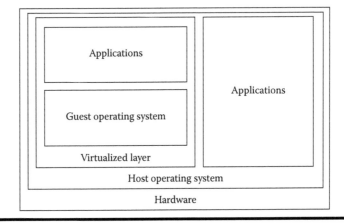

Figure 10.1 Virtualization architecture.

- Log files containing information such as virtual disk partitioning, virtual networking settings, or state configurations
- Dump files from random access memory (RAM) or paging files

Cloud Computing

Through the combination of several major technology concepts, cloud computing has evolved over several decades to become the next stage in computing models. As cloud computing continues to mature, providing organizations with an inexpensive means of deploying computing resources, it is driving a fundamental change in the ways technology is a common layer of service-oriented architectures. Cloud computing presents a unique challenge because of the dynamic nature in which information exists, and the shift to it means organizations have less control over physical infrastructure assets. This leads to the inherent challenge of maintaining best practices for cloud computing while continuing to enable digital forensic capabilities.

Cloud computing has revolutionized the ways ESI is stored, processed, and transmitted. There are numerous challenges facing the digital forensic community when it comes to gathering and processing digital evidence in cloud computing environments. These broadly categorized technical, legal, or organizational challenges can impede or ultimately prevent the ability to conduct digital forensics. While cloud computing possesses similarities to its predecessor technologies, the introduction of this operating model presents challenges to digital forensics.

With cloud-based systems managed by cloud service providers (CSP), organizations may not have direct access to the hardware to gather and process evidence following traditional methodologies and techniques. As a result, collection and preservation of cloud-based evidence that is relevant to a specific organization's investigation can be challenging where factors such as multitenancy, distributed resourcing (cross-borders), or volatile data are persistent.

Refer to Chapter 8 titled "*Cloud Computing Enablement*" for further discussion about enabling digital forensic capabilities with cloud computing environments.

Mobile Devices

From significant technology advancements made over the last decade, business has evolved into a much more dynamic and mobile workforce. Since its inception, the world of mobile technologies has evolved quickly: New devices, operating systems, and threats are emerging every day. Mobile devices present a unique challenge because of how quickly these technologies are changing and the shifting of traditional concepts, such as establishing a perimeter around systems and data. This leads to the inherent challenge of maintaining best practices for mobile device usage while continuing to enable digital forensic capabilities.

In today's world of technology, mobile devices (including smartphones and tablets) have allowed for businesses to transform into much more mobile and dynamic workplaces where employees can work anywhere at any time. However, with a mobile workforce it is quite common that mobile devices, both personally and corporate owned, have been used to access business information that may need to be gathered and processed during an investigation.

Since mobile devices became commonplace in the late 1990s, the digital forensic community has seen an increasing demand to gather and process digital evidence from these devices, presenting numerous challenges. With the proliferation of mobile devices with technologies designed for consumers and businesses alike, they increasingly contain much more potential for digital evidence that needs to be gathered and collected during an investigation.

Detailed discussions about mobile devices and enabling digital forensics capabilities can be found in Chapter 7 titled "*Controlling Mobile Devices.*"

External Sources

Aside from cloud computing environments, there will be cases where digital evidence exists beyond the boundaries of the organization's control that is both relevant and meaningful to an investigation. Understanding that the scope of what could constitute an external source, examples of where digital evidence can be found include, but are not limited to, collaboration and communication platforms (such as web-based email or social media platforms) or managed service providers (MSP), who provide defined sets of services to clients.

Within these external sources, much like the other sources of evidence, much of the same type of background and foreground digital evidence can exist, subjective to what ESI the systems or application within these sources create. Where digital evidence has been identified to exist in an external source, such as a cloud environment, it is not as easily or readily available for organizations. In most cases, it is necessary to involve law enforcement agencies to facilitate gathering digital evidence from external sources, which can prove to be a troublesome and challenging task. Alternatively, formalized legal contracts can be drafted as a mechanism for guaranteeing that third-parties will cooperate in gathering digital evidence when required by the organization.

While the above examples are by no means a definitive representation of every location where potential digital evidence can exist, because every organization is unique and will need to determine the relevance and usefulness of each data source as it is identified.

Additional information about different legal and regulatory governance around the proof of fact, as relates to evidence, can be found in Chapter 4 titled "*Laws, Standards, and Regulations.*"

Evidence Gathering Considerations

Digital evidence is gathered from many different sources that contain the data used to establish factual conclusions. However, it is important to remember that data is only one piece of the puzzle in answering the "who, where, what, when, how" questions of an investigation. The reality is there are several other factors that can be used to provide context and supplemental details about data content that can influence the meaningfulness, usefulness, and relevance of digital evidence during a forensic investigation.

Best Evidence Rule

Originating in British law in the eighteenth century, the best evidence rule is a legal principle that holds the original copy of a document, including both real (or physical) and electronic evidence (or logical), as the superior evidence. In most cases, this means that the verifiably authentic original document must be the one admitted into a court of law as evidence, unless it has otherwise proven to have been previously lost or destroyed. Additionally, the rule of best evidence states that secondary evidence, such as bit-level forensic image, will not be legally admissible if an original, authentic data exists and can be obtained. For example, the application of the best evidence rules can be equated to Federal Rules of Evidence (FRE) 1003, which states that "a duplicate is admissible to the same extent as the original unless a genuine question is raised about the original's authenticity or the circumstances make it unfair to admit the duplicate."

The best evidence rule only applies when a party (i.e., the defending organization) wants to legally admit a specific document, where the original is no longer available, and want to prove the contents to be evidence. If the courts rule that the producing part has demonstrated why the original document cannot be admitted, then the secondary evidence can be legally admissible.

Contextual Awareness

On its own, data contained within ESI can introduce challenges whereby it lacks relative and comparative traits. Bringing about these contextual characteristics requires preserving the supplemental information about ESI that can subsequently be used to correlate and associate digital evidence and help to answer questions about "who, where, what, when, how," so that factual conclusions can be established.

Commonly referred to as *background evidence*, this supplemental information comes in the form of a layered-stack model where each layer serves a purpose to the other layers above and below it. Illustrated in Figure 10.2, a layered model for contextual awareness is comprised of the following attributes:

- *Layer 1: Network*—An arrangement of interconnected hardware that support the exchange of data
- *Layer 2: Device*—A combination of hardware components adapted specifically to execute software-based systems

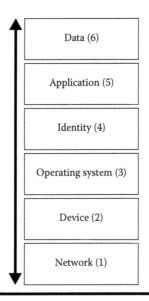

Figure 10.2 Contextual awareness model.

- *Layer 3: Operating System*—Variations of software-based systems that manage the underlying hardware components to provide a common set of processes, services, applications, etc.
- *Layer 4: Identity*—Characteristics that define subjects interacting with software-based systems, processes, services, applications, etc.
- *Layer 5: Application*—Software-based processes, services, applications, etc., that allow subjects to interface (read, write, execute) with the data layer
- *Layer 6: Data*—Structured and/or unstructured ESI that is gathered as foreground digital evidence in support of an investigation

By applying meaningful context to ESI content, factual evidence-based conclusions can be established in a more accurate and thorough manner because the questions of "who, where, what, when, why, how" can be answered with a higher level of confidence and assurance.

Metadata

Metadata is information used to describe how, when, and by whom ESI was collected, as well as how it is formatted; essentially, it is data about data that adds a supplemental layer of contextual information to ESI content. With an investigation, it can provide digital evidence with increased association traits with other ESI, and that can expose information that would be otherwise hidden, deleted, or obscured. Generally, metadata can be distinguished in one of the following categories:

- *Structural metadata* is used to describe the organization and arrangement of information and objects, such as database tables, columns, keys, and indexes.
- *Guide metadata* is used to assist with locating and identifying information and objects, such as a document's title, author, or keywords.

Metadata is commonly used during the processing phase of an investigation to reduce data volumes by adding meaning so that relevant evidence can be more accurately identified. For example, common types of metadata that can be used to supplement evidence during a forensic investigation include, but are not limited to:

- Date and time of when a file was modified, accessed, or created (MAC)
- Location of where a file is stored on an electronic storage medium
- Identity and profile information of user accounts
- Digital image properties, such as number of colors or the source camera model
- Document properties, such as author or the last save/print timestamp

Fundamentally, because metadata is still ESI, it is also subject to the same evidence preservation requirements that are imposed on ESI identified as digital evidence. As discussed later in this chapter, safeguards must be taken to maintain authenticity and integrity of metadata so that is can be effectively used during an investigation and meets legal and regulatory requirements for admissibility in a court of law.

Time Synchronization

Throughout most organizations today, there are many systems and technologies readily connected to a networked environment. Additionally, where an enterprise has an international presence, there is less chance that all systems and technologies will hold the same date and time values. Understanding that all systems and technologies have the potential to contain some form of relevant and meaningful evidence, time synchronization is a major concern when it comes to gathering and processing digital evidence.

Where a centralized log management solution will be used to preserve evidence long-term, such as an enterprise data warehouse (EDW),[6] date and time values from multiple regions can be identified, normalized into UTC, and recorded alongside of ESI as it is being gathered. By doing so, organizations will benefit from having a consistent and verifiable timestamp value allowing for much simpler correlation, corroboration, and association of digital evidence being gathered across all distributed systems and devices.

There are many mechanisms available to implement a synchronous timestamp across different systems and technologies, but, for the most part, these options are still considered a decentralized model for achieving time synchronization across distributed evidence sources. As a best practice, network time protocol (NTP) servers set to UTC allows organizations to establish a centralized location for all systems and technologies to obtain consistent date and time synchronization. While the NTP servers function as the authoritative source for date and time, it is important that time zone offsets are configured correctly on all distributed systems and technologies, based on the time zone the system or device physically resides in.

While NTP addresses the issue of centralized time synchronization, it does not account for the accuracy of time being published to connected data sources. Originally developed for military use, the global positioning system (GPS) provides real-time information about a system's or technology's position, elevation, and time. GPS receivers have a high rate of accuracy and are relatively easy to implement because they, for the most part, only need an antenna with unobstructed line of sight to several satellites for them to work correctly. Connecting a GPS receiver to the NTP device is a cost-effective way of ensuring accurate time signals are being received.

Although organizations might only conduct business in a single time zone, an incident will most often produce digital evidence on data sources that span across several time zones. Having a centralized solution to provide a distributed data source with accurate time synchronization is not something traditionally easy to challenge in a court of law.

Cause and Effect

A common challenge faced during a forensic investigation is identifying the root cause of an event that ultimately led to an effect on the evidence gathered. For example, when a user or process modifies any given file within a file system, the metadata properties of that file will change; specifically, one or more timestamp values will change depending on the modification made. Identification of a cause is generally viewed as one of the most important conclusions to establish during an investigation because nothing happens by chance. Without having facts that scientifically explain the relationship between cause and effects, questions can arise about the credibility of evidence being gathered and processed.

For quite some time, the *natural law of cause and effect*, also referred to as Newtonian causality, has been a guiding scientific principle for investigations. Under this principle comes the belief that all occurrences have a definitive, identifiable cause and a definitive effect, and that that cause and effect are proportionate. Essentially, the bigger the effect, the bigger the cause. Supporting this we also find the *Pareto principle*, sometimes referred to as the 80/20 rule, that states approximately 80% of all effects come from roughly 20% of the causes. Taking into consideration both ideologies, it is evident that distributions of cause and effect are rarely equal in any scenario.

It is not realistic for organizations to identify, understand, and catalogue all combinations of causality possible within their organizations. Instead, by referring to the business risk scenarios, as discussed in Chapter 6 titled "*The Business of Digital Forensics*," organizations can better reduce the unknown causality events applicable to their business environment. By doing so, organizations will be in a position where they can identify and consider additional ESI sources where digital evidence needs to be gathered to improve the enterprise investigative capabilities.

Correlation and Association

Evidence gathered during an investigation is the primary means of establishing fact-based conclusions. Historically, the scope of what would be used as digital evidence in a crime scene was limited to data gathered from the computer systems directly involved in the incident. However, resulting from the pervasiveness of technology today, most business environments consist of interconnected and distributed technologies where an event on one system is often related to events on other systems. Where this condition exists, it is necessary to broaden the scope of an investigation outward to ensure all systems and devices that have potential to be involved are considered as a source of evidence.

From an expanded investigative scope, establishing a relationship between multiple evidence sources is necessary to build credibility by helping to answer the questions of "who, where, what, when, why, how." Gathering evidence from these additional sources of evidence to build facts needs to consider links between both the content and context by which digital evidence exists. For example, the chain-of-evidence model, illustrated in Figure 10.3, is a methodology that depicts the groupings of discrete action and the level of authority required to execute them. Notably, each group of actions is directly linked to those groups above and below it, creating a complete chain of evidence.

Creating links between different data sources, while challenging in certain circumstance, is critical for building the credibility of evidence to establish factual conclusions. Following the chain-of-evidence model requires digital forensic practitioners to think in terms of gathering and processing evidence from throughout the enterprise to satisfy the entire chain rather than meeting only a specific phase of the investigation.

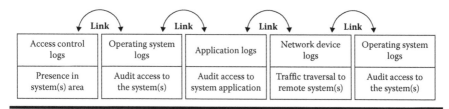

Figure 10.3   Chain-of-evidence model.

Corroboration and Redundancy

Technology has reached a point where it is pervasively distributed and embedded in both our personal lives and business operations. Independently, these individual sources of digital evidence do not offer much to an investigation in terms of piecing together a larger puzzle of what happened. Considering this, when it comes time to gather ESI from these technologies for an investigation there is a constantly growing amount of digital evidence that needs to be processed to establish facts and conclusions. However, when ESI from multiple data sources are being gathered for an investigation, there is the possibility that some level of duplication will be seen in relative to the digital evidence content. This duplication should not be viewed as a negative; it should be viewed as an advantage because it substantiates and helps to prove facts.

Generally, the goal of all digital forensic investigations is to use digital evidence as a means of establishing credible and fact-based conclusions. As stated previously, the credibility of digital evidence can be put into question when it cannot be scientifically proven. Achieving and maintaining this requires that ESI is gathered and processed as a complete chain of evidence because it is highly likely that indicators of the same cause and effect located in other data sources. Over time, as ESI continues to be gathered and processed across multiple data sources, there will be a sufficient volume of digital evidence available which will eventually minimize the need for extensive forensic analysis of systems to gather it. As a side benefit, gathering evidence from multiple data sources allows organizations to start leveraging consistent methodologies and techniques across the entire chain of evidence that can then be used to support other digital forensic supported function, such as incident response and eDiscovery, which is discussed throughout Section C: Integrating Digital Forensic Capabilities.

Data Security Requirements

Storing and preserving ESI as digital evidence can become problematic if data security controls are not implemented and continuously enforced. Preserving ESI to maintain legal admissibility, including authenticity and integrity, depends on the organization's diligence and attention to their legal and regulatory compliance requirements, awareness of the threat landscape, and identification of both the risk and value of preserving digital evidence.

Complimentary to the architectural design of an enterprise data repository for ESI, discussed later in this chapter, work must be done to incorporate industry best practices and standards for how to provide adequate security and reliability of digital evidence through its entire lifetime. To do this requires that ongoing assessments of ESI storage solutions are completed to identify and understand risks associated within its implementation, including:

- Understanding the value of ESI that needs to be preserved
- Interpreting legal and regulatory compliance, standards, and guidelines

- Assessment of the effectiveness of security controls and designs
- Documenting the architectural requirements to support ESI preservation

Data security requirements for preserving ESI are complimentary to the functional requirements of a log management solution whereby they collectively address the need to protect the solution, its data, and its users. While data security requirements are commonly sourced from legal and regulatory bodies (whether international, federal, or local), organizations should adopt industry best practices as a measurement of their due diligence to preserving digital evidence. For example, the following security principles can be applied to provide data security of ESI in a log management solution for the purposes of preserving digital evidence:

- *Confidentiality*: Applying data classification labels as a mechanism for enforcing access controls mechanisms, such as mandatory access control (MAC)[7]
- *Integrity*: Generating cryptographic hash values, such as the Message Digest Algorithm family[9] (i.e., MD5) or the Secure Hashing Algorithm family[10] (i.e., SHA-2), for collected data stored in the centralized repository
- *Availability*: Requiring backups are taken in support of disaster recovery capabilities
- *Continuity*: Building cold/warm/hot sites in support of business continuity capabilities
- *Authentication*: Leveraging existing centralized directory services for subject identification
- *Authorization*: Implementing role-based access controls (RBAC)[11] to objects
- *Nonrepudiation*: Use of cryptographic certificates to associate the actions of or changes by a specific subject, or to establish the integrity and origin of information

Data-Centric Security

Traditionally, enterprise defenses follow a methodology whereby a defined perimeter around the corporate network exists and internal resources are secured against external threats. This approach was very static in nature because technology required network connections to access corporate resources, which was easier to secure and manage. However, given the ever-increasing mobility and dynamic nature of the modern workforce that can be connected anywhere at any time, the traditionally static approach to securing corporate resources does not work as intended.

In today's business landscape, securing corporate resources needs to focus primarily on data so that when an incident happens, there are artifacts that can be investigated. Supporting this methodology, a data-centric security model is an approach that focuses on data rather than technology, users, or applications.

Assessing the requirements for providing data-centric security means having a good understanding of the data and the context by which it is used throughout the organization. At the core of this model, the following are four (4) general questions that every organization need to ask themselves:

Question 1: Where is the data?
With this question, it is important to consider that data not only exists in the logical sense, both also that it exists in the physical sense. Essentially, where data resides determines what type of security controls are required to safeguard it from threats and potential compromised. Considering this, regardless of the type of data, asking "where" must always be the starting point for applying a data-centric security model.

Question 2: What is the data?
Asking this question is an exercise in classifying data based on its content (the information it contains) and context (how information is contained). Answering this starts within the administrative controls of how an organization applies sensitivity, value, and criticality toward categorizing its information, essentially resulting in a data-classification schema. When establishing a data-classification schema, it is important to consider "where" the data resides because, depending on physical location, there might be specific legal or regulatory requirements for categorizing data.

Question 3: Who has access to the data?
Like the question of "where" data exists, there are both physical and logical aspects to consider when answering this question. In the physical realm, this could mean having a pass or key to enter a restricted area, or in the logical realm, being able to modify a file versus only being allowed to read it. Building off the responses from the previous questions, knowing what the information is and how access to it should be controlled is fundamental in answering this question.

Question 4: Why do they need access to the data?
When answering this question, it is important to be specific to prevent a generalized assessment from being done. By doing so, explicit use case scenarios can be properly defined and how each of these scenarios should be handled when accessing the data in question. Asking "why" exists far beyond the realm of security and often requires understanding how business operations are designed and intended to function. If done properly, having answers to this question before an incident occurs will provide established facts and conclusions earlier during forensic analysis.

Noticeably absent from the above questions are "how" and "when" data is accessed. The reason being that with a data-centric security model, the context gathered from the responses are applicable to any environment, both physical

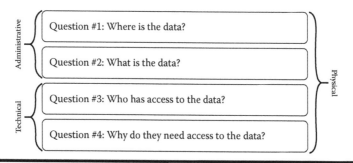

Figure 10.4   Data-centric security control associations.

and logical, and provide the necessary information for implementing a strategy to properly secure and manage the data in question.

Figure 10.4 illustrates how the four preceding questions relate to the implementation of administrative, technical, and physical controls to secure and manage information in a data-centric security model.

Preservation Strategies

Gathering ESI as digital evidence might not be as straightforward as we would like it to be. For example, where large organizations conduct business across multiple jurisdictions, they are ultimately bound to the legal and regulatory requirements for protecting and preserving their ESI. Refer to Chapter 4 titled "*Laws, Standards, and Regulations*" for additional information regarding the applicability of law and regulations to digital evidence.

Understanding the requirements and constraints around what, how, and where ESI can be gathered as digital evidence is necessary to develop strategies for addressing and maintaining the legal admissibility of ESI and to demonstrate compliance with applicable laws and regulations. It is important to keep in mind that as these strategies are being implemented, they need to encompass a holistic approach that includes complimentary administrative, physical, and technical solutions.

Enterprise Governance Framework

A common mistake is to turn toward technology first as the Swiss Army knife that will solve all challenges relating to digital evidence. The reality is that before any technology comes into play, there needs to be a foundation in place that outlines the business need for implementing any technologies. Therefore, first and foremost it is required that a foundational governance structure is established in the form of administrative controls that include the creation and approval of enterprise-wide policies, standards, and guidelines that support the requirements for preserving ESI as digital evidence.

Enabling the forensic viability of digital evidence through the enterprise governance framework, the following subject area should be addressed as part of the developed documentation:

Personnel

- Implement a continuous education program to ensure proper training and awareness if delivered to all stakeholder involved in the collection, preservation, and storage of digital evidence. Refer to Chapter 3 titled *"Education, Training, and Awareness"* for further discussion.
- Require enhanced background checks on a more frequent basis for personal who have access to and work with digital evidence.
- Mandate compliance to the enterprise governance framework by requiring stakeholders to sign necessary documentation as an indication of their understanding and acknowledgment.

Assurance Controls

- Mandate that routine audits or assessments are conducted on administrative, physical, and technical controls implemented to gather, process, and store digital evidence.

Evidence Storage

- Maintain the authenticity and integrity of digital evidence to its original source.
- Document all operational aspects of digital evidence management, including:
  - Storage solutions and facilities
  - Operational processes and procedures
  - Change management
  - Disaster recovery and business continuity
- Establish design and architecture specifications of desired business operations in accordance with legal or regulatory requirements.
- Enforce the principle of least privilege access and implement the use of multifactor authentication mechanisms, including:
  - Something you have (i.e., smart card)
  - Something you know (i.e., password)
  - Something you are (i.e., fingerprint)
- Apply a layered defense-in-depth approach of security controls using a combination of administrative, physical, and technical solutions to deter, detect, deny, and delay potential attackers and threats.

Evidence Handling

- Enforce the principle of least privilege access to only those personnel who are required to interact with digital evidence.
- Implement integrity monitoring to verify that digital evidence has not been tampered with or modified from its know-good and authenticated state.
- Prohibit the alteration or deletion of digital evidence using any form of storage medium that is write once read many (WORM).
- Restrict the storage of, transmission of, and access to digital evidence without the use of cryptographic encryption.
- Seal digital evidence in appropriate containers (i.e., evidence bag, safe) to preserve authenticity and integrity during long-term storage.
- Define the long-term retention and recovery strategies for digital evidence.

For further information about how the enterprise governance framework and its applicability to the organization's overall digital forensics capabilities, including specific documentation examples, refer to Chapter 6 titled "*The Business of Digital Forensics*."

Physical Security Controls

Although physical security controls may not always have direct interactions with ESI, generally providing more ancillary provisions, they are often implemented to control and protect information assets by reducing the risk or damage of loss. As part of the holistic approach to preserving digital evidence, physical security controls must be considered as contributing to maintaining the authenticity and integrity in any combination of the following:

- *Deter*: These controls convince potential intruders or attackers that the likelihood of their success is low because there are strong security defenses in place. Typically, there controls are found in any combined use of barriers (i.e., ballocks), surveillance (i.e., closed circuit television [CCTV]), or lighting (i.e., spotlights).
- *Detect*: These controls discover and interrupt potential perpetrators before an incident or event occurs. Typically, these controls are found in any combined use of surveillance (i.e., CCTV), sensors (i.e., alarm systems), or barriers (i.e., guards).
- *Deny*: These controls prohibit potential perpetrators from accessing controlled or restricted areas, such as server rooms or evidence lockers. Typically, these controls are found in any combined use of barriers (i.e., doors), access mechanisms (i.e., biometric scanners), or storage facilities (i.e., lockers).
- *Delay*: These controls are the last line of defense when other types of controls (deter, detect, delay) are unable to mitigate physical security risks. Typically, these controls are found in any combined use of barriers (i.e., inspection stations), access mechanisms (i.e., turnstiles), or storage facilities (i.e., lockers inside restricted areas).

Least Privilege Access

Although the current threat landscape has evolved to include a series of sophisticated and complex attacks, the delivery channels and attack vectors continue to prey on the absence or weakness in how physical, technical, or personnel security controls are implemented. If not addressed promptly, these deficiencies can become the catalyst for rendering digital evidence inadmissible in a court of law.

The unfortunate reality is that, throughout some organizations, access to information is typically granted beyond the scope of what is otherwise necessary for employees to perform their job duties. As one of the cornerstones within the information security discipline, least privilege access is illustrated in Figure 10.5, showing how it guarantees access to information is maintained at the minimal level required to allow for normal business operations.

Implementing rigid access controls over whom and what has access to ESI is critical in managing the legal admissibility of digital evidence. The absence of access controls, such as applying the principles of least privilege access, puts organizations in a position where they cannot effectively demonstrate their proper due diligence in managing the credibility of their digital evidence, putting into question its authenticity and integrity.

Integrity Monitoring

All ESI, whether technology-generated or technology-stored, is susceptible to issues of trustworthiness because, without properly controls in place, the data contained within cannot be easily validated, resulting in legal challenges to its authenticity and integrity. Ultimately, these issues of credibility are contributing factors that render ESI inadmissible as digital evidence in a court of law, which can make or break a legal proceeding.

Integrity monitoring solutions, also known as either host-based or file integrity monitoring, are technologies used to detect changes being made to and within a

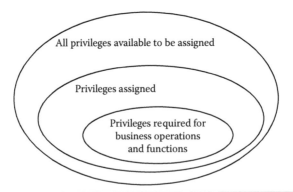

Figure 10.5   Least privilege access.

file system and that generate alerts based on defined policies. Integrity monitoring is deployed as an early warning indicator of potentially malicious activity and the presence of unwanted or unauthorized applications in a network environment. The basis of how integrity monitoring work comes with establishing what the known-good operating condition of a file system is. This known-good baseline preserves a snapshot of the file system in its approved and normal operational state, then uses the snapshot with any combination of attributes as part of continuous verification and validation for changes, such as:

- Permissions and entitlements
- Data content of files
- Metadata attributes (i.e., size, creation date/time)
- Cryptographic hash values (i.e., Message Digest Algorithm family, Secure Hashing Algorithm family)

Using the snapshot as the baseline, integrity monitoring solutions continuously monitor all changes to, and within, a file system (i.e., registry, files, directories, etc.). If later scans detect that an attribute of objects being monitored has changed, an event is generated, and depending on the policy action taken, such as generating an incident ticket for security to investigate, to remediate the change by reverting the file system back to the known-good snapshot.

In addition to using integrity monitoring technologies as a means of establishing authenticity and integrity of ESI, these solutions have also been identified as a requirement for several regulatory compliance objectives, such as:

- Payment Card Industry Data Security Standard (PCI-DSS)—Requirement 11.5
- Sarbanes-Oxley Act (SOX)—Section 404
- Federal Information Security Management Act (FISMA)—National Institute of Standards and Technology (NIST) Special Publication (SP) 800-53 Rev3
- Health Insurance Portability and Accountability Act (HIPAA) of 1996—NIST SP800-66

The online references to the above regulatory objectives can be found in the Resources section at the end of this chapter.

Cryptographic Verification

With every interaction or exchange involving ESI, there is an increased potential that changes, whether knowingly or unintentional, can be made. However, it is critical that any form of data modification is diminished so that the forensic viability of ESI, including authenticity and integrity, is maintained to guarantee its legal admissibility as digital evidence.

The goal for maintaining the authenticity of digital evidence is to demonstrate that it is the same data as what was originally seized. Supporting the need to establish authenticity, the goal for maintaining the integrity of digital evidence is to demonstrate that it has not been changed since the time it was first gathered. For example, the following are use cases where cryptographic algorithms are used to establish authenticity and integrity of digital evidence:

- Both the Message Digest Algorithm family (i.e., MD5) and the Secure Hashing Algorithm family (i.e., SHA-2) are commonly used to generate unique cryptographic identifiers of files and data streams.
- Cyclic redundancy checks (CRC)[12] are commonly used when gathering digital evidence to detect modification to underlying files and data streams. Using these calculations allows forensic investigators to use the duplicate data during analysis instead of risking potential contamination of the original evidence source.

The uniqueness of these cryptographic algorithms makes them an important technique for documenting the authenticity and integrity of digital evidence. When used as a control mechanism, cryptography provides the required level of assurance that the integrity of collected business records can be proven when authenticated to the original data source.

Enterprise Log Management

Log management across an enterprise environment is first and foremost a discipline that leverages technology to meet business, and, in some cases, legal and regulatory needs. Achieving a successful log management implementation requires organizations to follow a systematic and strategic approach that delivers positive return on investment (ROI)[13] that satisfies both business and technical needs.

Implementation Factors

Perhaps the most common reason why enterprise log management fails is because of improper planning prior to moving into the design and implementation phases. Therefore, before work begins to build any form of log management solution, careful consideration needs to be given to key factors that are essential to a successful implementation.

Business Driven, Not Technology-Centric

The use of technology within an enterprise environment must always be driven by business needs. Although this should be common knowledge, there continue to be instances where technology is implemented first and subsequently business requirements are retrofitted to make use of its features and functionalities. This approach most often results in failed implementations, which reinforces the need to establish business requirements well before any development or implementation occurs. Having business requirements established upfront, the focus can then be turned toward designing aspects of the log management solution to meet these needs.

With technology being driven by the business, there will be an expectation that value will be gained from the final solution. Identifying value expectations from technology, as related to business needs, means completing a *requirements analysis* to determine if implementing any given technology is worthwhile in terms of generating a positive ROI. For example, some considerations that should be noted when determining if a positive ROI exists include, but are not limited to:

- Level of integration with enterprise infrastructure (i.e., directory services)
- Increased EDW customization to fit business requirements
- Minimal compromises made on technology components
- Centralized management and support interface exchanges
- Lower total cost of ownership (TCO)[14]

Data Retention

Regardless of being identified as digital evidence, organizations need to keep their business records for a given period because of stipulations defined by either legal or regulatory bodies. Where it is mandated to have this level of governance over business records, formal documentation must be created to define an enterprise-wide policy and schedule for data retention. Not only does retaining this ESI meet the requirements of laws and regulations, but also it demonstrates due diligence in preserving potential evidence that might need to be gathered and processed for investigations. For example, a common requirement for data retention is to preserve email messages in a long-term, read-only archival solution that does not allow for subsequent modification of the ESI.

However, careful planning needs to go into the type of storage solution that will be used to support any data retention requirements. For example, where backup tapes are commonly used to provide long-term storage for information systems, over time the data can be susceptible to information loss as a result of external factors (i.e., magnetic fields) or even technology obsolescence. For these reasons, identifying a solution that meets the specific data retention needs for different types of business records needs to be part of the planning phase before any solution is implemented.

Adaptive Infrastructure

Since the 1960s, technology has significantly evolved in respect to storage capacities, which has certainly become one of the biggest challenges facing most organizations today. As technology continues to advance and storage capacities grows, so does the volume of potential evidence that needs to be gathered, processed, and preserved. Although digital forensic tools and techniques have also seen significant advancements alongside technology's evolution, to help reduce the time required to work with growing data volumes, there remains underlying concerns with how to manage and preserve the increasing volume of potential evidence.

Foremost, the first step in addressing this is to design an evidence storage solution that is adaptable to the continuously growing data volumes. For example, by using solutions such as an *enterprise data warehouse* or an *evidence storage network*, both discussed later in this chapter, data can be managed and preserved in a scalable manger that is dynamically adaptable to evolving capacity demands. Secondly, the continuously increasing amounts of data being stored has potential to impact the performance of data mining and analytics within the storage solution. As a preventative measure, the use of catalogs (types of data being stored) and indexes (properties about data being stored) are useful to quickly identify information and reduce the length of time required to retrieve potential evidence.

Log Management Solutions

When implementing any technology solution where evidence may exist, it is important that you consistently adhere to the principles, methodologies, and techniques of digital forensics. This means that, at all times, organizations must guarantee that the solutions they implement adhere to the best practices for maintaining the authenticity and integrity of digital evidence, and, at no time, introduce risk of spoilage that renders evidence legally inadmissible.

The purpose of this section is to provide an overview of log management solutions where organizations can preserve their digital evidence. Resources on the log management solutions outlined below can be found in the Resources section at the end of this chapter.

Enterprise Data Warehouse (EDW)

An EDW is a collection of integrated technologies that provides a centralized repository for storing information from multiple and disparate data sources. With an EDW, gathered data is historically maintained so that trends can be watched over longer periods to improve data mining, analytics, and reporting capabilities. Typically, EDW solutions have the following characteristics:

- *Subject oriented*: Data is gathered, stored, and organized as a set of information that can be used for a specific business need.
- *Integrated*: Data is consistently structured so it can always be associated to other gathered data without exception.

- *Nonvolatile*: Data is loaded and accessible in a write-once, read-only (WORM) method.
- *Time variant*: Data is accurate at specific points in time and is represented over a long period (such as 5–10 years).

An EDW is a living ecosystem built to deliver specific functionality that meets a business need. Developed using a combination of business and technical components that seamlessly work together, an EDW provides organizations with the ability to consume operational data (used to run the business—such as an order-entry system) and informational data (summarized, normalized, and optimized operational data) to improve the decision-making process. The methods by which the extraction, transformation, and loading (ETL) of data is performed depends on the business need for building the EDW. For example, the following architectural reference models can be used when designing and planning an EDW solution:

- *Basic* is a type of architecture that allows users direct access to data. This architecture requires data is preprocessed before being ingested into the EDW.
- *Staging* is a type of architecture that includes an intermediate area where data preprocessing is performed.
- *Data marts* are a type of architecture, like the basic model, where specific data are placed into separate structured sets.
- *Staging with data marts* is an architecture including a combination of an intermediate preprocessing area and separate structured sets.

Evidence Storage Network

With technology being so pervasive across both our personal and business lives, and the rate at which ESI proliferates across different technologies, it is safe to say that the days are gone when the scope of a digital forensic investigation is limited to a single computer system. The reality is that management of complex investigations where digital evidence is being extracted from multiple sources—such as traditional computer systems, networks, mobile devices, and cloud computing environments—has become a major challenge. In some cases, evidence only needs to be held for the duration of the investigation (or trial). In other cases, evidence needs to be held beyond the duration of the investigation (or trial). Where this is the case, the resulting cause is that organizations need to preserve and store these massive amounts of digital evidence for extended periods.

Traditionally, organizations have leveraged digital backup solutions, such as tapes or external hard drives, to preserve digital evidence long-term. However, digital media technology is constantly changing, and what is available now may not be accessible years from now. Also, digital media degrades over time and few, if any, can guarantee the integrity of stored digital evidence beyond a given period. Furthermore, in multinational enterprises, where digital forensic practitioners are in different geographies, digital evidence needs to be accessible to all those involved in the investigation to allow for collaboration. Continued storage of digital evidence in isolated or offline environments introduces challenges, given the massive amounts of evidence being gathered today. Ideally, what is needed is an efficient way for storing, preserving, and accessing the growing volumes of digital evidence from any location throughout the enterprise.

An evidence storage networks, like an EDW, is a centralized repository where digital evidence can be stored, preserved, and accessed over extended periods. It is designed to support secure access to digital evidence from throughout the enterprise, eliminating the need to maintain digital evidence backup systems. The primary technologies available today to implement network-based storage solutions include:

- *Network area storage (NAS)* is a scalable technology attached to a network and accessible via standard network protocols (i.e., transmission control protocol/ internet protocol (TCP/IP)). It comes embedded with an OS and, in some cases, comes prebuilt in appliances for increased ease of use.
- A *storage area network (SAN)* is a segmented area of the organizations network that is used to handle and store ESI. SAN removes the need for creating and maintaining any storage devices, because it is essentially a part of the enterprise network environment, but only dedicated to storage-heavy traffic.

Any combination of NAS and SAN can be used to achieve an evidence storage network for long-term storage of digital evidence. The decision to use any of these technologies for extended preservation of digital evidence goes back to the business need for implementing it as well as the cost-benefit analysis of selecting one over the other.

Summary

Evidence is the cornerstone from which fact-based conclusions are established. Guaranteeing that evidence remains legally admissible and forensically viable requires following consistent and repeatable methodologies and techniques throughout the entire lifecycle of evidence. Organizations must employ a complimentary series of administrative, physical, and technical controls to effectively maintain the authenticity and integrity of business records that could be used a potential digital evidence.

Resources

Data Warehousing

Jiang, Bin. *Constructing Generic Data Warehouses with Metadata-driven Generic Operators (In the Age of Big Data: Generically Data Warehousing)*, Vol. 1.
Kimball, Richard. *Kimball's Data Warehouse Toolkit Classics*, 3 vols., 2nd ed.

Log Management

Chuvakin, Anton A; Schmidt, Kevin J. *Logging and Log Management: The Authoritative Guide to Understanding the Concepts Surrounding Logging and Log Management.*

National Institute of Standards and Technology (NIST). *Guide to Computer Security Log Management.* http://nvlpubs.nist.gov/nistpubs/Legacy/SP/nistspecialpublication800-92.pdf.

Regulations

PCI-DSS: Requirements and Security Assessment Procedures v3.1. Requirement 11.5. https://www.pcisecuritystandards.org/documents/PCI_DSS_v3-1.pdf. PCI Security Standards Council, 2015.

SOX Act of 2002. Section 404. https://www.sec.gov/about/laws/soa2002.pdf. US Securities and Exchange Commissions, 2002.

FISMA SP800-53 R4. Requirement SI-7. http://csrc.nist.gov/drivers/documents/FISMA-final.pdf. NIST, 2013.

HIPAA SP800-66. Section 4.16. http://csrc.nist.gov/publications/nistpubs/800-66-Rev1/SP-800-66-Revision1.pdf. NIST, 2008.

Glossary

1. **Electronically stored information (ESI)** is information created, manipulated, communicated, stored, and best utilized in digital form, requiring the use of computer hardware and software.
2. **Hearsay evidence** is secondhand or indirect evidence that is offered by a witness of which they do not have direct knowledge but, rather, their testimony is based on what another person has said to them.
3. **Structured** data is information that resides in a fixed field within a record or file (i.e., databases, spreadsheets).
4. **Unstructured** data is information that does not reside in a traditional row-column arrangement (i.e., email, productivity documents).
5. **Backplane** is a group of electrical connectors in parallel with each other, so that each pin of each connector is linked to the same relative pin of all the other connectors to form a computer bus.
6. **Enterprise data warehouse (EDW)** is a central repository used to store amalgamated data from one or more disparate sources in support of analytics and reporting.
7. **Mandatory access control (MAC)** is a type of access-control mechanism where a subject's ability to access resource objects is controlled by the system or an administrator.
8. **Form factor** is commonly used in describing the specifications of a computing device, a computer case or chassis, or one of its internal components, such as a motherboard.

9. **Message Digest Algorithm family** is a suite of one-way cryptographic hashing algorithms that is commonly used to verify data integrity through the creation of a unique digital fingerprint of differing length based on version used

10. **Secure Hashing Algorithm family** is a suite of one-way cryptographic hashing algorithms that is commonly used to verify data integrity through the creation of a unique digital fingerprint of differing length based on version used.

11. **Role-based access control (RBAC)** is an approach where subjects have access to objects based on their associated roles.

12. **Cyclic redundancy check (CRC)** is an error-detecting calculation that is commonly used in digital networks and storage devices to identify accidental changes to raw data.

13. **Return on investment (ROI)** is the benefit to the investor resulting from an investment of some resource.

14. **Total cost of ownership (TCO)** is a financial estimate to determine the direct and indirect expenses and benefits of an investment.

Chapter 11

Digital Forensic Readiness

Digital forensic tasks are commonly performed in reaction to some type of security event or incident. By operating under this context, there is extreme pressure put on the investigative team to work quickly to gather digital evidence before it is modified or lost. Not only is digital evidence critical in establishing fact-based conclusions, but it can also be used to help organizations effectively manage different business-risk scenarios. Fortunately, within enterprise environments there is greater opportunity to proactively gather digital evidence before an incident occurs so that there is a greater chance that it will be available during an investigation.

Forensic Readiness 101

Digital forensic readiness places emphasis on the fact that security events and incidents will occur, instead of being concerned with the traditional responsive approaches. First proposed in 2001, the concept of digital forensic readiness is a methodology designed to allow for organizations to make appropriate and informed decisions about their business risks through effective use of their electronically stored information (ESI).[1]

Generally, the objective of digital forensic readiness can be summarized as the ability to maximize the potential use of ESI while minimizing investigative costs. In addition to this primary objective, other benefits realized from digital forensic readiness include:

- Legally gathering admissible evidence without interrupting business functions
- Gathering evidence required to validate the business impact of security events and incidents

- Permitting investigations to proceed at a cost lower than the cost of a security event or incident
- Minimizing the disruption and impact to business functions
- Guaranteeing evidence maintains positive outcomes for legal proceedings

Cost versus Benefit

Putting a digital forensic readiness program in place may not be a cheap venture, and it needs to be carefully weighed against the benefits an organization will realize once it has been fully implemented. To make an educated decision about whether benefits outweigh costs, a realistic and thorough assessment needs to be done so that all factors that will affect cost are identified.

Attributing Costs

Items contributing to the cost of digital forensic readiness must be both tangible and intangible in nature, spanning across administrative, technical, and physical elements throughout the entire enterprise. Starting with a service catalog, as discussed in Chapter 6 titled "*The Business of Digital Forensics*," each cost element will have been previously associated with an enterprise service where all costing was quantified.

Arriving at an informed decision on whether to include a service as a cost contributor is subject to each organization's interpretation of what is required to achieve readiness. Familiarity with enterprise services, including knowing where security controls have been deployed and both fixed or variable expenditures, are all aspects that need to be deliberated for demonstrating the value of implementing a digital forensic readiness program. While not all security controls contained within the service catalogue will be attributed to the cost of digital forensic readiness, the following are examples of those that will have direct influence on cost:

- *A governance document*—including policies, standards, guidance, and procedures—is continuously reviewed and revised to address changing business operations based on criteria, such as the evolving threat landscape and advancements in technology.
- *Education and awareness training* provides continuous improvements to all stakeholders with any level of involvement with the enterprise's digital forensic capabilities.
- *Incident management* involving the activities of identifying, analyzing, and mitigating risks to reduce the likelihood and potential of security events from reoccurrence.

- *Data security* includes the enhanced capability for the organization to systematically gather potential evidence and securely preserve it long-term.
- *Legal counsel* provides advice and assurance that methodologies, operating procedures, tools, and equipment used during an investigation will not impede legal proceedings.

Realizing Benefits

Even with a strong defense-in-depth strategy of administrative, physical, and technical security controls, organizations still need to operate under the mindset that security events and incidents will occur. Accepting this fact, the realization that taking a proactive approach against security events and incidents can lead to values, such as:

- Minimizing costs associated with disruption to business operations (during an investigation) and becoming more efficient and effective in responding to security event and incidents
- Expanding the capabilities and effectiveness of security controls to improve the notification, containment, and remediation of a much wider range of cyber and information security threats
- Deterring malicious or inappropriate activity through the continuous monitoring and analysis of user and entity behavior
- Establishing a high level of confidence with customers, shareholders, and regulators by exhibiting maturity in the ability to manage security incidents and safeguarding informational assets
- Encouraging better working relationships with law enforcement and regulatory agencies by demonstrating compliance with applicable laws and regulations and immediate disclosure of ESI when required
- Complying with rules governing the discovery and timely production of ESI relevant to litigation matters

Ten Steps to Forensic Readiness

Even if it has not been formally acknowledged yet, the reality is that every organization is already doing some activities that are contributing to the proactive nature of digital forensic readiness. Achieving a state of readiness is a win-win situation for enterprise environments, because it is complementary to and an enhancement of an organization's overall risk management strategies.

Making progress toward achieving digital forensic readiness requires following a systematic approach of multiple risk-based steps. Illustrated in the following sections, the ten steps required to achieve a state of digital forensic readiness must be executed.

Step 1: Define Business Risk Scenarios

First and foremost, organizations need to clearly understand why they are investing their time, money, and resources in digital forensic readiness capabilities. If a business risk exists where gathering and preserving digital evidence is necessary, and there is a positive return on investment (ROI)[2] by being proactive, then operating in a state of readiness is beneficial.

It is important to understand that every organization is unique and has different business risk profiles that require different needs for digital forensic readiness. Translating risks into business context, there are five major types of risk classifications that can be applied:

- *Strategic risk* is associated with the organization's core business functions and commonly occurs because of business interactions where goods and services are purchased and sold, supply and demand varies, competitive structures are adjusted, and the new or innovative technologies emerge. This includes transactions resulting in asset relocation from mergers and acquisitions, spin-offs, alliances or joint ventures, strategies for investment relations management, and communicating with stakeholders who have invested in the organization.
- *Financial risk* is associated with the financial structure, stability, and transactions of the organization.
- *Operational risk* is associated with the organization's business operational and administrative procedures.
- *Legal risk* is associated with the need to comply with the rules and regulations of governing bodies.
- *Other risks* are associated with indirect, nonbusiness factors, such as natural disasters and others as identified based on the subjectivity of the organization.

These business risk classifications, within the context of digital forensic readiness, are scenarios that organizations must identify and develop strategies to manage. Outlined in the following section are multiple business scenarios where digital forensics can be applied to manage business risk. While the applicability of business risk scenarios might not fit the profile of every organization, it is important that each is understood so that they can be considered for relevancy.

> *Reducing the impact of cybercrime*: With information technology (IT) playing an integral part of nearly every business operation, the evolving threat landscape continues to increase risks associated with organizational assets. Using a threat-modeling methodology, organizations can create a structured representation of the different ways threat actors can execute attacks and how their tactics, techniques, and procedures can be used to create an impact. The output of this exercise can be put to practical use by implementing countermeasures that create potential digital evidence.

Validating the impact of cybercrime or disputes: When a security event or incident occurs, organizations must be prepared to quantify and qualify business impact. To obtain a complete and accurate view of the entire cost from the impact, both direct and indirect contributors must be included in the impact assessment. This means identifying tangible and intangible elements from different types of controls (e.g., preventive, detective, corrective) or the overhead cost of managing the incident (e.g., personnel and technology expenses).

Producing evidence to support organizational disciplinary issues: A business code of conduct document promotes a positive work environment that, when signed, strengthens the confidence of employees and stakeholders by establishing an accepted level of professional and ethical workplace behavior. When this code of conduct has been violated, employees can be subject to disciplinary actions. Where disciplinary actions escalate into the legal realm, organizations must approach the situation fairly and reasonably by gathering and processing credible digital evidence to establish fact-based conclusions.

Demonstrating compliance with regulatory or legal requirements: Compliance is not a one-size-fits-all process. It is driven by factors such as an organization's industry (e.g., financial services) or the countries where business is conducted (e.g., Canada). The importance of how governing laws and regulations directly influence the way organizations operate must be clearly understood. Evidence documenting that compliance standards are met must be specific to the requirements of the regulations and laws of the jurisdiction.

Effectively managing the release of court-ordered data: Regardless of how diligent an organization is, there will always be a time when a dispute ends up before a court of law. With adequate preparation, routine follow-ups, and a thorough understanding of what is considered reasonable in a court of law, organizations can effectively manage this risk by maintaining the admissibility of ESI, such as the requirements of the U.S. Federal Rules of Evidence. Ensuring compliance with these requirements demands that organizations implement safeguards, precautions, and controls to ensure their ESI is admissible in court and that it is authenticated to its original source.

Supporting contractual and commercial agreements: From time to time, organizations are faced with disagreements that extend beyond disputes that involve employees. With most of today's business interactions conducted electronically, organizations must ensure they capture and electronically preserve critical metadata about their third-party agreements. This would include details about the terms and conditions or the date the agreement was cosigned. A contract-management system can be used to standardize and preserve metadata needed to provide sufficient grounds for supporting a dispute.

Defining the business risk scenarios that are the primary driver for establishing proactive investigative capabilities is the most critical aspect of practicing digital forensic readiness. Although each business risk scenario contains a series of unique use cases and requirements to proactively gather digital evidence, there remains a degree of commonalities in the justifications for why these data sources need to be readily available.

Refer to Chapter 4 titled *"Laws, Standards, and Regulations"* for further discussion about the U.S. Federal Rules of Evidence.

Refer to Chapter 13 titled *"Electronic Discovery and Litigation Support"* for further discussion about the production of court-ordered evidence.

Step 2: Identify Potential Data Sources

Understanding and defining which business risks are applicable, organizations now need to determine the potential sources of digital evidence that exist throughout their enterprise environment. The most common source of digital evidence can be found in traditional technologies, such as desktops, laptops, and servers. However, organizations must also consider the possibility that data sources also exist dispersed across many different sources.

Similar to how a service catalog provides organizations with a nontechnical understanding of how to locate and align security controls with enterprise digital forensic capabilities, each data source needs to be placed into a similar hierarchical structure. Maintaining an inventory of data sources where digital evidence exists, such as by using a data map, allows organizations to quickly identify it and determine its relevance for proactively gathering. The methodology for creating an inventory of potential evidence sources includes the following phases of activities:

> *Phase 1—Preparation*: Create an action plan to guarantee the strategies used to develop the inventory achieve the organization's goals, objectives, and vision. As a component of this action plan, the following details should be specified:
> - What tasks and activities need to take place to identify data sources?
> - What roles and responsibilities for ensuring the tasks and activities are completed are needed?
> - What are the specifics, such as when tasks and activities will take place, in what order, and for how long?
> - What resources (i.e., funding, people, etc.) are needed for successful completion?
>
> *Phase 2—Identification*: As data sources are identified, each must be categorized and recorded in a centralized repository. While the decision to include or exclude specific data source properties from the inventory belongs to each organization, there are a series of common elements that should be present, such as:
> - *Data format* describes the high-level grouping of how the information is arranged in the data source, such as structured[3] or unstructured.[4]
> - *Data origin* identifies the system and/or application where the information is generated, such as an email archive, an end-user system, a network share, and a cloud service provider.

- *Data category* illustrates the type of information available in the data source, such as multimedia, email messages, and productivity suite documents.
- *Data location* determines how the information persists within the data source, such as at-rest, in-transit, or in-use.

Phase 3—Deficiencies: While the inventory is being completed, there may be gaps in the completeness or availability of ESI. Resolving these deficiencies should be done separately from digital forensic readiness, because the activities required are different in scope. Determining whether a data source meets the requirements to provide ESI to support an investigation is based on the following groupings:

- *Content* are the elements that exist within ESI containing details about a security event or incident, and can be used as digital evidence to arrive at fact-based conclusions. Commonly categorized as foreground evidence, information gathered from data sources should contain content necessary to establish fact-based conclusions about the "who, where, what, when, and how" aspects of an investigation. By assessing the content of a data source, organizations will be able to determine if it contains information that is relevant and useful as digital evidence.
- *Context* is the circumstances whereby supplemental information is used to further describe a security event or incident. Commonly categorized as background evidence, supplemental information gathered from relevant data sources can help to establish fact-based conclusions about the "who, where, what, when, and how" aspects of an investigation. By applying meaningful contextual information to digital evidence, fact-based conclusions can be reached at a much quicker rate because the team can answer with a higher level of confidence.

Refer to Chapter 10 titled *"Digital Evidence Management"* for further discussion about common sources and different types of digital evidence.

Refer to Chapter 6 titled *"The Business of Digital Forensics"* for further discussion about a service catalog.

Refer to Chapter 13 titled *"Electronic Discovery and Litigation Support"* for further discussion about a data map. Additionally, a sample data map has been provided in the Templates section of this book.

Step 3: Determine Evidence-Collection Requirements

Having inventoried all available data sources where potential digital evidence exists, there now needs to be documented requirements for how ESI must be collected and preserved to guarantee forensic viability and legal admissibility. To ensure these evidence-collection requirements are consistently applied, they must be communicated out to those individuals (i.e., information technology (IT) system owners) who are responsible for operating and managing technology where digital evidence is located.

Creating evidence-collection requirements must be practical in terms of the organization being able to realistically implement what is outlined. Determining what level of requirement can be reasonably enforced (i.e., mandatory, recommended, optional), organizations need to answer the following questions:

> *Can a forensic investigation proceed at a cost in comparison to the cost of an incident?* As a result of the cost-benefit analysis to qualify and quantify this comparison, organizations will be able to determine the monetary benefits and impacts of creating collection-requirement statements.
>
> *Can the digital evidence be gathered without interfering with business functions and operations?* Where digital evidence can be proactively gathered, there will be reduce likelihood that resources will be pulled away from their day-to-day business operations to assist with the investigation. This improvement can reduce the impact on business operations, and mitigate lost productivity or degradation in service availability.
>
> *Can a forensic investigation minimize the impact or interruptions to business functions and operations?* The ability to minimize business impacts has a direct dependency on whether digital evidence can be gathered and processed quickly. If it can be achieved effectively, not only does it reduce the turnaround time for starting the investigation, but it can also enable proactivity.
>
> *Can the digital evidence make a positive impact on the likely success of any formal legal actions?* Producing digital evidence requires that forensic viability and legal admissibility of ESI is guaranteed throughout its lifecycle. As discussed in Chapter 10 titled *"Digital Evidence Management,"* rules governing the admissibility of ESI as evidence in a court of law can only be followed if the evidence demonstrates business "records of regularly conducted activity," such as an act, event, condition, opinion, or diagnosis. This means that relevance and usefulness of ESI needs to be determined before drafting evidence-collection requirements to avoid overcollection of downstream processing and review expenses.
>
> *Can the digital evidence be gathered in a manner that does not breach compliance with legal or regulatory requirements?* Laws and regulations can impose restriction on how organizations conduct business in different counties and regions. Understanding that these legal mandates govern how organizations conduct their business, and also influence controls for demonstrating adherence to regulations regarding managing digital evidence.

Refer to Chapter 10 titled *"Digital Evidence Management"* for further discussion about strategies for preserving digital evidence.

Step 4: Establish Legal Admissibility

Within most legal systems, there are rules that set precedence for governing when, how, and for what purpose ESI can be placed before a trier of fact[3] (i.e., judge). Traditionally, courts have viewed ESI as hearsay[4] evidence because its authenticity could not be proven factual beyond a reasonable doubt. However, exceptions exist that permit the legal admission of ESI as evidence if it has been demonstrated as authentic, reliable, and trustworthy. Achieving legal admissibility requires that all ESI being produced is worthy of acceptance in a court of law as evidence. This means that organizations must prove that digital evidence is both relevant (i.e., material, factual), and that it is not surpassed by invalidating factors (i.e., unfairly prejudicial, hearsay).

Yet, there is still potential that ESI will be challenged during legal proceedings, mostly in the form of contests to authenticity and that the ESI was not altered or damaged. Gathering ESI in a manner that meets legal admissibility requirements is not as straightforward as it might seem. Determining how to guarantee ESI will remain authentic, reliable, and trustworthy starts with asking two questions:

> *Can digital evidence be gathered without interfering with business operations?* Where data sources of potential evidence exist and have been identified as candidates for proactive gathering, an assessment of effort required needs to be done while not impeding normal business functions.
>
> *Can digital evidence be gathered legally?* In some countries and regions, there are laws, standards, or regulations surrounding the protection and privacy of information, such as what type can be collected and where it can be stored. Obtaining reasonable assurance that gathering ESI will not violate applicable rules should be done through consultation with legal and compliance teams.

Having answered these questions, and knowing constraints around gathering ESI, a series of administrative, technical, and physical strategies can be identified and developed to guarantee ESI remains authentic, reliable, and trustworthy.

Refer to Chapter 10 titled "*Digital Evidence Management*" for further discussion about strategies for preserving digital evidence.

Refer to Chapter 4 titled "*Laws, Standards, and Regulations*" for further discussion about legal precedence on digital evidence.

Step 5: Establish Secure Storage and Handling

Leveraging the strategies implemented to guarantee the forensic viability and legal admissibility of ESI, focus must now shift toward maintaining these qualities of ESI throughout its lifetime. As was done previously, the combination of complimentary administrative, technical, and physical controls needs to be implemented in a layered fashion, so that digital evidence will be handled correctly and stored securely, such as:

- Establishing a governance framework to address areas, including, but not limited to:
  - Personnel (i.e., background checks)
  - Evidence storage (i.e., security architecture and design)
  - Assurance controls (i.e., control assessment schedules)
- Applying the concept of least privileged access[5] so that subjects[6] only have access to the objects[7] required to perform their job.
- Deploying monitoring solutions to guarantee the authenticity and integrity of digital evidence.

Demonstrating authenticity and integrity of digital evidence being preserved long-term is the same as when it is being gathered and processed. Originally developed by the Association of Chief of Police Officers (ACPO) in the United Kingdom, the *Good Practices Guide for Computer Based Electronic Evidence* illustrates four principles that must be followed to guarantee authenticity and integrity of digital evidence:

1. No action taken by law enforcement agencies or their agents should change data held on a computer or storage media that may subsequently be relied upon in court.
2. In circumstances where a person finds it necessary to access original data held on a computer or on storage media, that person must be competent to do so, and be able to give evidence explaining the relevance and the implications of their actions.
3. An audit trail or other record of all processes applied to computer-based electronic evidence should be created and preserved. An independent third party should be able to examine those processes and achieve the same result.
4. The person in charge of the investigation (the case officer) has overall responsibility for ensuring that the law and these principles are adhered to.

Refer to Chapter 10 titled *"Digital Evidence Management"* for further discussion about strategies for preserving digital evidence.

Step 6: Enable Targeted Security Monitoring

Up until this point, the focus on proactively gathering digital evidence was based on supporting the organization's business-risk scenarios. However, while continuing to support digital forensic readiness, the objective of this step is to identify additional ESI that can be collected and used to detect potential threats. The goal of this step is not to locate other ESI and gather it for the sake of having it proactively available;

determining what additional information should be gathered derives from asking, "At what point should we be suspicious?"

As a starting point, organizations need to define in their enterprise governance documentation (i.e., corporate policies) what is deemed to be acceptable activity, so that there is a clear understanding when deploying targeted security monitoring. As with best practices for security management, a defense-in-depth approach must be followed using traditional controls, such as antimalware or intrusion prevention systems (IPS), and modern controls, such as mobile device management (MDM) and data loss prevention (DLP).

Targeted monitoring within all security controls should be applied using a combination of analytical techniques to ensure that differing patterns of acceptable use can be detected. For example, the following are considered the three major categories of analytical techniques that can be used with security-control monitoring:

- *Misuse detection* is a technique that applies correlation between observed activity and known unacceptable or known-bad behavior, including pattern matching, protocol analysis, and heuristics analysis.
- *Anomaly detection* is a technique that works from a baseline of acceptable behavior and, comparing observed activity to that baseline, identifies unacceptable or known-bad behavior that is not within the predefined baseline.
- *Specification-base detection* is a technique that uses behavior patterns, such as the principle of least privilege access, to detect unacceptable or known-bad behavior by machine learning.

Before implementing any type of security monitoring, it is important that organizations deploy their targeted capabilities under the following considerations:

- Ensure a criticality-based deployment to target high-value and high-risk assets (i.e., employees, systems, networks)
- Deploy a combination of different analytical techniques
- Use solutions that meet the desired service level objectives (SLO)[8] for responding
- Conduct regular reviews of security controls to ensure accuracy
- Refer to Chapter 14 titled *"Information Security and Cybersecurity"* for further discussion about integrating digital forensic with enterprise security capabilities.

Step 7: Define Investigative Workflows

No two security events are identical in content and context. Although technology can facilitate the decision-making process, human intervention is needed to appropriately assess risk level and make informed decisions about whether further actions are necessary, such as initiating a digital forensic investigation.

A digital forensic investigation can be initiated due to a variety of different triggers, including continuous security monitoring, customer complaints, or management escalations. Organizations must be able to demonstrate an acceptable level of due diligence by ensuring they have workflows in place to respond to different types of security events and incidents when they occur. From the time an event occurs there needs to be a repeatable process in place that response teams can use to ensure steps involving information gathering (i.e., preserving digital evidence), information sharing (i.e., stakeholder reporting), and documentation (i.e., standard operating procedures [SOP]) are consistently followed.

Ultimately, clear, concise, consistent, and repeatable workflows are needed to reduce the potential for rushed and uninformed decisions. Also, keeping in mind that every organization is different in how they build workflows, developing them should provide enough flexibility so that the best and most-educated decisions can be made for what actions are needed. As a starting point, it is recommended to leverage industry best practices for defining workflows, such as the *Computer Security Incident Handling Guide*, published by the National Institute of Standards and Technology (NIST).

Refer to Chapter 2 titled *"Investigative Process Methodologies," "Incident Management and Response,"* and Chapter 13 titled *"Electronic Discovery and Litigation Support"* for examples of investigative workflows where digital forensic capabilities are integrated.

Step 8: Establish Continuing Education

A successful digital forensic readiness program, let alone enterprise digital forensic capabilities, cannot be achieved without all stakeholders having the necessary level of knowledge about what is required of them. Foundationally, without proper training and education about digital forensic principles, methodologies, and techniques, the people factor, not technology, becomes the weakest link of all digital forensic capabilities, including proactive readiness.

Providing different levels of knowledge for all stakeholders, depending on the nature of their involvement with the enterprise's digital forensic capabilities, is an effective way of disseminating information about the benefits and value of proactive readiness.

Refer to the chapter titled *"Education, Training, and Awareness"* for additional information on the different level of knowledge organizations can offer or support depending on the various roles stakeholders may have before, during, or after an investigation.

Step 9: Maintain Evidence-Based Reporting

The purpose for conducting an investigation is not to place blame on individuals, but instead to establish fact-based conclusions as demonstrated through credible digital evidence. By applying an evidence-based methodology, organizations will be positioned to establish credibility in answers to questions of "who, where, what, when, and how," as they arise.

As a best practice, all investigations should be conducted on the basis that it will proceed into a court of law. Therefore, reporting should not only be done as a means of sharing information within the organization, but also create with the intention of presenting evidence as legal testimony. Where verbal reports are delivered, it is important to speak directly to the facts of the investigation and to avoid making assumptions without supporting facts. With written reports, at a minimum, they should be created with the following standards consistently applied:

- Accurate description of all event and incident details is provided.
- The report content is clear, concise, and understandable to relevant decision-makers.
- The content is deemed admissible and credible in a court of law.
- The content does not portray opinions or information that is open to misinterpretation.
- The content contains sufficient information to establish factual relevance of conclusions.
- The report is completed and presented in a timely manner.

Regardless of whether evidence demonstrates guilt or innocence, when reporting investigative findings, it is important that with any type of report (written or verbal), focus is placed on credible fact-based conclusions.

Step 10: Ensure Legal Review

At any time during an investigation, it may be necessary to obtain legal advice to provide a level of assurance that there is sufficient credible evidence to support legal proceedings or that evidence gathered does not support factual conclusions. For the legal team to provide an educated and accurate advisement, they need to be knowledgeable in applicable laws, regulations, and standards.

If the legal team is knowledgeable in applicable laws, regulations, and standards, they can readily provide the required level of advisement needed to determine if evidence is credible and will likely hold up in a court of law. For example, the legal team could be called upon to advise and facilitate decision-making relating to the following areas:

- Constraints imposed over the proper and effective use of evidence during an investigation, such as reasonable disclosure timeframes or legal admissibility
- Disputes over contractual commitments and obligations between external entities (i.e., suppliers, customers) to advise and work toward resolution
- Liabilities stemming from breaches where guidance on the best course of action is needed (i.e., customer information exposed)
- Prosecution of perpetrators for restitution of any losses experienced or to ensure claims (i.e., insurance) are properly substantiated

Refer to Chapter 4 titled *"Laws, Standards, and Regulations"* for additional information about legal and regulatory governance.

Achieving Forensic Readiness

Digital forensic readiness is an organization's ability to proactively maximize their prospective use of ESI while reducing investigative costs and gains in operational efficiencies. Following the systematic approach outlined in the ten preceding steps, organizations will realize the benefits of being proactive in gathering and preserving digital evidence.

Recognizing that there is significant effort involved in successfully enabling a state of digital forensic readiness throughout the enterprise, working through the implementation does not need to be overly complicated. Although working through the steps can be complex, organizations should keep the following in mind:

- *Maintain a business-centric focus*: A significant barrier to a successful implementation comes from ineffective communication about business risk to those stakeholders who work directly with and support technologies. Essentially, a successful implementation requires following a risk-based approach that is balanced in terms of understanding the business reasons of having this program in place, who should be involved under what circumstances, and being able to support technical elements in how the organization conducts digital forensics.
- *Do not reinvent the wheel*: Identifying and integrating the administrative, technical, and physical aspects of digital forensic readiness does not means organizations need to start from the ground up. Investment in time, effort, and resources must be focused on what is required to guarantee a successful implementation by leveraging materials that are readily available for use.
- *Understand costs and benefits*: Decisions to skip, substitute, or not invest the required time, effort, and resources can result in failed, incomplete, or misaligned implementations. It is critical that proper planning and investment into digital forensic readiness is allocated so that the goals of the program, such as mitigating business risk, are achieved at a reasonable cost.

Summary

Digital forensic readiness is the ability to proactively maximize the use of electronic stored information (ESI) to reduce the cost of the investigations. The continued practice of waiting for a security event or incident to happen before addressing is it both disruptive to business operation and significantly riskier in terms of guaranteeing digital evidence will not be altered, lost, or incorrectly handled. Organizations that understand the importance of implementing proactive mechanisms to maintain forensic viability and legal admissibility of digital evidence have a much greater chance of surviving and prospering in the continuously evolving threat landscape.

Glossary

1. **Electronically stored information (ESI)** is information created, manipulated, communicated, stored, and best utilized in digital form, requiring the use of computer hardware and software.
2. **Return on investment (ROI)** is the benefit to the investor resulting from an investment of some resource.
3. **Trier of fact,** or finder of fact, is any person or group of persons in a legal proceeding who determines whether, from presented evidence, something existed or some event occurred.
4. **Hearsay evidence** is secondhand or indirect evidence that is offered by a witness of which they do not have direct knowledge but, rather, their testimony is based on what others have said to them.
5. **Least privileged access** is the practice of limiting subject access to objects at the minimal level required to allow normal operations and functions.
6. **Subject** is an active element that operates on information or the system state.
7. **Objects** are passive elements that contain or receive information.
8. **Service level objectives (SLO)** are specific quantitative characteristics used to measure service delivery in terms of availability, throughput, frequency, response time, or quality.

INTEGRATING DIGITAL FORENSIC CAPABILITIES

With cybercrime becoming more pervasive, organizations are continuously grappling with the need to implement control mechanisms to effectively manage their business risks. In response, digital forensic capabilities provide the necessary support to build enterprise-wide control mechanisms to manage these risks. But the reality is that not only can digital forensics be applied toward acquiring evidence to validate the impact of cybercrime, disputes, or other disciplinary issues, but it can also be used in cases where evidence is required for matters not related to digital crime.

Aside from cybercrime, most organizations also have a need to gather and process electronically stored information (ESI) to support other business risk scenarios where digital evidence must be produced consistent with the principles, methodologies, and techniques of digital forensics, such as to support the legal team with electronic discovery (eDiscovery) collections or within the incident response (IR) team to facilitate incident recovery tasks. In all cases, the execution of digital forensics in terms of integrating its fundamental principles, methodologies, and techniques in a broader scope of business risk management will bring about an enhanced ability to produce legally admissible evidence.

There are still some organizations that are not aware of the risks they face, how harmful they can be, or the controls by which they can effectively mitigate their exposures. Integrating digital forensic capabilities into key business operations at an enterprise-wide level allows organizations to better manage these business risk by building both defensive and offensive strategies involving digital evidence. Essentially, integrating an enterprise's digital forensic capabilities is a strategic measure that not only guarantees the integrity and authenticity of ESI, but also enables a proactive readiness that positions an organization to best demonstrate their ability to manage business risks.

Regardless of whether the digital forensics team is supported in-house or through external managed services, the ability to integrate their digital forensic capabilities depends on whether the organizations recognize the importance for doing so. In this section, we will discuss different business services where integrating digital forensic capabilities provides significant return on investment.

Chapter 12

Incident Management and Response

Resulting from strategic integrations through the enterprise, digital forensic capabilities can be invoked to support several key business functions. Like the principles, methodologies, and techniques found within the digital forensics discipline, the incident management lifecycle provides organizations with a consistent, repeatable, and structured framework to manage and handle security events and incidents. As a component of the framework, digital forensic practitioners will be called upon to provide their subject matter and technical expertise during the incident-response activities. Because of the close integration, it is imperative that digital forensic practitioners know their role, what to expect, and when to interject so that critical pieces of evidence are gathered to facilitate root cause analysis.

Understanding the Incident Response Workflow

Illustrated in Figure 12.1, the incident response workflow consists of four major phases where subsets of specific activities are performed to manage the incident.

The major phases of the incident response workflow are performed in sequence and, like the high-level digital forensic process model discussed in Chapter 2 titled "*Investigative Process Methodologies*," requires that preceding phases are revisited as new events or findings are detected, making it very much a lifecycle.

Phase 1: Preparation

Like digital forensics, the workflow begins with activities that enable the overall management and handling of an incident. This is by far the most critical phase of the lifecycle because it establishes the foundation that all other phases will be executed.

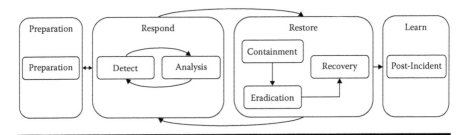

Figure 12.1   Incident management lifecycle.

Effective incident response capabilities require that formal policies, plans, and procedures be documented and implemented for all of the following activities to be successful. Included within the scope of incident response policies, the following must be implemented.

Policies

Policies are blueprints that describe the specific goals for having incident management capabilities. These documents, intended to be high-level and not contain details, commonly contain the following:

- Management's statement of commitment
- Purpose and objective for creating the policy
- Scope of whom, how, and when the policy applies

Plans

Plans build off policies to outline the focused and coordinated approach of incident management. These documents need to meet the organization's unique requirements and provide a roadmap for how incident-response capabilities will be realized. These documents, intended to contain specifics, commonly include the following:

- Mission, strategies, and goals for incident management
- Prioritization or severity ranking of incidents
- Communication and escalation management
- Contact information
- Team structure and models
- Stakeholder approval

Procedures

Procedures should be comprehensive and detailed with technical processes, checklists, and forms that will be used throughout the incident-response workflow. These documents establish the consistent and repeatable methodology that is applied to all phases and activities. Suggested components for including requirements of digital forensics throughout the incident handling and response phases are contained within each of the phases following.

Phase 2: Respond

Perhaps the most challenging aspect of incident response is to accurately detect that a security event or incident has occurred, largely because of the broad scope for where an event or incident can occur. Although appropriate documentation has been implemented to enable a consistent and repeatable incident-response workflow, the way in which organizations handle incidents can vary on a case-by-case basis. Within this phase of the incident management lifecycle, the following activities are performed.

Detect

Before an incident becomes an incident, there must be an observable occurrence that takes place, referred to as an "event," such as a user accessing a restricted area or a firewall blocking a network connection. Events, either physical or technical in nature, can originate from many different internal and external sources.

If left unaddressed, an event can turn into an "incident," which are any violation or imminent threat of violating the organizations, that can result in greater risk and potential for more serious business impact. Generally, indicators of an incident can be placed into one of the following groups:

- *Precursor incidents* are those events that indicate an incident may occur in the future.
- *Indicator incidents* are those events that signify that an incident has occurred or is occurring now.

Analysis

Assessing the validity and severity of an incident would be a relatively simple task if all events were guaranteed to be accurate. However, the reality is that even when confirmed, it does not always warrant that an incident has or is about to happen. For this reason, it is imperative that those responsible for the initial triage of events have sufficient information available so that they can properly assess whether the event(s) is a true-positive[1] or false-positive.[2]

The validation done in this initial triage is an important step in determining which incident-response activities will be performed afterward. For example, where the incident has been invalidated, tuning and adjustment to security controls must be done to reduce the likelihood of the false-positive detection reoccurring. Alternatively, where an incident is confirmed, the incident response team (IRT) must be invoked to prioritize and appropriately manage the incident. As a rule of thumb, incidents should be handled based on priority and not on a first-in-first-out (FIFO) basis; like how a hospital's emergency room (ER) operates.

At the end of this phase, the IRT should have established facts about the incident that can be used to answer the following questions:

- What is the nature of the incident?
- What is the point of origin?
- What is the motive behind the attack?
- What systems, business operations, or informational assets are affected?

Phase 3: Restore

Once the incident has been formally acknowledged and the IRT is invoked, appropriate actions must be taken to mitigate further impact and begin repairing any affected business operations.

Containment

Subjective to an organization's business profile, it is most likely that every incident will be unique, and there will be no single means of universally managing an incident. Because of this, a decision needs to be made as to which countermeasures will be implemented, or deployed, to control the impact beyond the assets and resources currently affected. Ultimately, deciding what strategy best suits the incidents means that organizations must understand the context under which the incident occurred. For example, the following should be used when deciding which containment strategies are most appropriate for a specific incident:

1. Protection of human life
2. Protection of classified and sensitive informational assets
3. Protection of other informational assets
4. Protection of systems and infrastructure
5. Minimal disruption of business operations (i.e., effectiveness, time to implement)

Understandably, the primary goal at this point in the incident-response workflow is to select a containment strategy that will help control impact and eventually facilitate the complete restoration of business operations. Throughout these activities, digital forensic practitioners will be relied upon to give consideration as to what is required to preserve any potential digital evidence before it is lost, altered, or otherwise made unavailable.

The more volatile data that needs to be gathered presents increased challenges to guarantee that this evidence will remain forensically viable as containment efforts proceed. However, it is important to remember that if the ability to collect and preserve any digital evidence before containment strategies are implemented comes with inherent risks. For example, the longer it takes to decide whether evidence is required, the greater the risk of the incident intensifying and further impacting the organization.

If a decision is made to gather evidence before containment activities are performed, it is important to do so by targeting sources of evidence that are at a higher risk of being lost, altered, or otherwise made unavailable. Illustrated in Table 12.1 is the order of volatility for digital evidence, listed from most volatile to least volatile.

Table 12.1   Order of Volatility

Lifespan	Storage Type	Data Type
As short as a single clock cycle	CPU storage	Registers
		Caches
	Video	RAM
Until host is shut down	System storage	RAM
	Kernel tables	Network connections
		Login sessions
		Running processes
		Open files
		Network configurations
		System date/time
Until overwritten or erased	Nonvolatile data	Paging/swap files
		Temporary/cache files
		Configuration/log files
		Hibernation files
		Dump files
		Registry
		Account information
		Data files
		Slack space
	Removable media	Floppy disks
		Tapes
		Optical disc (read/write only)
		Optical disc (write only)
Until physically destroyed	Outputs	Paper printouts

Eradication and Recovery

With containment strategies implemented, the IRT can begin activities to remove and eliminate all indicators and artifacts of the incident from their environment. During this work, all affected assets and resources need to be thoroughly identified and remediated to guarantee that when the containment measures are removed, if they are going to be removed, that the incident does not resurface or propagate.

Recovery efforts involve restoring any affected asset or resource to its normal and fully operational state, which can include activities such as resetting credentials, restoring data backups, or installing patches and updates. Recovery efforts should be completed following eradication activities, not in parallel, so that prioritized focus is on eliminating the threats from the environments as quickly as possible, then refocusing efforts towards restoration.

Phase 4: Learn

Most often when an incident happens, it is a result of a new threat, attack vector, or perpetrator that was not previously accounted for as part of the defense-in-depth security control strategy, as discussed in Chapter 14 titled *"Information Security and Cybersecurity."* Regardless, the most commonly overlooked phase of the incident-management lifecycle is the activities where we reflect on what happened so we can learn and improve our defenses.

As part of this "lessons learned" exercise, which should include a representative stakeholder from each team or department involved during the incident, additional security controls to improve the overall security posture—and mitigate future incidents of the same nature—should be identified so that a feasibility assessment of their effectiveness in mitigating future incidents can be determined. As part of this exercise, the specific details of the incident should be revised to properly close off the incident, including:

- What happened and at what time(s)?
- How well did stakeholders and the IRT deal with the incident?
- Were incident-management processes and procedures followed?
- Did incident-management documentation contain adequate information?
- Did any activities, steps, or actions inhibit restoring business operations, functions, or services?
- How could notification, escalation, and information sharing be improved?

At the end of this phase, the incident-management lifecycle resets back to the preparation phase. Now, outputs from postincident activities will be carried forward so that future incident-response capabilities can be enhanced to reduce the likelihood of new incidents reoccurring.

The Incident Response Team (IRT)

Within the incident response team (IRT), there will most likely be a combination of technical and business representatives who all have interests in mitigating the business impact. An IRT should always be readily available to respond and work to mitigate potential business impact from an incident. Generally, the IRT is responsible for:

- Developing appropriate incident-management documentation
- Retaining resources necessary to perform incident management activities
- Investigating the root cause of detected incidents
- Managing digital evidence gathered and processed from the incident
- Recommending countermeasures and security controls (administrative, technical, or physical)

The ways in which the IRT is implemented depends largely on the organization's makeup, such as geography, size, and business functions. For example, in some enterprises, the IRT might be contained to one centralized location where all incident-response capabilities are managed. Alternatively, some organizations may decide to implement regional IRTs across different locations to support geographical needs, while maintaining a single coordinated governance structure. In either case, it is important that the IRT consists of stakeholders representing different key business functions so that the necessary expertise, skills, and decision-making capabilities can be fully utilized. For example, depending on the organization, the following matter expertise may be needed in the incident-management lifecycle:

- *Management* are responsible for establishing documentation, providing funding, and allocating resources. Ultimately, they are accountable for coordinating incident-response capabilities among all stakeholders and for the distribution of information.
- *Information security (IS)* provides supplementary support throughout the incident-response workflow, such as validating security controls (i.e., firewall rules, intrusion-prevention signatures).
- *Information technology (IT)* has the most intimate knowledge of systems and the potential impact on them from incident-response activities, such as the sequence for shutting down critical systems.
- *Legal* should review all documentation to ensure the organization is compliant with applicable laws, regulations, standards, and the right to privacy. Additionally, these individuals must be engaged when there is potential for some type of legal ramifications associated with the incident, such as prosecution of perpetrators.
- *Public and corporate affairs* facilitates, depending on the incident, communications and information sharing with external parties (i.e., media).

- *Human resources and employee relations* mediate disciplinary proceedings where violation of corporate governance (i.e., business code of conduct) has occurred and an employee is involved.
- *Business continuity planning* ensures documentation is aligned and consistent with the organization's ability to continue its business operations. Their expertise can be used to help minimize operational disruptions and assist with communication.

In addition to having stakeholder representation from key business functions, every successful IRT has clearly defined roles for critical functions during an incident. For example, every IRT should have individuals placed in the following roles:

- *Team lead* oversees all activities performed during the incident. This role is also responsible for coordinating the review of all actions taken during Phase 4, which can lend to changes in documentation and how incidents are handled going forward.
- *Incident lead* has ownership over the immediate incident and oversees coordinating all incident-response activities. All communications about the incident are coordinated through this role to ensure accurate and timely dissemination of information.
- *Associate members* are those individuals who form the IRT as representatives from different business functions. Their involvement and roles can vary depending on the nature of the incident.
- *Scribes* are people who track all activities and document the actions taken throughout the incident. Depending on the nature of the incident, multiple scribes might be necessary to capture a comprehensive register of all activities and actions taken.

The Role of Digital Forensics During an Incident

Digital forensic individuals are those with knowledge of the scientific principles, methodologies, and techniques of the discipline. They are equipped with knowledge, experience, and tools necessary to ensure that activities performed during the incident-response workflow preserve the forensic viability and legal admissibility of digital evidence.

The role of digital forensics within the IRT is twofold: the first is that of an advisor (or consultant) to ensure the team addresses concerns of preserving digital evidence, and the second is the technical professional who leads the activities to gather and process digital evidence. Whether these roles are held by a single individual or split among multiple people is dependent on the nature of the incident, size of the organization, and overall maturity of the organization's incident-response capabilities. In circumstances where the incident necessitates having the role of digital forensic resources separated, the following must be considered during the incident-response workflow.

Practitioner

People in this role are hands-on when it comes to gathering digital evidence during an incident. These individuals must demonstrate the knowledge and skills necessary to apply the principles, methodologies, and techniques of digital forensics on gathered evidence is forensically sound and legally admissible.

Advisor

People in this role are hands-off with all activities directly involving the gathering of digital evidence. These individuals must demonstrate a thorough understand of the principles, methodologies, and techniques so that they can correctly instruct and influence key decision-making during the incident-response workflow.

In circumstances where there is only a need to have a single digital forensic resource assigned to the incident, this individual will be responsible for switching between practitioner and advisor roles. In this situation, the role demands for these individuals to guide the IRT through decision-making processes become hands-on when it comes time to gathering digital evidence. At times, playing both roles can be daunting and cumbersome when trying to ensure that the IRT does not make rash and uninformed decisions that could potentially impact digital evidence. To mitigate this, it is recommended that the advisor and practitioner roles are performed individually through any combination of internal (i.e., employees) and external (i.e., professional services) resources based on cost, skills, response time, and data sensitivity.

Further discussions about education and training relating to digital forensics can be found in Chapter 3 titled *"Education, Training, and Awareness."*

What to Expect During an Incident

Incidents can be stressful. Most often, there is going to be a great number of questions being asked, from people such as executive management, and pressure to resolve the situation as quickly as possible. When present, these factors can lead to the IRT feeling a sense of urgency and anxiety that can lead to rash, uneducated, and uninformed decisions. Preventing this from happening requires the IRT to have a structured approach to incident response and to consistently follow the policies, plans, and processes implemented previously discussed in Phase 1. Examples of specific types of incidents contained in the following may require the IRT to be invoked to perform incident-response actions.

Denial of Service

Although not intended to destroy or steal informational assets like other types of attacks, a denial of service (DoS) attack is effectively used to degrade the availability of a network, system, or service to its legitimate users. Taking DoS a step further, a distributed denial of service (DDoS) occurs when intermediary computer, also referred to as agents or zombies (which can number in the hundreds or thousands), are simultaneously activated to launch a DoS attack against a network, system, or service.

When such an attack occurs, the digital forensic practitioner can be called upon to help the IRT determine the origin and identify of the attacker. Foremost, the question "Is the attack originating from inside or outside the organization?" needs to be answered to guide the IRT in the direction the investigation needs to take. Tracing back the attacks locale requires analyzing technology-generated log files to identify activities and events that confirm the attack locale. Depending on the evidence-based conclusions established from this analysis, the investigation can go in one of two directions:

Attack Originated Internally

In cases where evidence confirms the attack is originating from inside the organization's network boundary, tracing back the attacker's origin requires analysis of technology-generated log files to establish the extent to which systems, networks, and services are being targeted or even used to perpetrate the attack. In some cases, specialized tools and techniques must be used to capture network activity between the attacker and a target, so that details about the attack can be gathered and used to supplement further processing of information relating to the incident. Combining the network forensic evidence with the use of metadata and other equivalent characteristics within log files is valuable to correlate and corroborate information across multiple data sources, so that factual conclusions can be established. Refer to Chapter 10 titled *"Digital Evidence Management"* for further discussion about technology-generated log files and contextual awareness.

As output from analyzing all available information, evidence might identify that the attack is a result of misconfigured information systems or technologies within the organization's environment. While this might come as a relief that there is no malicious intent behind the attack, it is still generating a DoS, and work must be done to address the technical issues to mitigate future occurrences. On the other hand, if evidence identifies malicious code on internal systems as the cause of the attack, the scope of the investigation from being about a DoS attack changes into an investigation into malware infection, discussed in the following section.

Attack Originated Externally

In cases where evidence confirms the attack originated outside the organization's network boundary, tracing back the attack's origin may require the involvement of several external parties to provide information relevant to the attack, such as internet service provider (ISP), managed services provider (MSP), and, in most cases, law enforcement agencies.

Investigating these attacks involves Internet-based networks and systems that are not as straightforward as investigating attacks contained within the organization's span of control. The reality is that these investigations can prove challenging because obtaining relevant evidence is going to encounter several legal issues where varying degrees of law enforcement agencies or court systems will need to intervene. Refer to Chapter 4 titled *"Laws, Standards, and Regulations"* for further discussion about jurisdictions and governing laws.

Before starting an investigation into these Internet-based attacks, organizations need to assess the feasibility and probability that relevant evidence can be obtained from all parties required in a reasonable time in contrast to the incident's impact. For example, if an attack impacted an organization's online platforms for about one hour, and no data breach resulted from the incident, it may not be worth the time, effort, and resources to proceed further with the investigation. However, if an attack brought all business operations to a halt for an extended period, and significant information asset loss was experienced, the organization might decide to engage law enforcement to facilitate obtaining relevant evidence to prosecute their attackers. Where this is the case, the digital forensic practitioner will be called upon to ensure that evidence obtained from external parties is forensically viable and legally admissible.

Malware Infections

Traditionally, mitigating security controls against malicious code or malware involves implementing blacklisting[3] technology (i.e., antivirus solutions) to detect and mitigate known hostile and intrusive software from executing on host systems. However, current antivirus solutions suffer from a low detection rate, due to the rate at which new malware is being released, and thus are suffering from reduced effectiveness to protect information systems and assets from malicious attacks.

Failure to respond to a malware compromise carries the risk of infections spreading quickly and manifesting into a potentially significant outbreak. When any severity of malware infection is identified, digital forensic practitioners can be brought in to provide evidence-based answers to essential questions, such as:

- *How did the malicious code circumvent perimeter defenses?*
  Threat actors[4] are constantly assessing weaknesses within security controls to identify ways of delivering their payload and executing their attacks. Most likely, evidence of what channels were used to deliver and execute an attack will be found in the log files that are created through the normal course of system operations, which is discussed further in Chapter 10 titled *"Digital Evidence Management."* The objective of analyzing these log files is to locate indicators that point to which security controls failed to stop the attack. Based on the facts gathered from this analysis, there can be conclusions drawn that no further action is needed for this portion of the investigation, meaning that

focus needs to be placed on internal security controls for identification of where the attack originated from.

■ *What system changes does the malicious code make?*
Malware's objectives can include such things as disrupting communications, stealing informational assets, accessing private networks, or hijacking systems. All malware infections result in some type of change to host systems, which can be captured and reverse engineered to restore compromised systems back to a known-good state. The challenge with establishing facts to answer this question comes with the frequency by which malware is distributed and pinpointing the exact variant involved with infection. Once isolated, the digital forensic practitioner will reverse engineer to identify indicators of compromise.

■ *What informational assets and systems were affected or compromised?*
Reverse-engineering activities will produce indicators of compromise that can be applied to scan and assess the scope of impact to informational assets and systems across the organization. This exercise often produces a list of systems where malware infection has occurred so that an impact assessment can be completed. Establishing facts about which business systems are infected changes the scope of the investigation from being about malware infection to either a data-breach investigation, or a disaster-recovery and business-continuity exercise.

The preceding are not an exhaustive list of questions you need to ask to determine the impact of a malware infection or outbreak. As stated previously, it is important that the digital forensic practitioner understands and knows what they are doing, why they are doing it, and what value their involvement in malware infections brings to the IRT. As a strategy, when establishing facts to answer investigative questions relating to malicious code, it is recommended to conduct analysis of all potentially malicious code in a controlled and isolated environment, so the outputs and actions do not generate any impact to the business environments. That way, the baseline used for analysis will be in a known-good state that allows for system changes to be captured and highlighted for use in containment or eradication activities.

Data Breaches

A data breach occurs when informational assets or systems have been accidentally or maliciously disclosed to unauthorized parties. The reality is that breaches are certain, and many organizations have already suffered from a data breach in one form or another. When a breach does happen, there will be a tremendous amount of pressure to assess and contain impact, as well as there being increased scrutiny on which controls failed, allowing the breach to occur.

When a breach does occur, time is of the essence to reduce the likelihood of further loss and to limit the extent to which breached data is available to unauthorized parties. As the digital forensic practitioner, you can be brought in to provide evidence-based answers to essential questions, such as:

- *How did the attacker gain access through the perimeter defenses?*
  Evidence needs to be gathered from relevant data sources to identify the point of entry. Most likely, evidence of entry will be found in log files that are created through the normal course of system operations. The objective of analyzing these log files is to find indicators that point to where access was gained through the security controls. Based on the facts gathered from this analysis, there can be conclusions drawn that no further action is needed for this portion of the investigation, meaning that no access was gained from outside the organization's network.
- *How did the attacker obtain access to the informational asset(s)?*
  The fact that access to informational assets or systems was gained is an indicator that sufficient permissions/privileges were obtained to get access. Activities showing the movement between the point of entry and the location of the informational asset or system must be captured in the log files for subsequent analysis. The challenge with establishing facts to answer this question comes with guaranteeing that all relevant evidence has been captured in log files throughout all technologies where movement occurred. Additionally, demonstrating which accounts were affected at all points throughout the movement, accompanied by the level of access within each technology, is necessary to answer this question.
- *How was the informational asset(s) exfiltrated outside the organization?*
  Information assets can reside in different states depending on whether it is being actively used, including being in a volatile (i.e., resident in random access memory [RAM]) or nonvolatile (i.e., dormant in a data object) condition. Beginning with knowing all the informational assets or systems that were breached, the flow of data in its entirety needs to be understood so that additional assets and systems can be included within the scope of the investigation. Establishing facts to answer this question requires that all channels where data flow occurred, along with the state and conditions by which that data exists throughout its lifecycle, must be known.

The preceding questions are by no means exhaustive or a representation of all answers needed to determine the impact of a data breach. It is important that the digital forensic practitioner knows what they are doing, why they are doing it, and what value answering these questions brings to containing and remediating data breaches. When establishing facts to answer investigative questions relating to data breaches, it is best to break down the larger, more general questions into smaller, more manageable pieces. Then it will be easier for both the digital forensic practitioner and the IRT to decompile the breach incidents, and better narrow down the focus on what digital evidence is meaningful and relevant to the investigation.

Unauthorized Access

One of the cornerstones in the information security discipline is the principle of least privileged access, which implies that subjects[5] should only have access to the objects[6] that are necessary as part of normal business operations. For example, financial analysts do not need access to human resource records, and human resource personnel do not need access to quarterly results. However, resulting from malware infections or data breaches, attackers or perpetrators can come into possession of credentials (i.e., of network domain administrators) that can be used to gain further access to informational assets or systems across the enterprise.

When unauthorized access does occur, the extent to which the attacker or perpetrator used these credentials to access (and potentially compromise) information assets and systems must be identified. As the digital forensic practitioner, you can be brought in to provide factual evidence-based answers to essential questions, such as:

- *How did the perpetrator come into possession of the credentials in question?*
  For unauthorized access to be gained, there needs to have been an opportunity for the perpetrator of the unauthorized access to come into their possession. For example, if through the investigation, it is concluded that the perpetrator is not malicious, and came into possession of the credentials through nonmalicious disclosure (i.e., colleague providing via email), then the investigation will most likely not proceed down this path further. However, if it is concluded that the perpetrator gained access through unsanctioned actions (i.e., key logger), then, most likely, the investigation will expand to determine how the breach occurred.
- *What informational assets were accessed?*
  Depending on what credentials were stolen, they will carry with them different levels of access to varying information systems and data. Regardless of how access to the credentials was gained, the individual who came into possession was not authorized to have them and is not permitted to access the information he or she can read or write (principles of least access privilege). Because the informational assets were disclosed to an unapproved subject, the organization may have a legal or regulatory duty to report the unauthorized data, to governing bodies and any persons (i.e., law enforcement, privacy commissioner) whose information was affected as result of the access. It is important that an impact-assessment analysis is completed as quickly, but as thorough and accurate, as possible so that any potential for harm to persons is mitigated (i.e., fraud).

The questions above are by no means exhaustive or a representation of all answers needed to determine the extent and impact to which unauthorized access was gained. As with previous incident types, it is important that digital forensic practitioners understand the scope to which answering these questions is needed to determine what actions are necessary as part of the investigation. As a strategy, when establishing facts to answer investigative question relating to unauthorized access, it is recommended to break down the larger and more general questions into smaller, more manageable pieces. By doing so, it will be easier for digital forensic practitioners and the IRT to itemize the unauthorized access, and focus on what digital evidence is meaningful and relevant to the investigation.

Regardless of what type of incident has occurred, the IRT is expected to function as a cohesive unit. When key stakeholders and matter experts can effectively collaborate and communicate , they become the voice of reason, bringing about a sense of calmness and rationality to the situation. There must not be individual decisions made without consensus from the collective IRT members, so actions are taken based on informed group decisions.

For further discussion about preservation, collection, and retention of digital evidence, including common sources of digital evidence that can be found, refer to Chapter 10 titled *"Digital Evidence Management."*

Investigative Techniques

There is no magic involved when it comes time to integrating digital forensics as a component of the incident-management lifecycle. The fact is that it is just as much an art as it is a science where digital forensic practitioners apply their experience, intuition, and knowledge of the proven scientific methodologies, principles, and techniques. By combining digital forensics with incident-management capabilities, organizations will be able to maximize their ability to gather digital evidence before it is lost due to containment or remediation efforts. The following are examples of techniques frequently used by digital forensic practitioners to establish fact-based conclusions in different incident-response scenarios.

Network Forensics

As mentioned previously, there are times when communications between systems and devices need to be observed to understand what is being transmitted. Network forensics refers to using these technologies to effectively gather information from networks in support of an incident-response or a digital forensic investigation.

Within most organizations today, there exists many security controls and technologies that work together to support network forensic capabilities. Network-based technologies, such as sensors (i.e., intrusion prevention systems [IPS]), access control devices (i.e., firewalls), and sniffers (i.e., NetFlow), all provide a layer of contextual awareness to digital forensic investigations that helps to identify relevant and meaningful digital evidence.

Network traffic data is commonly stored in log files, but, in some instances, it may be required for practitioners to perform a *packet capture*. Although using packet captures to collect network traffic is typically a straightforward task, the volume of information that needs to be processed can be overwhelming and time consuming to gather. Overcoming this means having a good understanding of the organization's computing baseline, such as typical usage patterns of systems and networks, so that anomalous network traffic patterns can be easily identifiable, in turn, reducing the volume of information that needs to be processed. However, before performing any network forensic activities, it is important that digital forensic practitioners consider the following:

- Networks can span across multiple geographical regions, where different time zones are used. As network-based information is captured, it is important that the time-zone offset is captured, and that time is synchronized using a common provider (i.e., network time protocol [NTP] server). Further discussion about time synchronization can be found in Chapter 10 titled *"Digital Evidence Management."*
- Networks can span multiple geographical regions where different legal and regulatory jurisdictions govern the access to, transmission of, and storage of electronically stored information (ESI).[7] Where there is more than one jurisdiction involved, it is important that all parties collaborate on the gathering and processing of network-based information. Further discussion about legal and regulatory jurisdictions can be found in Chapter 4 titled *"Laws, Standards, and Regulations."*
- Rates by which network-based information is captured, such as off-line (after information is transmitted) or real-time (while information is transmitted), determines how quickly it can be accessed, processed, and used as digital evidence. Depending on the business-risk scenario and the profile of the network being monitored (i.e., data center, call center), different collection rates can be applied to make the most effective use of the captured information.
- Increasing network bandwidth is creating larger quantities of information that can be transmitted simultaneously. With that, the potential size of network-based information that exists can be very large and the ability to effectively capture and store it can become problematic. Depending on the business-risk scenario and the profile of the network being monitored (i.e., data center, call center), an assessment of what type of information need to be collected (i.e., network protocols), and the extent to which the information will be collected (i.e., metadata or full-capture) should be done.

Although digital forensic practitioners will need to use technology tools to help gather and process network traffic data, these tools cannot compensate for the need to have knowledgeable individuals who are properly trained and experienced in conducting network forensic investigations. For example, not only do practitioners need to understand the tools and techniques used for conducting network forensics, it is also necessary for them to have comprehensive knowledge of networking principles, commonly used network protocols and services, security controls and technologies, and network-based threats and attack vectors.

Reverse Engineering Malware

Reverse engineering is about taking a product and dissecting it to uncover and better understand its design, so that similar or better products can be made. It is the opposite of engineering, where knowledge of structures, schemas, and interrelationships are extracted without the use of preexisting specifications or models.

Depending on the nature of an incident, many pieces of malicious code could be identified that need to be reverse engineered so that their behaviors can be uncovered and better understood, such as what changes are made to systems they infect. When this happens, digital forensic practitioners can be called upon to assist or lead in reverse engineering malicious code and come up with answers to contain and eradicate the threat, or to assist in subsequent investigation activities (i.e., data breach assessment).

Specific to malicious code, there are many different approaches that work for reverse engineering, such as system-level or code-level, but at the end of the day it comes down to technology tools. The tools used to reverse engineer malicious code (i.e., disassemblers, debuggers, decompilers) were created to support software development but proved to be valuable for figuring out malicious code. However, before reverse engineering any malicious code, it is important that digital forensic practitioners consider the following:

- Reverse engineering requires a great deal of manual processing to be done because there is currently a lack of automated tools available. This shortage in automated tools is not because they cannot be created, but because, unlike digital forensics, there is no consistency in how malicious code is developed, packaged, or released. Because manual efforts are required, reverse engineering should be performed by individuals who know which and when certain techniques or methodologies should be used.
- Authors of malicious code know that their software will inevitably be the subject of reverse-engineering activities. As a means of making the task more challenging, most malicious code authors incorporate some form of antiforensic features into their software to conceal their source code. Using specialized tools such as program packers, sometimes referred to as software packers or runtime packers, authors can compress their malicious code into a form of encrypted self-extracting archive that helps avoid

disassembly. Further discussion about antiforensic techniques, detection, and countermeasures can be found in Chapter 9 titled *"Combatting Antiforensics."*

■ Executing malware samples on computer systems that are not isolated or protected from the rest of the enterprise is extremely dangerous. To mitigate the risk of the malware propagating and causing further impact, using a controlled environment is necessary to conduct any reverse engineering or malicious code assessments. Achieving this can be done using sandbox technologies, which are security mechanisms used to isolate the execution of unverified, untested, and untrusted software applications or code. However, these technologies most commonly use virtualized environments to assess malicious code. Authors know this and, much like the program packers, have incorporated awareness to detect the presence of a virtual environment so that their malicious code behaves differently than it would under normal circumstances.

Reverse engineering is perhaps one of the most complex and intriguing practices in digital forensics, because it combines a practitioner's technical skills (i.e., computer systems, software development, and forensic science) with an integrated artistic approach (i.e., code breaking, puzzle solving). Of course, the way in which the technology threat landscape evolves, and the complexity and involvement to reverse engineer needs to be assessed on a case-by-case basis.

Timeline Analysis

Digital evidence gathered during an incident can originate from many disparate sources each having its own relevancy and meaningfulness to the investigation; refer to Chapter 10 titled *"Digital Evidence Management"* for examples of common sources of digital evidence. On their own, these sources of evidence offer little value because they lack context in the bigger picture of the investigation. However, as a collective dataset, the aggregate of digital evidence provides a complete perspective on the events that occurred during the incident.

With this aggregated data set, the events need to be sorted so that the sequence of events (from all sources) can be chronologically analyzed. Timeline analysis should be a key technique for any investigation, because the timing and chronology of events is always relevant. That said, it is important to note that there is no one best way that describes exactly how a forensic timeline must be built. However, the process can be quite tedious if not completed using some degree of automated tools.

File systems commonly track different date and time stamps of activities relating to files, much like a log file maintains date and time stamps of when an event occurred. These date and time stamps, as a form of supplementary metadata, are the primary source of data that will be used to construct a timeline; including:

- *Created date* refers to the date and time when a specific data object in a file system was created.
- *Last written date* refers to the date and time when the content of a specific data object in a file system was changed.
- *Last accessed date* refers to the date and time when a specific data object in a file system was accessed (i.e., read) by a user, application, or system.
- *Last modified date* refers to the date and time when a file system property of a specific data object in a file system was changed (i.e., renaming the data object's name).

However, before reverse engineering any malicious code, it is important that digital forensic practitioners consider the following factors:

- The date and time stamps used and retained vary depending on the file system being used. For example, the last modified date only exists in file systems where a master file table (MFT) is used (i.e., New Technology File System [NTFS]) or the ability to turn off tracking last accessed date within NTFS. With each data source being used to build a forensic timeline, it is important that the practitioner is familiar with the underlying file system of each source, and how date and time stamps are tracked and retained.
- Date and time stamps can be recorded in different data sources and may not be synchronized using a common provider (i.e., network time protocol [NTP] server). In these cases, the practitioner needs to know the time-zone offset for each data source and then standardize the data and time stamps, so the forensic timeline can be built. Further discussion about time synchronization can be found in Chapter 10 titled *"Digital Evidence Management."*
- With each additional data source, the potential volume of information that will be added into the forensic timeline can become overwhelming for practitioners to manually analyze for relevant and meaningful evidence. Additionally, the structure and content of each data source will most likely be inconsistent, making it more difficult to perform the timeline analysis. Overcoming these concerns means investing in tools and technologies that can accommodate expanding volumes of data while programmatically sorting through the masses, and extracting the information needed to support the timeline analysis.

Summary

The integration of digital forensic capabilities into an incident-response program provides organizations with a consistent, repeatable, and structured framework to manage and handle security incidents. As a strategic component of the incident-management framework, the expertise of digital forensic practitioner helps ensure considerations for gathering digital evidence are properly met and that, when required, it is gathered in a manner that guarantees legal admissibility.

Glossary

1. **True-positive** occurs when results properly indicate the presence of a condition.
2. **False-positive** is an error in which results improperly indicate the presence of a condition when it should not be.
3. **Blacklisting** is an access-control mechanism that permits all access (read, write) to objects and execution of functions, except those that are explicitly defined.
4. **Threat actors** identify and/or characterize the malicious adversary with intent and observed behaviors that represent a threat.
5. **Subject** is an active element that operates on information or the system state.
6. **Objects** are passive elements that contain or receive information.
7. **Electronically stored information (ESI)** is created, manipulated, communicated, stored, and best utilized in digital form, requiring the use of computer hardware and software.

Chapter 13

Electronic Discovery and Litigation Support

The scope of what can be digital evidence encompasses any form of electronically stored information (ESI),[1] such as email messages, audio and video, pictures, office productivity documents, and more. A time will come when the organization needs to locate digital evidence to support a legal or regulatory requirement (i.e., demonstrate compliance, contractual dispute). As a component of the larger electronic discovery (eDiscovery) program, which can be thought of as a data-mining exercise to gather ESI, digital forensic practitioners will be called upon to provide subject matter and technical expertise to assist in discovering and producing relevant ESI. Because of the close integration between digital forensics and eDiscovery, it is imperative that digital forensic practitioners know the role they play with eDiscovery, what to expect, and where their services are needed so that evidence is gathered in a timely manner.

What is Electronic Discovery (eDiscovery)?

The term eDiscovery was first used in the United States and United Kingdom to describe the legal process known as disclosure. Since then, the term has been used internationally to reference the process of discovering relevant ESI that has been court ordered during litigation. During discovery, ESI identified as relevant is placed on legal hold to guarantee that it is preserved in its current state without further modification, deletion, or other interferences. ESI is then collected and processed using technologies that search, tag, and flag based on the keywords and search terms outlined during the scoping of the litigation.

Sometimes, eDiscovery is used interchangeably with digital forensics, which is misleading. EDiscovery is a legal term used to describe disclosure of evidence during a litigation, whereas digital forensics describes the scientific principles, methodologies, and techniques to gather and process digital evidence. Although the two are distinct things, it is important to understand that digital forensic capabilities are fundamental to guarantee that evidence produced during eDiscovery is legally admissible.

Rules and Governance

In the context of eDiscovery, digital evidence is referred to as ESI. Discussed further in Chapter 10 titled *"Digital Evidence Management,"* rules have been established to govern the legal admissibility of any ESI as digital evidence, such as the Federal Rules of Evidence (FRE).

One of the principle rules with eDiscovery is that organizations have a duty to take reasonable steps to identify and preserve relevant ESI, in a timely manner, when any form of litigation is anticipated. To ensure organizations take reasonable steps to not delay legal proceedings, the following series of rules and principles have been established to govern eDiscovery and legal proceedings.

Federal Rules of Civil Procedure (United States)

Within the United States, the Federal Rules of Civil Procedure (FRCP) governs all civil actions and proceedings to secure a just and speedy procedure. These rules apply to the processes followed to prepare and produce ESI during the eDiscovery process. Specifically, the following sections of the FRCP have implications if not followed during eDiscovery.

Rule 16: Pretrial Conferences; Scheduling; Management

This section states that it is the expectation of the courts that organizations take reasonable steps to ensure they are ready for the proceedings. This includes being confident in the sources of relevant ESI, so that pretrial meetings can establish what is discoverable.

Rule 26: Duty to Disclose; General Provisions Governing Discovery

Under this section, Rule 26(a) allows for the scope of discovery requests to include "documents, ESI, and tangible things." However, within Rule 26 there are other provision that have been established to protect against excessive or expensive discovery requests, including:

- Rule 26(a)(1)(C) requires that, unless there is an objection or another time set by court order, initial disclosures must be made no later than 14 days after the meet and confer (Rule 26[f]).

- Rule 26(b)(2)(B) introduces the notion of "not reasonably accessible," where a party does not need to produce ESI from sources because of undue burden or cost.
- Rule 26(b)(5)(B) provides the courts with procedures for settling matters where ESI has been produced when it should not have been.
- Rule 26(f) requires all parties to hold a meet and confer either 1) within 99 days of the filing, or 2) at least 21 days before a scheduled conference.

Rule 33: Interrogatories to Parties

Defined in this section is that discoverable business records, created or stored in electronic format, are given to the requesting parties to examine, audit, compile, abstract, and summarize.

Rule 34: Producing Documents, Electronically Stored Information (ESI), and Tangible Things, or Entering onto Land, for Inspection and Other Purposes

Within this section, Rule 34(b) establishes a structured protocol for resolving disputes about how documents are produced for requesting parties. In some instances, parties may not have the necessary equipment or expertise to read the produced ESI. Through negotiation, the production format is agreed upon, which often is for documents to be produced in a native file format because they review the most detail and have broader support.

Rule 37: Failure to Make Disclosures or to Cooperate in Discovery; Sanctions

Included in this rule is the power for judges to impose penalties against a party "who fails to obey an order to provide or permit discovery." However, Rule 37(e) outlines the certain conditions and circumstances where, if met, provide safety from penalties if they did not preserve ESI and can no longer discover it.

Rule 45: Subpoena

This rule protects those who are nonparty to discovery from the costs or burdens that parties must typically pay or undergo.

The Sedona Conference

Founded in 1997, the Sedona Conference is a group of lawyers and industry professionals dedicated to the advanced study of many law and policy areas, including eDiscovery.

The Sedona Principles

Deriving from the efforts of the Working Group on Electronic Document Production and Retention (WG1), the Sedona Principles were first published in 2004 (last revised in 2017) to address the production of ESI for legal discovery.

Primarily, WG1 was concerned with how the rules and concepts established for discovery of physical documents would be adequate to establish similar governance over electronic documents. Although these principles are not specifically referenced as a component of international law, many of the states in the U.S. and Canada have amended their rules to adopt them as a guide for court decisions.

Contained within the 2017 publication, the following fourteen statements comprise version 3 of the Sedona Principles:

- Principle 1: "Electronically stored information is generally subject to the same preservation and discovery requirements as other relevant information."
- Principle 2: "When balancing the cost, burden, and need for electronically stored information, courts and parties should apply the proportionality standard embodied in FRCP 26(b)(1) and its state equivalents, which requires consideration of the importance of the issues at stake in the action, the amount in controversy, the parties' relative access to relevant information, the parties' resources, the importance of the discovery in resolving the issues, and whether the burden or expense of the proposed discovery outweighs its likely benefit."
- Principle 3: "As soon as practicable, parties should confer and seek to reach agreement regarding the preservation and production of electronically stored information."
- Principle 4: "Discovery requests for electronically stored information should be as specific as possible; responses and objections to discovery should disclose the scope and limits of the production."
- Principle 5: "The obligation to preserve electronically stored information requires reasonable and good faith efforts to retain information that is expected to be relevant to claims or defenses in reasonably anticipated or pending litigation. However, it is unreasonable to expect parties to take every conceivable step or disproportionate steps to preserve each instance of relevant electronically stored information."
- Principle 6: "Responding parties are best situated to evaluate the procedures, methodologies, and technologies appropriate for preserving and producing their own electronically stored information."
- Principle 7: "The requesting party has the burden on a motion to compel to show that the responding party's steps to preserve and produce relevant electronically stored information were inadequate."
- Principle 8: "The primary sources of electronically stored information to be preserved and produced should be those readily accessible in the

ordinary course. Only when electronically stored information is not available through such primary sources should parties move down a continuum of less accessible sources until the information requested to be preserved or produced is no longer proportional."

- Principle 9: "Absent a showing of special need and relevance, a responding party should not be required to preserve, review, or produce deleted, shadowed, fragmented, or residual electronically stored information."
- Principle 10: "Parties should take reasonable steps to safeguard electronically stored information, the disclosure or dissemination of which is subject to privileges, work product protections, privacy obligations, or other legally enforceable restrictions."
- Principle 11: "A responding party may satisfy its good faith obligations to preserve and produce relevant electronically stored information by using technology and processes, such as sampling, searching, or the use of selection criteria."
- Principle 12: "The production of electronically stored information should be made in the form or forms in which it is ordinarily maintained or that is reasonably usable given the nature of the electronically stored information and the proportional needs of the case."
- Principle 13: "The costs of preserving and producing relevant and proportionate electronically stored information ordinarily should be borne by the responding party."
- Principle 14: "The breach of a duty to preserve electronically stored information may be addressed by remedial measures, sanctions, or both: remedial measures are appropriate to cure prejudice; sanctions are appropriate only if a party acted with intent to deprive another party of the use of relevant electronically stored information."

The Sedona Canada Principles

In 2006 a small group of lawyers, judges, and technologists met to begin working toward developing a set of principles, based on the existing Sedona Principles and Canadian law, that would govern discovery processes by the Canadian bar. Deriving from the efforts of the Working Group on Sedona Canada (WG7), the Sedona Canada Principles were first published in 2008 (last revised in 2015) to address the production of ESI for legal discovery.

Contained within the 2015 publication, the following nine statements comprise version 2 of the Sedona Canada Principles:

- Principle 1: "Electronically Stored Information is discoverable"
- Principle 2: "In any proceeding, the parties should ensure that steps taken in the discovery process are proportionate, taking into account: (i) the nature

and scope of the litigation; (ii) the importance and complexity of the issues and interests at stake and the amount in controversy; (iii) the relevance of the available electronically stored information; (iv) the importance of the electronically stored information to the Court's adjudication in a given case; and (v) the costs, burden and delay that the discovery of the electronically stored information may impose on the parties."

- Principle 3: "As soon as litigation is reasonably anticipated, the parties must consider their obligation to take reasonable and good-faith steps to preserve potentially relevant electronically stored information."
- Principle 4: "Counsel and parties should cooperate in developing a joint discovery plan to address all aspects of discovery and should continue to cooperate throughout the discovery process, including the identifications, collection, processing, review, and production of electronically stored information."
- Principle 5: "The parties should be prepared to produce relevant electronically stored information that is reasonably accessible in terms of cost and burden."
- Principle 6: "A party should not be required, absent agreement or a court order based on demonstrated need and relevance, to search for or collect deleted or residual electronically stored information that has been deleted in the ordinary course of business or within the framework of a reasonable information governance structure."
- Principle 7: "A party may use electronic tools and processes to satisfy its documentary discovery obligations."
- Principle 8: "the parties should agree as early as possible in the litigation process on the format, content and organization of information to be exchanged."
- Principle 9: "During the discovery process, the parties should agree to or seek judicial direction as necessary on measures to protect privileges, privacy, trade secrets and other confidential information relating to the production of electronically stored information."

Rules of Civil Procedure (Canada)

The basic presumption with litigation is that the producing party will bear the cost of producing evidence. In Canada, like the United States, eDiscovery is also used as a weapon to force a settlement because of potential costs imposed on producing parties associated with discovery requests. However, unlike the United States court system, Canadian courts almost always consider whether costs should be awarded at the end of a litigation proceeding.

For example, within the province of Ontario, the Ontario Rules of Civil Procedure have given the courts power to make awards of costs by setting out factors that mitigate excessively broad discovery requests where the cost is greater than the award. Specifically, within Rule 57.01(1)(f)(i) there are considerations of whether any steps taken was "improper, vexatious, or unnecessary," which were taken to include excessively costly discovery requests. The fear that eDiscovery requests could be used to threaten and force parties to settle has encouraged the creation of rules to govern civil procedures like those already existing within the United States.

When the Sedona Canada Principles were being created by WG7, they considered rules for discovery that already existed within both the Ontario Rules of Civil Procedure and the Quebec Civil Code. Appreciation for differences between electronic and paper documents allowed for the relevance of case law to be applied to achieve the fundamental objective of securing the "just, most expeditious and least expensive" resolution of litigation. For example, in different Canadian provinces, the definition of what is considered an electronic document varies:

- Alberta Rules of Court defines a "computer generated document" as "a document that a party to proceeding files with, or causes to be issued by, the Clerk or Registrar that (a) is more than 10 pages long, and (b) was generated by computer."
- British Columbia Court Rules Act defines a "document" as "a photograph, film, recording of sound, any record of a permanent or semi-permanent character and any information recorded or stored by means of any device."
- Ontario Rules of Civil Procedure defines a "document" as "data and information in electronic form" and sets out standards for the format of electronic documents in Rule 4.01(3).
- Prince Edward Island Rules of Civil Procedure defines a "document" as "data and information in electronic form." Also, it defines "electronic" as "[that which is] created, recorded, transmitted or stored in digital form or in other intangible form by electronic, magnetic or optic means or by any other means that has capabilities for creation, recording, transmission or storage to those means."

Guided by the work of the Sedona Canada Principles, the Ontario E-Discovery Implementation Committee (EIC) created a checklist, as guidance for parties preparing a discovery plan, which has now become part of Canadian procedural law to support the "proportionality, reasonableness, efficiency and defensibility of the discovery process."

In 2010 the province of Ontario amended its rules of civil procedure to formalize the requirements for parties involved in litigation to agree upon and file a written discovery plan within 60 days after the closing plea. Additionally, the *Guidelines for the Discovery of Electronic Documents in Ontario* was issued as a best practices manual to aid parties performing electronic discovery.

The online resources for the *Checklist for Preparing a Discovery Plan* and the *Guidelines for the Discovery of Electronic Documents in Ontario* have been provided in the Resources section at the end of this chapter.

Possession, Custody, or Control

In addition to FRCP 26(a) and 34 noted above, within FRE 34(a) and 35(a), discussed in Chapter 10 titled *"Digital Evidence Management,"* there are rules obligating respondents to produce "documents, ESI, and tangible things" that are within that party's:

- *Possession*: the ownership and occupation of an object or asset
- *Custody*: the care and holding of an object or asset
- *Control:* the power to direct and manage an object or asset

If a party has "possession, custody, or control" of ESI, then they have a legal duty to preserve it and produce it when requested. However, in today's technology-driven world where digital content is created, transferred, stored, and accessed across an interconnected and geographically distributed network of systems, what does it means to have "possession, custody, or control?"

In 2016 the Sedona Conference published commentary on these rules and the foundational principles that apply when establishing "possession, custody, or control" of ESI:

- Principle 1 states that responding parties will be deemed in "possession, custody, or control" of ESI when they have legal rights to obtain and produce it on demand.
- Principle 2 states that parties opposing the preservation or production of ESI outside its control generally bear the burden of proof that they do not have actual possession or legal rights to obtain the requested ESI.
- Principle 3 includes:
  - 3(a) that outlines when a challenge is raised over the respondents "possession, custody, or control" of ESI, the court should apply modified "business judgment rule" factors.
  - 3(b) that outlines to overcome presumptions of modified "business judgment rule" factors, the requestor bears the burden to demonstrate their ESI concerns (e.g., location, format, access, etc.).
- Principle 4 includes the notion that "possession, custody, or control" should never be interpreted in a way that overtakes conflicting laws or statutes.
- Principle 5 states that respondents to a specifically tailored request for ESI, but do not have actual possession or legal right to obtain the requested ESI because it is in the "possession, custody, or control" of a third party, should notify the requester so that the requester can obtain the ESI from the third party.

Understanding the eDiscovery Workflow

In a technology-driven world where a large majority of business records are being produced, stored, and retained digitally, the amount of evidence made of ESI that needs to be gathered for legal or regulatory purposes can be staggering. This presents a challenge for both legal entities and organizations, because they need take what was done traditionally, with filing and boxing of paper-based evidence, and translate those processes and procedures digitally.

Generally, eDiscovery is the process of applying these traditional legal processes and procedures throughout the digital world. Originally created in 2005, the Electronic Discovery Reference Model (EDRM) framework was designed as guidance for discovering, gathering, and integrating ESI as part of traditional legal processes and procedures. Illustrated in Figure 13.1 is Version 3 of the EDRM framework published in 2014. The online reference has been provided in the References section at the end of this chapter.

Designed to be cyclical in nature, not linear, the EDRM is an iterative process that involves engaging different stakeholders (i.e., legal teams, digital forensic practitioners) at different phases, sometimes numerous times, to produce ESI as required. Working through the EDRM framework, the goal is to cull[2] the overall volume of available ESI down to a relevant subset that will be produced as evidence. To do so, specific activities are performed in support of the following EDRM stages.

Information Governance

While a significant contributor, the discipline of managing adequate and proper recording of information throughout an enterprise environment is a much larger task than just supporting eDiscovery capabilities. Information (or data) governance, as a component of an organization's overall enterprise-governance framework, is a requirement in guaranteeing to the confidentiality, availability, preservation, and accessibility of information.

A major component of information governance is to support the organization's capability to comply with the rules governing litigation procedures and the discovery of ESI as required. However, it is important to note that while information

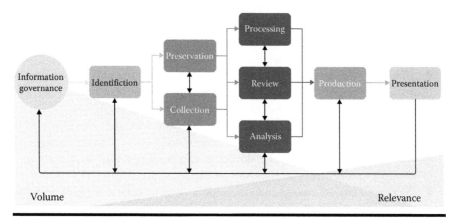

Figure 13.1 Electronic discovery reference model.

governance plays an important role in enabling the discovery of ESI, it is not necessarily a step taken directly as part of the eDiscovery workflow. Understanding that information governance is essential to eDiscovery, the following principles are best practices that all organizations need to implement:

- *Executive sponsorship* is necessary to the success of all information-governance capabilities. As the sponsor who is ultimately accountable and responsible for the organization's information-governance program, they are key to driving efforts to completion by communicating goals and objectives throughout the enterprise on what the information-governance program will address.
- *Governance framework* consists of clear policies, standard, and guidance documentation that outlines the appropriate access and use of informational assets throughout the enterprise. It is vital that this documentation is communicated regularly and concisely to all employees that they not only know the business value the information-governance program brings, but also the consequences for violating it.
- *Information integrity* considers the consistency and repeatability of the methods and techniques used to create, retain, preserve, distribute, and track information. By following good information governance practices, organizations can readily demonstrate assurance that their informational assets are accurate, correct, and authentic, mitigating the risk of data alteration, tampering, deletion, or spoliation.
- *Data classification* is the means of organizing and categorizing information based on its structural format, content, and the relationship (links) to it. Also, it means creating a retention and destruction schedule to define how long the information will be kept (e.g., 10 years) and how it is to be archived and disposed of.
- *Information security* implements measures to safeguard information against damage, theft, or alteration in three states: data-at-rest,[3] data-in-transit,[4] and data-in-use.[5]
- *Information control* are mechanisms deployed to control the access to, creation, modification, and printing of information. When declared a record, information must be properly retained and disposed of as required to comply with legal and regulatory requirements, such as applying legal holds.
- *Monitoring and auditing* of compliance to the enterprise governance framework must be done to guard against spoliation of information and track the access, use, and modification to information across the enterprise.
- *Stakeholder consultation* involves working closely with the individuals who know best about why information is needed and how to properly manage it. This allows organizations to make better and more informed decisions about how to closer adhere with legal and regulatory requirements.
- *Continuous improvement* includes ongoing reviews to account for gaps or shortcomings in the overall program. Additionally, it allows for changes in business environment, technology usage, or organizational strategy to be incorporated.

Identification

Identifying of relevant ESI begins when a litigation is reasonably anticipated. At that time, the team will begin conducting comprehensive searches for sources of potentially relevant information (i.e., paper files, information technology [IT] system) to determine the scope, breadth, and depth of discovery. The team should anticipate that a change in scope could occur at any time, such as the nature of the dispute itself or the custodians[6] involved, and be prepared to respond in very short time frames so as to not impede the production of court-ordered evidence. Operating in a state of proactive preparedness allows organizations to demonstrate their ability to respond accordingly to discovery requests.

Understandably, it can be challenging to always be prepared when enterprise operations are in a constant state of evolution where new systems and types of discoverable business records pop up frequently. Going back to the information-governance work done previously, as new systems and associated data are created, it must be onboarded so that the team's ability to locate ESI can be done in a timely manner. An essential component to this is building a data map to maintain an accurate and up-to-date inventory of systems and applications found throughout the enterprise where potential ESI is created and stored.

The most common descriptive elements that organizations should use in the data map, as provided in the Templates section of this book, should include:

- *Overall status* provides a visual representation of maturity related to the gathering of digital evidence for the overall business scenario, including the following labels:
  - Green = Fully Implemented
  - Blue = Partially Implemented
  - Orange = In Progress
  - Yellow = Plan in Place
  - Red = Not Implemented
- *Business scenario* indicates which of the business scenarios, as discussed in Chapter 6 titled "*The Business of Digital Forensics*," the data source contributes to as digital evidence.
- *Operational service* aligns the data source to the operational service it is associated with as documented in the organization's service catalog, which is discussed further in Appendix D: Service Catalog, and including things such as digital investigations and litigation support.
- *Data format* describes the high-level grouping of how the information is arranged in this data source, such as structured[7] or unstructured.[8]
- *Data origin* identifies the system and/or application where the information is generated, such as email archive, end-user system, network share, cloud service provider.
- *Data category* illustrates the exact type of information available in this data source, such as multimedia, email messages, and productivity suite documents.

- *Data location* determines the state of how the information persists within the data source, such as data-at-rest, data-in-transit, and data-in-use.
- *Data owner* documents the specific individual who is responsible for the data.
- *Business use case* identifies the high-level grouping representing the motive for why this information exists, such as data loss prevention, data classification, and intrusion prevention.
- *Technology name* documents the organization who created and provides ongoing support of the solution where the data source persists.
- *Technology vendor* documents the organization who created and provides ongoing support of the solution where the data source persists.
- *Technology owner* documents the specific individual who is responsible for the solution where the data source persists.
- *Status* provides a visual representation of maturity related to the gathering of digital evidence for the specific data source, including the following labels:
  - Green = Fully implemented
  - Blue = Partially implemented
  - Orange = In progress
  - Yellow = Plan in place
  - Red = Not implemented
- *Status details* provide a justification for the status assigned to the maturity rating for the specific data source.
- *Action plan* describes the activities required for the organization to improve the maturity rating for the specific data source.

Although some of the preceding descriptive elements are beyond the information required for eDiscovery, inclusion of these elements will benefit digital forensic capabilities by creating a data source inventory of potential evidence throughout the enterprise. As a best practice, organizations should follow a systematic methodology for creating a data map as discussed in Chapter 11 titled "*Digital Forensic Readiness.*"

Typically, identification of ESI requires direct involvement from both business users and their IT support teams because, combined, they are most intimately familiar with where ESI exists. Subjective to the organization's eDiscovery program, digital forensic practitioners might be involved to provide their knowledge and expertise about where ESI exists. Further discussion on the role of digital forensic practitioners can be found in subsequent sections of this chapter.

Preservation and Collection

Once there is a reasonable anticipation of litigation, organizations need to take the necessary steps to preserve and collect relevant ESI identified in the previous phase. Ultimately, organizations are held accountable for guaranteeing that their duty to preserve court-ordered evidence is completed. As part of this responsibility, organizations need to notify custodians (i.e., employees, IT departments) who have "possession, custody, or control" of relevant information that they have become subject to legal discovery and that their information must be preserved, something referred to as a legal hold. As part of the legal hold, relevant information is isolated from subsequent access, and safeguards are implemented to avoid risk of modification or loss. Legal holds are issued in all litigation matters regardless of whether evidence is only preserved or is produced to the courts.

Gathering ESI, and guaranteeing that it is protected against alteration or destruction, is necessary for further use in the eDiscovery process. When doing so, guaranteeing legal admissibility of ESI requires following the principles, methodologies, and techniques of digital forensics. While portrayed as individual phases in the EDRM, the collection and preservation of digital evidence are closely related; therefore, they are represented simultaneously. Further discussion on the collection and preservation of digital evidence can be found in Chapter 2 titled *"Investigative Process Methodologies."*

Digital forensic practitioners will be directly involved throughout this phase of the eDiscovery workflow to guarantee that ESI remains forensically sound and that it is gathered following legal requirements for admissibility. Subjective to the organization, IT support teams can also be involved to preserve specific pieces of ESI (i.e., backup tapes) under the direct supervision of digital forensic practitioners. Further discussion on the role of digital forensic practitioner can be found in subsequent sections of this chapter.

Processing

With all identifiable ESI collected and preserved, the sum of what has been gathered can now be reduced in volume, both in terms of the total number of responsive documents and the overall data size. Additionally, ESI might have been collected and preserved in various formats (i.e., backup tapes, individual files, email messages) that need to be restored and, where required, converted into suitable formats to facilitate further cataloging and searching. Before progressing further in the eDiscovery lifecycle, ESI must be processed at an item level to:

- Record ESI metadata properties as it exists before processing
- Distinguish the data content contained within the ESI
- Defensibly reduce the volume of ESI based on relevance

Processing the total sum of ESI cannot be achieved without the use of technologies to programmatically cull all data and ultimately reduce the volume that needs to be subsequently reviewed. The following four subphases are followed when processing ESI:

1. *Assessment* determines what ESI does and does not need to progress further through the eDiscovery lifecycle. During this phase, samples may be used to identify data types and determine potential relevance for further processing.

Critical elements for successful assessment, including following a consistent methodology, defining goals and expectations, and handling exceptions.

2. *Preparation* involves executing activities against ESI (i.e., extraction, indexing, hashing) for subsequent processing. During this phase, samples are used to determine what activities are needed to prepare the ESI, such as decompressing archives (i.e., ZIP). With these activities completed, a determination can be made as to what ESI needs to progress further.

3. *Selection* applies criteria (i.e., deduplication, searching, analytics) to identify what ESI needs to progress further. From these activities, the volume of ESI will be reduced into a subset for review.

4. *Output* allows for selected ESI to be moved into the review phase. This is the last opportunity to identify and correct any issues or exceptions that arose during the processing phase of the eDiscovery lifecycle.

Subjective to the organization's eDiscovery program, digital forensic practitioners can be directly involved to preprocess ESI as a means of reducing volumes before being ingested into eDiscovery review platforms. If not required, digital forensic practitioners must still be readily available to provide technical expertise to cull and process ESI. Further discussion on the role of digital forensic practitioner can be found in subsequent sections of this chapter.

Review

Reviewing ESI is a critical step in most litigation proceedings. During this phase of the eDiscovery workflow, responsive ESI will primarily be analyzed so the team can get a greater appreciation for developing facts, reducing (legal) risk, and facilitating the collaboration between parties. Additionally, parties will also be evaluating responsive ESI for:

- Data that is considered privileged, private, contains trade secrets, or other confidential information
- Key patterns, topics, custodians, and other search terms relevant to the discovery request

However, the reality is that there may still be an enormous volume of ESI that needs to be reviewed, which can seem daunting. The good news is that with the continuous integrations between vendor offerings and increasingly efficient options for handling the volumes of data there have been significant advancements in eDiscovery solutions. Additionally, eDiscovery technologies continue to emerge to bring about new feature sets, such as concept-based searching, machine learning, linguistic pattern recognition, and other functionalities that allow for review capabilities beyond the traditional culling of data.

Technology Assisted Review (TAR)

Technology assisted review (TAR) is the method of leveraging technology to programmatically review ESI, based on expert reviewer input, to expedite the production of court-ordered evidence.

Perhaps the earliest discussion on the topic of using technology to facilitate ESI review was in a 2005 article titled "Automated Document Review Proves Its Reliability," in which analysis revealed that a human review team identified approximately 51% of relevant ESI, where automated assessment technologies identified more than 95%. This finding incited further discussions and research into how technology could provide for a more efficient, less costly, and more proactive review process.

Over the next decade, many agencies contributed to the development of computer-assisted review and predictive-coding solutions, including the National Institute of Standards and Technology (NIST), United States Department of Defense (DoD), the Sedona Conference, and many other independent researchers. From all the work done by these pioneers, it was proven that using technology-assisted review can and does produce more accurate results compared to exhaustive manual review efforts.

Today, TAR has become an essential component of litigation review because of its ability to prioritize ESI and reduce the amount of time and cost for review. It has become such an integral component of the discovery process that many jurisdictions have declared it to be black letter law.[9]

Typically, digital forensic practitioners are not directly involved in reviewing ESI; this is normally left to the legal teams. Although, it is important that digital forensic practitioners are readily available to provide technical expertise to construct and execute searches. Further discussion on the role of digital forensic practitioner can be found in subsequent sections of this chapter.

Analysis

For litigation teams to make informed decisions, they need reliable methods for establishing facts—this phase sets out to achieve this. However, it is important to recognize that although this phase appears after the review phase, it is a recurring activity that must occur throughout many different phases during and before the eDiscovery workflow. Analyzing ESI should be performed throughout the eDiscovery lifecycle as new evidence is obtained, and the litigation evolves.

The analysis phase involves evaluating ESI, in terms of both content and context, by applying search criteria such as key patterns (i.e., phrases and search terms) and custodians (i.e. people). The goal here is to determine relevance and meaningfulness of ESI to help parties with important decision-making strategies, but making sense of evidence requires more than technology. As discussed in Chapter 2 titled "*Investigative Process Methodologies*," if technology is relied on too much as the catchall way to find all evidence, there might still be misleading or incomplete facts established. Being able to perform analysis means having the experience and mindset that escapes scientific or technology foundations and move into the realm of art and perception.

Analytics is about sorting through ESI, finding hidden patterns and correlations, and then extracting meaning to get closer to the facts. Typically, the analysis of ESI is the responsibility of the legal teams and does not require work from digital forensic practitioners. Although, it is important that digital forensic practitioners are readily available to provide technical expertise where required. Further discussion on the role of a digital forensic practitioner can be found in subsequent sections of this chapter.

Production

With the entirety of ESI having been analyzed, the litigation team must now deliver all relevant evidence to the opposing party. However, because of the potential cost and risk associated with producing ESI (i.e., authenticity, integrity), the mechanism and format by which ESI is delivered must be agreed on by all parties during the initial meet and confer.

Typically, producing ESI in the agreed-upon method and format does not require the direct involvement from digital forensic practitioners. Although, it is important that digital forensic practitioners are readily available to provide technical expertise when delivering ESI. Further discussion on the role of digital forensic practitioner can be found in subsequent sections of this chapter.

Presentation

Before ESI existed, evidence was presented to applicable audiences (i.e., judge, jury) in paper form. However, due to the nature of ESI and the increase in production volumes, displaying ESI has proven to be challenging for litigation team and some litigation matters require exhibits to be presented in near-paper (native) formats. Fortunately, developments in technology solutions have made it easier to convert different types of ESI formats into near-native document productions.

As part of the litigation team's strategy for presenting evidence, there needs to be attention to maintaining evidentiary requirements for ESI to remain legally admissible. For example, included within this strategy, there must be safeguards to guarantee authenticity and chain of custody are dealt with appropriately; refer to Chapter 10 titled *"Digital Evidence Management"* for further discussion.

Typically, this phase of the eDiscovery workflow does not directly require involvement from digital forensic practitioners. Although, it is important that digital forensic resources are readily available to provide technical expertise when displaying exhibits (i.e., expert witnesses). Further discussion on the role of digital forensic practitioner can be found later in this chapter.

Managing Litigation Discovery

Most commonly, those involved in eDiscovery will feel a sense of urgency for getting to the end of the job and producing all court-ordered evidence as quickly as possible. While this is quite natural, it is important that the team stays calm and does not let the pressure get the better of them, because if they do, it can lead to errors. Managing a litigation matter requires that the team has strong working knowledge and experience in the methodologies and techniques needed to execute each phase of the eDiscovery workflow. For example, a litigation cannot be effectively managed if the legal team has limited technical knowledge or if the digital forensic team does not have a reasonable grasp on litigation concepts and procedures.

In the past, after litigation was formally started, the matter would progress until discovery was exchanged between parties. When discovery was requested in this time, parties would gather all available documents, assign them a Bates number,[10] and review for relevancy. However, when ESI came into the scope of discovery, the litigation landscape increased in complexity leaving parties searching throughout their enterprise for relevant information, both physically and logically.

As guidance for navigating (complex) discovery requests, EDRM has published a project management guide as a framework to simply the eDiscovery workflow and maximize the success of discovery projects. The EDRM project management process model is an extraction of core eDiscovery elements separated into the following seven distinct activities:

1. *Scoping* defines the success criteria by aligning resources toward a common set of objectives and goals that are used to establish a foundation for the following phases.
2. *Preliminary planning* produces a simple project plan that contains enough details for the team to determine resources, such as an external vendor, required.
3. *Team and vendor selection* formally engages either or both internal and external resources to support the project.
4. *Detailed planning* develops a comprehensive project plan which includes in-depth details about how the project will be executed.
5. *Startup* initiates project workflows, technology setup and configuration, user training (where required), and sample data exchanges for validation.
6. *Execution* focuses on ensuring the project does not deviate from the documented plan and making adjustments where needed.
7. *Closeout* formally concludes the project, as outlined in the plan, where data is archived or disposed of, reporting and metrics distributed, and lessons learned documented.

The EDRM project management guide was designed to be easily implemented and adaptable to handle a broad range of discovery projects. The online resource for the project management guide' has been provided in the Resources section at the end of this chapter.

Preservation Orders

Litigation matters complete each phase of the eDiscovery workflow right through to completion. However, subject to the nature of the litigation, an order could be placed by the courts that requires ESI to only be preserved from destruction and not actually produced. Where this occurs, parties for whom the discovery request is sought against will only work through the eDiscovery workflow up to the point of preserving ESI. In some cases, when seeking a preservation order, it is not uncommon for all parties involved to not yet have a thorough understanding of the extent to which ESI is readily available, and the mechanisms by which ESI can be placed on preservation.

For example, there are quite often assumptions made as to the cost and ease for a party to preserve backup tapes. When in reality, every backup system is unique and without having detailed specifications about the backup system, it can be quite difficult for parties to determine what steps are appropriate or inappropriate to meet the preservation requirement. As a safeguard against unreasonable preservation, FRCP Rule 26(b)(2)(B) establishes that "a party need not provide discovery of electronically stored information from sources that the party identified as not reasonably accessible because of undue burden or cost." Demonstrating undue burden or cost is the responsibility of the party for whom the discovery request is sought against.

Preservation orders should only be issued in circumstances where it can be first demonstrated that there is a genuine risk to a party's evidence being destroyed, which are quite routine for litigations involving ESI. However, before issuing a preservation order, parties should hold their initial meet and confer to ensure the scope of ESI requiring preservation is relevant and that it will not unduly interfere with the party's normal business operations. For example, FRCP Rule 26(f) establishes that although there is a requirement for parties to discuss preservation, this does not imply that a preservation order should only be issued in exceptional circumstances, and that courts should routinely enter these orders.

Legal Holds

As part of a preservation order, parties have an obligation to guarantee that relevant ESI belonging to identified custodians is not destroyed. To achieve this, a formal notification, known as a legal hold notice, is sent from the organization's legal team to each custodian instructing them not to delete, discard, or otherwise destroy any ESI that is relevant to the litigation. Legal holds are the first line of defense against the deletion of potentially relevant ESI and should be issued immediately after a litigation commences or is reasonably anticipated.

The Role of Digital Forensics in a Litigation

Digital forensic practitioners might play different roles throughout an enterprise depending on what is being asked of them (i.e., investigate, recover data, incident response, etc.). The reality is that digital forensic practitioners are quite frequently called upon to support eDiscovery efforts because legal team(s) are increasingly more knowledgeable about the need to gather and process ESI in a forensically sound manner.

In terms of an organization's eDiscovery program, digital forensic practitioners have a vital role in the success of every litigation. They are specially equipped with knowledge and tools to ensure that relevant ESI is discoverable and that its integrity will be maintained so that it will not be subject to challenges when produced to the courts.

Civil Matters

Outlined previously in this chapter, there are several rules governing civil procedures, such that if litigation is imminent, parties have a duty to begin preserving ESI (applying legal holds) immediately. Discovery in civil litigation matters is made in one of the following ways:

- *Requests for admission* are written documents asking opposing parties to confirm or deny certain facts, such as producing a written statement about whether a person has logged into a specific computer system.
- *Requests for production* is a written document requesting opposing parties for information (discovery) to be produced.
- *Deposition* is an oral statement made under oath by witnesses.

Whether establishing facts for admission, gathering ESI for production, or attesting to the processes used for preserving ESI, digital forensic practitioner can become involved throughout many phases of the eDiscovery lifecycle.

Criminal Matters

Digital forensic activities relating to a criminal matter are performed by commissioned agencies or law enforcement officers. This is because they are under strict protocol for the way in which these investigations are conducted (i.e., scope of the search warrant).

Like how parties have a duty to preserve when litigation is imminent, in exigency circumstances, where law enforcement believes evidence could be destroyed, evidence can be preserved in the interest of the investigation. Within enterprise environments, digital forensic practitioners can be called upon to assist law enforcement in preserving this evidence and, in some cases, helping to establish facts relating to the investigation.

Expert Testimony

Whether done through a written statement, such as an affidavit or will-say statement, or presented orally during trial, digital forensic practitioners are often required to give testimony during a litigation about specific aspects of the digital forensic work conducted to gather and process ESI. As an expert witness, you will be asked to demonstrate your credentials and then a judge will determine whether these qualifications are sufficient for you to provide expert testimony.

There has been an ongoing debate about whether it makes sense that legal systems (i.e., judges and juries) are qualified to decide whether an expert is an expert. Under the FRE Rule 702, any person is qualified as an expert if he or she possesses "knowledge, skill, experience, training, and education" on the subject relating to his or her testimony beyond common experience. However, determining if a person qualifies as an expert in a legal proceeding depends on whether his or her "scientific, technical, or other specialized knowledge will help the trier of fact to understand the evidence or to determine the fact in issue."

Expert testimony is allowed when it is provided from a reasonably reliable individual and is provided in a manner that assists the judge or jury in understanding facts about the litigation matter. When delivering expert testimony, it is important to avoid in-depth technical details that may not be readily understood or accurately interpreted by nontechnical individuals, such as the judge, jury, or opposing counsel. While not an easy task, it is highly recommended that digital forensic practitioners can translate their technical knowledge into a common language that judges and juries can understand. Refer to Chapter 3 titled *"Education, Training, and Awareness"* for further discussion about the educational roadmap for a digital forensic practitioner.

Regardless of whether the organization is faced with a criminal of civil matter, it is critical that a consistent and repeatable methodology is used to gather and process ESI. Rather than reinventing processes to support eDiscovery, it is recommended to leverage what was previously developed to support digital forensic investigations; refer to Chapter 2 titled *"Investigative Process Methodologies"* for additional information.

It is important to remember that each enterprise is different, and, as a result, the role played by digital forensic practitioners throughout the eDiscovery lifecycle can vary. In 2009 the EDRM Jobs Project was started as a means of building a framework for evaluating personnel needs or issues to support the requirements of the eDiscovery lifecycle. Within this framework, a matrix was created to illustrate the different enterprise stakeholders (i.e., legal, forensics, IT) and align the appropriate level of involvement required of them (i.e., responsible, accountable, consulted, informed). The online resource for the EDRM Talent Task Matrix has been provided in the Resources section at the end of this chapter.

Discovering Electronically Stored Information (ESI)

From the discussions at the beginning of this chapter, many international juris-dictions have supported the discovery of ESI for years, realizing that it is simply a matter of keeping pace with technology advancements and its adoption within enterprise environments. When it comes time to discover ESI for legal proceedings, there is no predefined list of ESI because of the wide variety of computer systems and technologies currently in use and the expansive nature of different types of information that is now stored electronically. For example, while not intended to be an exhaustive list, different types of ESI that may be requested during discovery, including, but not limited to:

- Electronic communications (i.e., email messages, instant messages, chat files, etc.)
- Multimedia content (i.e., graphics, audio, video)
- Technology-generated data (i.e., audit trails, logs, and registers)
- Productivity suite documents (i.e., spreadsheets, presentations)

Regardless of type, ESI can be found on many possible storage mediums, devices, and locations throughout an enterprise. For example, while not intended to be an exhaustive list, different types of storage mechanisms where ESI can persist include:

- Storage media:
  - internal drives (i.e. hard drives)
  - *magnetic tapes (i.e. backup tapes)*
  - *optical disk (i.e. Digital Video Disk (DVD), Blu-ray)*
  - portable drives (i.e. smart cards, Universal Serial Bus (USB) sticks)
- Storage devices:
  - Personal computing device (i.e., desktop, laptop)
  - Network attached storage (NAS) or storage area networks (SAN)
  - Mobile device (i.e., smartphone, personal digital assistant [PDA])
  - Cameras and camcorders
  - Input and output (I/O) devices (i.e. printers, scanners, copiers)
- Storage locations:
  - Enterprise internal network
  - Internet service providers (ISP)
  - Cloud service providers (CSP)
  - Managed service providers (MSP)

The reality is that there are many different data types and storage mechanisms that may contain electronic information relevant to a litigation that need to be discovered and produced. It is important to keep in mind that with every different data type and storage mechanism, there are different levels of effort and costs associated with discovery requests. Generally, understanding what the effort and cost will be to discover and produce ESI is divided into five categories as illustrated in Table 13.1.

Table 13.1 ESI Discovery Categories.

Category	Data Types	Tier	Accessibility
Online	ESI that is quickly and frequently accessed (i.e., hard drives, network shares)	One	Reasonably accessible
Near-line	ESI accessed via automated or programmatic systems (i.e., optical disks, portable drives)	One	Reasonably accessible
Offline	ESI located in long-term storage that is accessed manually (i.e., magnetic tapes, optical disks)	One	Not reasonably accessible
Backups	ESI located in long-term storage where proof of burden must be demonstrated (i.e., magnetic tapes)	Two	Not reasonably accessible
Fragmented	ESI that has been erased, overwritten, or corrupted and requires significant processing to access	Two	Not reasonably accessible

Discussed previously in this chapter, an essential component of the eDiscovery lifecycle includes building a data map to maintain an accurate and up-to-date inventory of systems and applications found throughout the enterprise where potential ESI is created and stored. The most common descriptive elements that organizations should use in the data map, as provided in the Templates section of this book, can be found previously in this chapter.

Summary

With electronic discovery (eDiscovery) and the duty organizations have in responding to litigation matters, digital forensic practitioners must have the subject matter and technical expertise to assist in discovering and producing relevant ESI. Understanding that digital forensic principles, methodologies, and techniques are critical to guarantee the legal admissibility of ESI, it is imperative that organizations adhere to proven eDiscovery best practices and have clear and concise governance documentation for stakeholders, technologies, and where their enterprise services are needed to discover and produce court-ready evidence.

Resources

Checklist for Preparing a Discovery Plan. https://www.oba.org/cbamedialibrary/cba_on/pdf/e-discovery/md9-checklistforpreparingdiscoveryplan-v-2-1(2).doc
Electronic Discovery Reference Model (EDRM) Model. http://www.edrm.net/frameworks-and-standards/edrm-model/.
EDRM Project Management Guide. http://www.edrm.net/frameworks-and-standards/edrm-model/project-management/.
EDRM Talent Task Matrix. http://www.edrm.net/frameworks-and-standards/talent-task-matrix/.
Federal Rules of Civil Procedure (FRCP). https://www.law.cornell.edu/rules/frcp.
Guidelines for the Discovery of Electronic Documents in Ontario. https://ciaj-icaj.ca/wp-content/uploads/documents/import/2005/696_-_Campbell.pdf%3Fid%3D1251%261493994416&usg=AFQjCNE5_8AIQlcuRaTZlcTFFwq4gjdmJw

Glossary

1. **Electronically stored information (ESI)** is information created, manipulated, communicated, stored, and best utilized in digital form, requiring the use of computer hardware and software.
2. **Cull** is to reduce or control the size of digital evidence by removing ESI that is of no relevance.
3. **Data-at-rest** refers to the protection of inactive data that is physically stored in any digital form (i.e., database, enterprise data warehouse, tapes, hard drives, etc.).

4. **Data-in-transit** is the flow of information over any type of public or private network environment.
5. **Data-in-use** applies to data that is actively stored in a nonpersistent states, such as memory, for consumption or presentation.
6. **Custodians** are individuals having administrative control and ownership of specific ESI.
7. **Structured** data is information that resides in a fixed field within a record or file (i.e., databases, spreadsheets).
8. **Unstructured** data is information that does not resides in a traditional row-column arrangement (i.e., email, productivity documents).
9. **Black letter law** refers to basic principles of law that have become well-established technical legal rules that are generally known and free from doubt or dispute.
10. **Bates number** (also referred to as Bates stamping, branding, coding, or labeling) is an identification system used to place markers on documents as they are gathered and processed during discovery.

Chapter 14

Information Security and Cybersecurity

Ever since information technology (IT) made its way into the enterprise, there has been a need to deploy security controls to safeguard informational assets from attacks and adversaries. However, security events and incidents are inevitable regardless of how good an organization thinks its defense-in-depth security strategies are, which then lends to the need for investigations to be performed in response. Leveraging the information and cybersecurity capabilities throughout the enterprise, organizations need to understand how best to integrate their enterprise security program to best enable their digital forensic capabilities.

Information Security vs Cybersecurity

Naturally, every organization is going to speak their own language when it comes to their respective business operations. While this is expected, it is important that every organization speaks the same language of what information security means versus what cybersecurity means. Contrary to common perception, whether done inadvertently or not, the terms *information security* and *Cybersecurity* are not the same. So, this begs the question, What is the difference between information security and cybersecurity?

Since the use of computer systems back in the 1960s, as discussed in Chapter 1, information security has been a discipline focused on the security of informational assets or systems, regardless of its state (i.e., physical paper, logical databases). As a means of safeguarding informational assets or systems, various technologies, processes (i.e., runbooks), and physical countermeasures (i.e., security checkpoints) are implemented in a defense-in-depth approach to protect physical and electronically stored information from unauthorized access, disruption, modification, or destruction.

With the introduction of interconnected computer systems and the Internet, the growing need to safeguard information grew beyond stand-alone computer systems and expanded into the digital realm. What has evolved into what is now referred to as cybersecurity involves the security of informational assets or systems, but only in a digital state (i.e., database, financial system). Safeguarding electronically stored information (ESI)[1] involves making use of various technologies and processes to protect networks, information systems, and data from attacks, damage, or unauthorized access.

The reality is, taking a closer look at these disciplines, it is evident that there are distinctively unique characteristics between the two. Illustrated in Figure 14.1, not only is it reasonable to say that the cybersecurity discipline is a subset of the information security discipline, with significant overlap in control functions, except where physical security comes into play. Also there are key characteristics shared across other information-centric operational functions (i.e., business continuity). What also becomes evidence is that information technology only encompasses a portion of risk management, because there needs to be complimentary administrative and physical controls in place to effectively manage business risk, not just technology.

Industry Frameworks

Rather than starting from the ground up, organizations should turn to the global security industry for guidance on how to build out an enterprise security program. Before any industry framework is selected, a thorough assessment must be done to ensure that it meets the organization's specific needs, including maturity, with coverage across applicable information and cybersecurity domains, such as incident

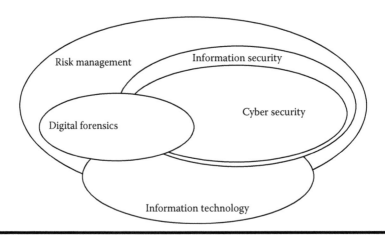

Figure 14.1   Information Security and cybersecurity.

management, security operations, and cryptography. As a reference, the following industry frameworks provide a general outline for organizations to enable effective information and cybersecurity capabilities. It is important to note that while the list of frameworks below may not be complete, the inclusion of one over another does not suggest it is better or recommended over those not referenced.

Information Security Forum (ISF) Standards of Good Practice for Information Security
The ISF Standards of Good Practice for Information Security provide organizations with comprehensive guidance for enabling security capabilities. The goal of these standards is to identify how regulatory and compliance requirements can be met while appropriately managing their business risks to an acceptable level of assurance.

International Organization for Standardization (ISO) 27001
The ISO 27001 is an international standard that provides a methodology for the implementation of security capabilities within an organization. The goal of this standard it to describe how organizations can manage their enterprise security program and achieve certification in recognition of their capabilities.

National Institute of Standards and Technology (NIST) Cybersecurity Framework
The NIST Cybersecurity Framework was drafted from the collective efforts of industry specialists, academic professionals, and government agencies. The goal of this voluntary, risk-based framework is to establish common language by which organizations can address and manage their business risk in a cost-effective means.

Open Web Application Security Project (OWASP) Open Cyber Security Framework Project
The OWASP Open Cyber Security Framework Project provides organizations with a practical structure for enabling or improving their security capabilities. The goal of this open community project is to establish a best practices[2] framework that both public and private organizations can readily adopt.

Understanding that every organization has different requirements for information and cybersecurity capabilities, there is no one-size-fits-all framework that unanimously aligns to every organization's needs. Therefore, the best approach is to use a combination of frameworks and standards to structure enterprise security capabilities. Online resources for the frameworks mentioned can be found in the Resources section at the end of this chapter.

Kill Chain

The term "kill chain" is a military concept describing an integrated, end-to-end, and systematic way to target and engage adversaries to create a desired effect, with the idea that breaking any one deficiency will ultimately interrupt the entire process.

In 2011 computer scientists at Lockheed-Martin applied the kill chain concept to the realm of information and cybersecurity.

What is now branded as the "intrusion kill chain," illustrated in Figure 14.2, this framework for defending computer networks has been adopted by organizations internationally as a management tool to continuously improve their enterprise security program. Contained within this kill chain, the seven stages an adversary moves through as they plan and execute their attacks are as follows:

1. *Reconnaissance*: Adversaries conduct research, identify, and select their targets by crawling[3] publicly available content (i.e., social networking, mailing lists) to harvest information, such as email addresses and details on specific technologies.
2. *Weaponization*: Adversaries combine malicious code or applications (i.e., remote access tools) with an exploit into a deliverable payload (i.e., productivity document).
3. *Delivery*: Adversaries transmit the weapon into the targeted environment using available business channels (i.e., phishing emails, universal serial bus (USB) devices).
4. *Exploitation*: Exploits incorporated within the delivered weapon is triggered and executed against the target.
5. *Installation*: Payload (i.e., malicious code or applications) resulting from exploitation is persistently installed on target systems allowing adversary access into the environment.
6. *Command and control (C2)*: Malicious code or applications installed on the target system establishes remote communications with adversaries so that they can have "hands-on-the-keyboard" access inside the target environment.
7. *Actions on objectives*: Adversaries locate informational assets of value, harvest it, and extract it from their target's environment.

Throughout the kill chain, organizations can develop different and appropriate defense-in-depth strategies for safeguarding their informational assets and systems. With each stage of the kill chain, it is important to contextualize

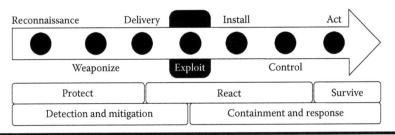

Figure 14.2 Intrusion kill chain.

			Detect	Deny	Disrupt	Degrade	Deceive	Destroy
Detection and mitigation	Protect	Reconnaissance						
		Weaponization						
		Delivery						
Containment and response	React	Exploitation						
		Installation						
		Command and control (C2)						
	Survive	Actions on objectives						

Figure 14.3   Kill chain course of action.

how information and cybersecurity capabilities will be implemented with the goal of breaking the chain as early as possible. As illustrated in Figure 14.3, the kill chain can be expanded into a multidimensional representation where the range of information and cybersecurity capabilities can be implemented with the methodology that, under different scenarios, a different course of action may be required. Illustrating the range of capabilities organizations can deploy, the matrix can include traditional security controls such as antimalware solutions to disrupt the installation of payload, firewall access control lists (ACL) to deny transmissions outside the network, or data execution prevention (DEP) to disrupt exploitation if it is initiated.

The goal of working with this matrix is to achieve a state of resilience by implementing strategic security capabilities that span multiple stages of the kill chain while aligning with different courses of action. That said, capabilities in any given quadrant doesn't signify complete resilience to intrusions; the performance and effectiveness of these security controls need to be measured against their ability to break or mitigate adversaries.

Digital Forensics in Enterprise Security

As discussed in Chapter 1, the evolution of cybercrime has accompanied advancements made in technology. However, with the increasing pervasiveness of technology in both the personal and business contexts, it is extremely important for organizations to have an effective and efficient enterprise security program in place.

In today's modern threat landscape, many organizations have established their enterprise security program with applicable governance models, security architectures, and strategies to effectively manage their business risks and to mitigate the compromise (losing, exposing) of their informational assets belonging to or entrusted to them. Most commonly, organizations will reference and, where feasible, adopt industry best practices for developing their enterprise security program which, if not suitably tailored to their respective business risks or needs (i.e., legal, regulatory), may not consider the importance of implemented defense-in-depth (administrative, technical, and physical) controls to increase the success rate of digital forensic investigations.

Because digital forensics is considered a subdiscipline of information security, it only seems natural that there is a close relationship between the two. Theoretically, if the defense-in-depth security was impenetrable, the possibility of an organization's informational assets and system to be compromised would be zero. But the reality is that security can never be completely effective, and, therefore, digital forensic capabilities are essential when security events occur. Generally, when a security event does occur, it is critical that immediate and appropriate actions are taken to reduce impact, recover business functions, and ultimately investigate. If not, there is an increased potential that relevant digital evidence will be damaged, dismissed, or simply overlooked.

Although digital forensics, information security, and cybersecurity are viewed as different enterprise disciplines, there are commonalities among them that present opportunities for enhancing digital forensic capabilities across the enterprise. As part of the enterprise security program, a primary objective is to achieve assurance that the damage or loss of information assets or system is minimized to within an acceptable level of business risk. One aspect of this comes from having proactive digital forensic capabilities that are intended to maximize the use of potential ESI while reducing the cost of investigations. Supporting this, examples of controls that can be implemented throughout the enterprise include, but are not limited to:

■ Evidence management framework (i.e., policies, standards, guidance)
■ Administrative, technical, and physical control mechanisms (e.g., operating procedures, tools and equipment, specialized technical skills)
■ Education and training programs (i.e., knowledge, skills)
■ Organizational, regulatory, and legal compliance requirements

For example, a primary objective of an enterprise security program is to achieve assurance that the damage or loss of informational assets or systems is minimized to an acceptable level of risk. Alternatively, a primary goal of reactive digital forensic capabilities is to establish fact-based conclusions based on credible evidence.

Examples of controls supporting both disciplines that can be implemented throughout the enterprise include, but are not limited to:

- Incident response capabilities, such as a security incident response team (SIRT) or computer (security) incident response team (CIRT/CSIRT)
- Disaster recovery planning
- Business continuity planning
- Gap analysis and recommendations
- Standard operating procedures (i.e., run books)

A proper balance needs to be reached so that industry best practices are adopted, and the necessary principles, methodologies, and techniques of digital forensics are incorporated so that activities, such as containment and recovery, account for proper evidence gathering and processing requirements. As an enterprise's technology footprint changes over time, it is important that the ways in which digital forensics capabilities are integrated evolves alongside. Naturally, it can be a constant struggle for organizations to effectively enable their required enterprise security capabilities while determining how to continuously improve their digital forensic capabilities at the same time. Fortunately, digital forensic principles, methodologies, and techniques have been clearly defined, well established, and scientifically proven over several decades, which allows organizations to integrate them relatively seamlessly into most enterprise architectures.

Within an enterprise environment, digital forensic practitioners play a vital role in the protection of informational assets and systems. Depending on their level of knowledge and experience gained, discussed further in Chapter 3 titled "*Education, Training, and Awareness*," they can often be viewed as a jack of all trades because of the way their role has allowed them to develop skills across many different fields, such as systems development, information technology (IT) architecture, or information and cybersecurity.

As result of their involvement in enterprise investigations, digital forensic practitioners can become deeply immersed in the detailed inner workings of many different aspects of an enterprise's business operations. With this exposure, they have an increased line of sight into areas of the organization where information or cybersecurity gaps exists and that may have otherwise not been uncovered until after a security event or incident had occurred. Contained in the sections below are examples of subject matters within the enterprise where digital forensic practitioners can bring added value and further strengthen an organization's enterprise security program.

Forensic Architectures

Traditionally, investigations have been performed in response to a security event or incident to determine root cause or assess business impact. Generally, the objective for performing any investigation is to establish factual evidence-based conclusions from relevant data sources (i.e., mobile devices, computer systems) across dissimilar architectures (i.e., corporate, cloud) in varying states (i.e., volatile, persistent). Ever since the formalization of the digital forensic discipline, there have been ongoing efforts to strategically integrate its foundational principles, methodologies, and techniques throughout an organization's security capabilities so that there is a higher level of assurance that credible digital evidence will be available when required.

Within the realms of information and cybersecurity, the CIA Triad (Confidentiality, Integrity, and Availability) describes the fundamental components for implementing security controls to safeguard informational assets. Likewise, following this CIA methodology, security architectures contain design principles that consider relationships and dependencies between various technology architectures with the goal of protecting informational assets and system. Naturally, this approach introduces complications for enabling digital forensic capabilities, because potential evidence may be unavailable due to improper design and implementation of security architectures.

As the starting point, the design of security architectures that proactively support digital forensic capabilities can be accomplished through the development of reference architecture templates. By having these templates readily available, organizations will have common frameworks with a consistent glossary of terms as reference for stakeholders (i.e., development teams) to understand digital forensic requirements. For example, organizations can outline the following components of their digital forensic requirements for security architectures:

- Regularly performing system and application backups and maintaining it as defined in the organization's enterprise governance framework
- Enabling auditing of security information and events for corporately managed assets (i.e., end-user systems, servers, network devices) into a centralized repository
- Maintaining records of known-good and known-bad signatures for systems and applications
- Maintaining accurate and complete records of network, system, and application configurations
- Establishing an evidence management framework to address the control of evidence to guarantee authenticity and integrity throughout its lifecycle

Systems Lifecycle

Traditionally, technical security requirements fell within the responsibility of network or system administrators to accurately identify and successfully implement. However, given the dynamic and mobile nature of today's workforce, coupled with the continuously evolving threat landscape and expanded scope of potential digital evidence, it has become apparent that assurance for adequate security standards needs to be integrated as part of the organization's overall security assurance.

This does not mean that organizations need to reinvent the wheel by developing new processes by which they can effectively integrate digital forensic requirements into their security architectures. Rather, they should look to incorporating reference architectures for digital forensics into existing life-cycle systems and applications. It is important to note that the word "development" was not included in the previous sentence because security is concerned with not only the development phases, but also with the ongoing operations and maintenance phases after the system or application has been developed.

Waterfall and Agile Models

Traditionally, the system or application life cycle has followed a waterfall methodology where each phase of the process is performed in a steady, noniterative downward sequence. With this approach, the next phase is only executed once the preceding phase has been completed. While there are many iterations of the waterfall methodology, each with its own variations, the following illustrate the high-level phases of the model:

- *Requirements* is the initiation point where the concept is captured and requirements are documented.
- *Design* analyzes requirements to create models and schemas resulting in the system architecture.
- *Implementation* includes product coding, proving, and testing.
- *Operations* involves the installation of the completed product, including ongoing support and maintenance

Under the waterfall model, incorporating security requirements must be systematically achieved from the beginning of the process. This way, when it comes time to design and implement the system or application, due diligence has been completed to minimize the attack surface and reduce risk associated with security flaws. However, with the velocity of technological advancement and the rate at which technology is being consumerized, it became apparent that customers expected greater functionality to come at a much faster pace. Because the waterfall model is linear in nature, which can result in an extended time until a completed product is delivered, organizations began looking to the agile methodology as an alternative.

With the agile model, work products are delivered through incremental and iterative phases known as "sprints." Unlike the waterfall model, the agile model continually revisits development requirements throughout the lifecycle, which can result in the direction of a project changing suddenly. Considering how the agile model enables organizations to follow a continuous integration and development approach, security has an important place in this methodology because of the extreme risk in original requirements and design changing. Generally, with each iteration of agile development, security needs to be incorporated by documenting and understanding:

- The current state; including:
  - Affected systems, applications, user, etc.
  - Data flows, interchanges, and communications between systems, applications, and users
  - Review of previously documented security concerns and findings to prevent reoccurrence
  - Impact assessment of change against enterprise security program
- What product will be delivered, including:
  - Business operations and service involved
  - Threat and risk assessment of informational assets and systems requiring protection
- How to securely delivery the product, including:
  - Apply the principle of least access privilege
  - Incorporate proactive capabilities (as described in the previous sections)

Ensuring security requirements are incorporated as a component of either methodologies is easier said than done. Without security being interwoven throughout the system's and application's life cycle, the organization's digital forensic capabilities will be hindered when it comes to the availability of potential digital evidence. Also, the absence of security within the system's and application's life cycle will result in digital forensic capabilities being impeded from become more proactive methodologies in terms of maturity, rather than continuing to operate as reactive.

Information Technology Governance

It is clear there is a strong relationship between digital forensics and enterprise information security and cybersecurity. However, as illustrated in Figure 14.1 at the beginning of this chapter, it is important to note that an enterprise security program also has a relationship with IT. Therefore, if the relationship between digital forensics and enterprise security exists, and enterprise security is related to IT, then there is a logical relationship that exists between digital forensics and IT governance. For any organization that wants to create effective digital forensic capabilities, it is necessary to understand the relationships between digital forensics, enterprise information security and cybersecurity, and IT governance.

Without an interface between these disciplines, there is potential for a significant amount of duplicated and overlapping governance documentation (i.e., policies, standards, procedures) to exist. For example, a common source of digital evidence is found within backups and archives of data and informational assets throughout the organization. Governance documentation most likely already exists within the organization's enterprise security program outlining how backups and archives are to be performed, lending to the importance for taking the interdependencies of these disciplines into account.

Generally, conducting audits is a cornerstone of ensuring that implemented security controls are performing as expected with the aim of reducing business risk to acceptable levels. Foremost, it is necessary to understand how the IT governance reference framework influences and intersects with digital forensic capabilities. For example, the Control Objectives for Information and Related Technology (COBIT) framework provide a good basis for comparing how the aspects of COBIT associate to aspects of digital forensics. The goal behind COBIT is to divide IT governance into several high-level processes, otherwise known as control objectives, so that organizations can develop detailed actions, which must be managed for compliance.

The first step in aligning IT governance with digital forensics is to build a taxonomy[4] of language that can be used for the comparison and framework alignment. A taxonomy is a living document that might never be considered finished because it is constantly evolving alongside changes to the organization's business operations and functions. A good taxonomy should be developed to be flexible enough that it can be adapted to any organizational changes, so it does not have to be recreated following the three stages below:

1. *Research and assess*: In this stage of the methodology, a team of key individuals is assembled to manage the entire development process. Once established, the team focusing on gathering information throughout the organization specific to the relevance of the taxonomy, the role it will have, and where there is existing information to be consumed.
2. *Build and implement*: In this stage of the methodology, the team conducts a series of interviews and surveys with subject matter experts to gather information necessary to develop the taxonomy. Using the aggregated results, the hierarchical classification scheme is built, evaluated, and implemented throughout the organization.
3. *Govern and grow*: In this stage of the methodology, the team is focused on planning the long-term stability and sustainability of the taxonomy. With the final revision implemented, the team must develop a governance structure focused on the continued life cycle including the:
    a. Creation of policies and procedures for implementation and maintenance
    b. Definition of the roles, responsibilities, and accountabilities
    c. Establishment of training and awareness programs for stakeholders

Working with the taxonomy as a basis for comparing and aligning digital forensics, five control groupings have been developed with refinement into 66 detailed control objectives. Tables 14.1 through 14.5 illustrate the groupings and control objectives.

Table 14.1 Grouping 1: Digital Forensic Readiness (DFR)

Control Objective 1: Planning Information Retention Requirements	
DFR1.1	Define business scenarios that require digital evidence.
DFR1.2	Identify available sources and different types of potential evidence.
DFR1.3	Determine the evidence collection requirement.
DFR1.4	Establish a policy for secure storage and handling of potential evidence.
DFR1.5	Establish a capability for securely gathering legally admissible evidence.
DFR1.6	Synchronize all relevant devices and systems.
DFR1.7	Gather potential evidence.
DFR1.8	Prevent anonymous activities.
Control Objective 2: Planning the Response	
DFR2.1	Ensure monitoring is targeted to detect and deter major incidents.
DFR2.2	Implement intrusion detection systems.
DFR2.3	Specify circumstances when escalation to a formal investigation should be done.
DFR2.4	Establish a computer emergency response team (CERT).
DFR2.5	Establish capabilities and response time for external digital forensic capabilities.
Control Objective 3: Digital Forensic Training	
DFR3.1	Train staff so that roles in digital evidence management are known.
DFR3.2	Develop in-house investigative capabilities (if required).
DFR3.3	Enhance capabilities for evidence gathering.
Control Objective 4: Accelerating the Digital Forensic Investigation	
DFR4.1	Document and validate an investigation protocol against best practices.
DFR4.2	Acquire appropriate digital forensic tools and systems.
DFR4.3	Ensure legal review to facilitate action in response to an incident.
DFR4.4	Define responsibilities and authority for CERT and investigative teams.
DFR4.5	Define circumstances for engaging professional investigative services.

Table 14.2   Grouping 2: Evidence Preservation (EPV)

Control Objective 1: Incident Response	
EPV1.1	Initiate incident response plan.
EPV1.2	Activate the CERT.
Control Objective 2: Secure Evidence	
EPV2.1	Secure the physical environment of a crime scene.
EPV2.2	Secure all relevant logs and data.
EPV2.3	Secure volatile evidence.
EPV2.4	Secure hardware.
EPV2.5	Label and seal all exhibits.
EPV2.6	Preserve chain of custody.
Control Objective 3: Transport Evidence	
EPV3.1	Securely transport evidence.
EPV3.2	Preserve chain of custody during transport.
Control Objective 4: Store Evidence	
EPV4.1	Store evidence in safe custody room.
EPV4.2	Control access to evidence.
EPV4.3	Preserve chain of custody in storage.

Table 14.3   Grouping 3: Forensic Acquisition (FACQ)

Control Objective 1: Ensure Integrity of Evidence	
FACQ1.1	Follow established digital forensic investigation protocols.
FACQ1.2	Write-protect all evidence source media.
Control Objective 2: Acquire Evidence	
FACQ2.1	Acquire evidence in order of volatility.
FACQ2.2	Acquire nonvolatile evidence.
Control Objectives 3: Copy Evidence	
FACQ3.1	Make forensic copies of all evidence.

(Continued)

Table 14.3   Grouping 3: Forensic Acquisition (FACQ) (*Continued*)

Control Objective 4: Authenticate Evidence	
FACQ4.1	Authenticate all evidence as identical to the original.
FACQ4.2	Time stamp all copies of the authenticated evidence.
Control Objective 5: Document Acquisition Process	
FACQ5.1	Document all actions through chain-of-custody documentation.

Table 14.4   Grouping 4: Forensic Analysis (FAN)

Control Objective 1: Plan Investigation	
FAN1.1	Review all available information regarding the incident.
FAN1.2	Identify expertise required.
FAN1.3	Identify most suitable tools to be utilized.
Control Objective 2: Develop Hypothesis	
FAN2.1	Develop a hypothesis to cover most likely scenarios.
FAN2.2	Define criteria to provide or disprove the hypothesis.
Control Objectives 3: Acquire Evidence	
FAN3.1	Acquire evidence using the most suitable tools available.
FAN3.2	Analyze evidence using the most suitable tools available.
FAN3.3	Conform to the requirements of the best evidence rule.
Control Objective 4: Test Hypothesis	
FAN4.1	Reconstruct sequence of events.
FAN4.2	Compare evidence with other known facts.
Control Objective 5: Make Findings	
FAN5.1	Make a finding that is consistent with all the evidence.
FAN5.2	Document the finding.
Control Objective 6: Document Case	
FAN6.1	Document all aspects of the case.
FAN6.2	Enter documentation into safe custody.

Table 14.5 Grouping 5: Evidence Presentation (EP)

Control Objective 1: Prepare Case	
EP1.1	Determine target audience (court, disciplinary hearing, inquiry).
EP1.2	Assemble evidence required for presentation.
EP1.3	Prepare expert witnesses.
EP1.4	Prepare exhibits.
EP1.5	Prepare presentation aids (graphics, slides, hardware).
EP1.6	Preserve chain of custody.
Control Objective 2: Present Case	
EP2.1	Present evidence in a logical, understandable way to ensure that the court can critically assess all information and understand the relevance of the case.
EP2.2	Make use of graphics and physical examples to illustrate difficult or critical concepts, if needed.
EP2.3	Ensure that a digital forensic specialist is on hand to assist in providing expert testimony.
Control Objectives 3: Preserve Evidence	
EP3.1	Preserve the evidence after the case has been presented, as it may be needed in case of appeal or if new evidence is obtained.

The digital forensic reference framework in the preceding tables is intended to provide organizations with a sound and practical basis for aligning digital forensic capabilities with IT governance. For further discussion about the above groupings of control objective, refer to Chapter 2 titled *"Investigative Process Methodologies,"* Chapter 7 titled *"Controlling Mobile Devices,"* Chapter 8 titled *"Cloud Computing Enablement,"* Chapter 10 titled *"Digital Evidence Management,"* Chapter 11 titled *"Digital Forensic Readiness,"* and Chapter 12 titled *"Incident Management and Response."*

Positive Security

Traditional approaches to managing information security through checklists, rules, and compliance cannot keep up with the modern threat landscape or increasing volumes of cyber-related threats and attacks. Essentially, continuing to play the cat-and-mouse game with cybercriminals is not feasible when they have invested significant effort into understanding the strengths and weaknesses of targeted security controls. For example, the current antivirus solutions, which follow a blacklisting approach, suffer from a low detection rate and, as a result, suffer from reduced effectiveness to protect information systems and assets from malicious attacks.

As the effectiveness of blacklisting solutions creates greater opportunities for cybercriminals to be successful in their attacks, attention needs to turn toward security strategies that reduce the overall attack surfaces by following a risk-based approach. With a risk-based-approach, rather than being concerned with identifying and managing threats through specific technology functionalities, the organization's overall attack surface is reduced by implementing agnostic solutions that employ a deny-by-default mechanism in a whitelisting approach.

Through a risk-based methodology, or a positive security approach, organizations will begin to realize several business benefits with respect to the protection of their information systems and assets, such as:

- Displacing security controls (such as antivirus solutions) that are becoming less effective or are contributing little value to the organization overall defense-in-depth strategy
- Improving overall performance of network and information systems by eliminating blacklist signature databases that consume significant resources
- Reducing the strain on supporting infrastructures for deploying blacklist signature updates across remote locations
- Enhancing operational efficiencies by lessening the work effort required to reactively maintain security technologies

Adopting a strategy that follows a positive security methodology aligns with the proven principles of least privilege by enforcing a deny-by-default approach to securing information systems and assets. In modern environments where cyberattacks and threats are constantly evolving and moving targets, implementing attack-agnostic solutions that reduce the organization's overall attack surface is a much more effective and sustainable strategy.

Defense-in-Depth

Traditionally, security controls are deployed and implemented throughout the enterprise following an overall defense-in-depth strategy. Illustrated in Figure 14.4 are the different layers found throughout a defense-in-depth strategy where security controls are implemented so that different views into information assets can be seen across the enterprise. Essentially, at the center of the defense-in-depth strategy is where data resides. Moving outward from data through the layers is where

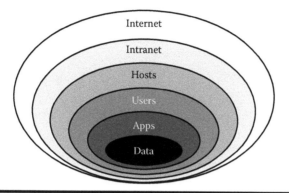

Figure 14.4   Defense in depth layers.

different interactions and the need for deploying appropriate security controls come into play.

As modern technologies, such as mobile devices, virtualization, and cloud computing, continue to proliferate as tools for conducting business, organizations are increasingly faced with the need to expose their business records and applications beyond the borders of their traditional network perimeter. With this, deployment of security controls needs to be placed closer to the actual data, as discussed previously in the section on the data-centric security model, to ensure adequate protection of information assets. Illustrated in Figure 14.5 are examples of security controls that should be considered part of a defense-in-depth strategy that aligns to the methodology of data-centric security:

- Network devices, such as routers/switches and firewalls, with access controls lists (ACL) to regulate data flows between different security zones (i.e., Demilitarized Zone (DMZ), between regional offices)
- Host-based hardening and vulnerability scanning to reduce the potential attack surface by applying configuration changes and software updates
- Subject authentication and authorization to maintain the principles of least privileges for access to objects
- Signature-based technologies, such as whitelisting or blacklisting, to detect and mitigate risk of threat actors[5] in both endpoint and network devices, such as antimalware solutions or intrusion prevention systems (IPS)
- Next-generation (next-gen) firewalls combine the traditional deep-packet inspection capabilities with an application's awareness to better detect and deny malicious or unacceptable activity
- Data loss prevention (DLP) uses classifiers to detect and prevent potential data exfiltration through data-at-rest[6], data-in-transit[7], and data-in-use[8] scenarios

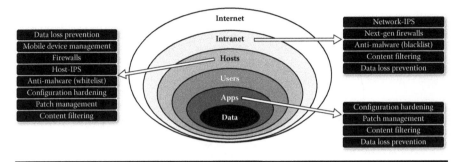

Figure 14.5   Defense-in-depth security controls.

- Mobile device management (MDM) allows remote administration and enterprise integration of mobile computing devices, such as smartphones and tablets
- Content filtering monitors activity and enforces compliance with defined acceptable use policies and standards

Australian Signal Directorate (ASD)

First published in February 2010, the Australian Signal Directorate (ASD) developed a series of prioritized security controls that, when used strategically, help to mitigate against cybersecurity incidents and intrusions, ransomware and external adversaries with destructive intent, malicious insiders, and a breach of business records. The guidance was generated as result of the ASD's experience in operational security, incident management, vulnerability assessments, and penetration testing. With this guidance, it is important to note that there is no single security control that can be implemented to mitigate the risk of a cybersecurity incident. However, the ASD has proven the effectiveness of implementing the following top four strategies, which are considered essential in mitigating approximately 85% of cybersecurity incidents, including:

- *Application whitelisting* to permit and trust "known-good" applications while restricting the execution of malicious or unapproved applications
- *Patch applications* to mitigate the risk of application vulnerabilities being exploited
- *Patch operating system* vulnerabilities to mitigate the risk of operating system vulnerabilities being exploited
- *Restrict administrative privileges* to the principle of least privilege access for individuals permitted access to only those objects required to perform their duties

While these top four strategies have been deemed essential security controls and have been declared mandatory for Australian government agencies as of April 2013, organizations can selectively implement any of the top 30 security controls to address specific security needs. Subsequently, in February 2017 the ASD issued a revision to the list, which illustrated further breakouts of top-four mitigation strategies across multiple risk areas, including the following:

1. Mitigate Strategies to Prevent Malware Delivery and Execution:
   a. *Application whitelisting* of permitted/trusted applications to prevent the execution of malicious/unapproved applications.
   b. *Patch applications* to mitigate the risk of application vulnerabilities being exploited.
   c. *Configure Microsoft Office* macro settings to block embedded execution to trusted locations (i.e., digitally signed) with limited write access.
   d. *User application hardening* to block, disable, or remove unneeded third-party applications featured in productivity suites (i.e., Microsoft Office), web browsers, and viewers (i.e., Flash).
2. Mitigation Strategies to Limit the Extent of Cybersecurity Incidents:
   a. *Restrict administrative privileges* to the principle of least privilege access for individuals permitted access to only those objects required to perform their duties.
   b. *Patch operating system* vulnerabilities to mitigate the risk of operating system vulnerabilities being exploited.
   c. *Multifactor authentication* for remote access services (i.e., virtual private networks [VPN]) and for all privileged access or actions (i.e., access to sensitive data).
3. Mitigation Strategies to Detect Cybersecurity Incidents and Responses:
   a. *Continuous incident detection and response* using automated analysis across centralized and time-synchronized log repositories; refer to Chapter 10 titled *"Digital Evidence Management"* for further discussion on security logging.
4. Mitigation Strategies to Recover Data and System Availability
   a. *Daily backups* of data, software, and configuration setting that are retained in offline repositories as per the enterprise's defined retention period(s).

Incorporating these essential mitigation strategies are proven to be effective in preventing a wide range of cybersecurity risks. Additionally, while not directly related to enabling digital forensic capabilities, the technology-generated logs outputted from these security controls can be useful as potential digital evidence during an investigation.

Security Investigations

Having capability to conduct a security investigation following digital forensic principles, methodologies, and techniques is necessary for every successful enterprise-security program. As a component of this capability, it is important to remember that business will continue to operate normally, which requires that digital forensic practitioners ensure there is minimal impact or interruptions as a result of their investigative activities. Ensuring minimal impact to business operations, organizations need to be in a state of preparedness so that when a security event or incident occurs, they are readily equipped to take appropriate action. Not only does this involve technical abilities, but it also involves administrative (i.e., processes) and physical (i.e., people) elements.

The Investigative Workflow

The digital forensic profession has evolved alongside the advancements in technology to become a mature discipline where the existing common body of knowledge (CBK)[9] consists of proven scientific principles, methodologies, and techniques, and has brought about a level of standardization and formal structure to the digital forensics profession. With the evolution of digital forensics over the decades, there have been consistent advancements made in areas such as education, technologies, and processes. Collectively, this progress painted a picture that bypassing, switching, or not following proper processes can lead to missed, incomplete, or inadmissible evidence, resulting in a failed investigation.

From this realization, several groups and individuals started working on developing models that would function as a framework for digital forensics processes to be consistently applied. Since then, there have been several authors who have taken on the task of proposing process models by which practitioners can follow as assurance that evidence has been gathered, processed, and preserved following repeatable methodologies and techniques.

Over the years, several different process models were proposed to formalize the digital forensic discipline and transform ad hoc tasks and activities into tested and proven processes. Yet, there is no single best process model that can be universally adopted as the one-size-fits-all methodology for all digital forensic investigations. Primarily, this is attributed to influences on the authors before and during the development of their process model. For the purposes of describing the activities and tasks performed during a digital forensic investigation, the stage illustrated in Figure 14.6 are as follows:

- *Preparation* includes activities to ensure administrative, technical, and physical provisions are in place.
- *Gathering* involves following proven techniques to identify, collect, and preserve evidence.
- *Processing* reveals data and reduces volumes based on the contextual and content relevancy.
- *Presentation* includes preparing reporting documentation.

Further discussion about the investigative process methodologies can be found in Chapter 2 titled "*Investigative Process Methodologies.*"

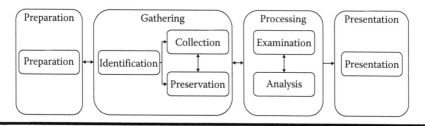

Figure 14.6 High-level digital forensic process model.

The Digital Forensic Team

In a corporate environment, there can be several individuals involved in supporting digital forensic capabilities, spanning well beyond just digital forensic practitioners. People, such as system support personnel and management, can have separate roles and responsibilities during the digital forensic life cycle to ensure the organization operates within the established principles, methodologies, and techniques, so evidence will be admissible in court.

For example, the digital forensic team consists of many people who are the core individuals responsible for executing the digital forensic activities and tasks. Titles used to describe the roles specific to the digital forensics team can be subjective (based on organizations or region) and are commonly used interchangeably. Fundamentally, the ability to create distinct roles with respect to an organization's digital forensic program is subjective to factors such as the size or arrangement of the organization.

Depending on the ability to create these distinct roles, there will be individuals throughout the organization who will play a different role and have varying involvement throughout the digital forensic life cycle. With every role, there's a need for training and awareness that aligns with the defined responsibilities. However, it is not expected that every role will be provided with the same type of education, because the knowledge required for each role varies. Organizations need to consider an effective way to ensure that different forms of education, training, and awareness about digital forensic principles, methodologies, and techniques are appropriately provided to all stakeholders.

Refer to Chapter 3 titled *"Education, Training, and Awareness"* for further discussion about digital forensic training and education roadmaps.

Types of Security Investigations

Conducting digital forensic investigations in the private sector is not much different from conducting one in the public sector. For example, in both the private and public sectors, digital evidence can be gathered and processed to support some type of criminal allegation. However, in the private sector there can also be a need for digital evidence based on corporate-asset abuse or policy violations.

Generally, most security events and incidents that require organizations to conduct a forensic investigation involve the misuse or abuse of informational assets or systems where potential sources of evidence can be located across many disparate technologies.

Typically, there are several business scenarios where digital forensics can be leveraged to effectively manage an organization's business risk; refer to Chapter 6 titled "*The Business of Digital Forensics*." Depending on how an organization implements and integrates their digital forensic capabilities, the following are examples of different security investigations that can be encountered:

- *Data breach* involves the access to and dissemination of informational assets to unauthorized entities.
- *Email abuse* involves the transmission of content that is outside the scope of acceptable usage as defined by the organization's enterprise governance framework (i.e., acceptable use policy).
- *Inappropriate activity* involves the access to and rendering of contraband content (i.e., pornography, pirated media).
- *Internet abuse* involves the access to and transmission of content that is outside the scope of acceptable usage as defined by the organization's enterprise governance framework (i.e., acceptable use policy).
- *Intrusion attempts* involve efforts to gain unauthorized access to informational assets or systems.
- *Malware infections* involve the installation and execution of malicious code.
- *Unauthorized access* involves the access to informational assets or systems without approval or delegated privilege.

As the investigation proceeds and evidence is processed, it is important to know how to distinguish between civil and criminal violations. Because any civil investigation can become a criminal investigation, it is critical that all digital evidence is handled following documented, repeatable, and consistent methodologies and techniques. Refer to Chapter 10 titled "*Digital Evidence Management*" for further discussion.

Investigative Techniques

As stated previously, digital forensics is built on an extensive CBK of well-established and proven scientific principles, methodologies, and techniques. As any security investigation progresses into the processing (examination and analysis) of digital evidence, work done by the digital forensic practitioners starts moving away from the scientific foundations and more into the realm of art and perception. A practitioner's ability to sort through masses of data, find hidden patterns and correlations, and extract meaning to get closer to the facts requires a level of intuition and insight gained through experience.

On one hand, if practitioners rely too much on subjective points of view based on experience, they could potentially overlook evidence. On the other hand, if they rely too much on technology as the catchall way to find evidence, they could be led into making incorrect or incomplete conclusions. It is not that practitioners conjure up magic when they are determining what constitutes order (evidence) versus chaos (clutter), it is more that this phase of the investigative workflow is an art than it is a science.

Balancing this equation lies within the use of technology that helps to automate the effective and timely processing of digital evidence, but practitioners cannot solely rely on technology to analyze and examine evidence. The other part of the equation is building analytical skills that have been learned and refined from their professional education, training, and past experiences.

Detailed discussion about the different forms of education, training, and awareness an organization should require of their people can be found in Chapter 3 titled "*Education, Training, and Awareness.*"

Machine Learning

As early as the 1980s, advancements in technology powered a realization that new algorithms used as part of artificial intelligence and machine learning could eventually help in decision-making processes. In the context of digital forensics, the application of machine learning is the process of applying multiple techniques and technologies to better interpret and gain knowledge about evidence from multiple data sources.

Making effective use of machine-learning capabilities requires understanding which approach is best suited to the needs of the investigation, including:

- *Inductive machine learning* involves self-learning based on techniques such as cluster analysis, link analysis, and textual-mining analytics.
- *Deductive machine learning* involves supervised learning[10] based on rule generators and decision trees.

Machine-learning forensics is the capability to recognize patterns across potential digital evidence to reduce or validate the impact of cybercrime; further discussion about applying digital forensic capabilities to mitigate business-risk scenarios can be found in Chapter 6 titled "*The Business of Digital Forensics.*" When using machine learning, digital forensic practitioners need to consider using any combination of both inductive and deductive approaches so the fact-based conclusions are established during the investigation.

Extractive Forensics

Extracting data from unstructured data sources has become increasingly challenging because of the way in which technology is rapidly advancing and the volume by which data is growing. Extractive forensics involves any combination of techniques that are used to uncover relationships and associations between individuals and ESI (i.e., documents, email messages). For example, the following are techniques commonly used as part of extractive forensics techniques.

Link Analysis   Link analysis is used to understand context, such as "who knew what, when, and where." Link analysis assists digital forensic practitioners in discovering relationships by directing them to specific relevant evidence (and other information) of interest that requires further analysis, rather than identifying large data patterns independently.

With link analysis, entities (e.g., individuals, systems) are represented as objects (i.e., circles) and are referred to as *nodes*. Connecting the nodes are lines, known as *edges*, that apply weighting to represent the strength of relationships between nodes, with stronger links having thicker connection lines. With link analysis technologies, graphs used to visualize the relationships between nodes, their associations, and, in some cases, the counts and direction of the connections and relationships.

As with any technique and technology, there are limitations with the use of link analysis during a security investigation. For example, while link analysis is great for discovering associations and relationships, its main limitation becomes noticeable as the number of nodes grows too large, and graphs become cluttered. Because of this, the use of link analysis during an investigation should be assessed to ensure that its application will simplify and narrow the scope of an investigation.

Text Mining   Text mining is a technique used to discover content (and context) hidden within the massive volumes of data sources. As technology continues to advance, organizations are increasingly generating and storing their informational assets in unstructured formats. This tendency has become increasingly important because of how it allows digital forensic practitioners to sort and organize large volumes of unstructured ESI through tasks such as taxonomy categorization, concept clustering, and summarization.

Using technology, analyzing substantial amounts of unstructured ESI can be automated to improve pattern and concept identification. Without the use of these tools, digital forensic practitioners could potentially miss hidden patterns or concepts because of how difficult, if not impossible, it can be to discover these by applying manual investigative techniques.

Text mining applies three approaches to sort, organize, and prioritize unstructured ESI: information retrieval, information extraction, and natural language processing. By using these approaches, digital forensic practitioners can convert the massive amounts of unstructured ESI into structured models that can be used to enhance analysis of and make correlations between digital evidence during an investigation.

Inductive Forensics

Creating visual representations and predictive models based on investigative evidence helps digital forensic practitioners establish their fact-based conclusions. Inductive forensics are a form of unsupervised learning[11] that involve performing cluster analysis to group a set of objects into smaller groups based on digital similarities, including:

- *Hierarchical clustering* builds multileveled orders using a tree structure.
- *Mean clustering* partitions data into distinct groups based on the point by which all data within a cluster intersect.
- *Gaussian mixture* models different clusters as a combination of two or more variables.
- *Self-organizing maps* use models to learn the topology and distribution of data.
- *Hidden Markov models* apply observed data to recover the sequence of data states.

For digital forensic practitioners, the use of unsupervised learning and cluster analysis provides a way of making observations that can lead to establishing evidence-based facts and conclusions about the investigation. While this type of unsupervised fact discovery can be useful for exploratory analysis, it can lead to a deductive type of analysis that can now be used to establish facts around differences and uniqueness among different clusters.

Deductive Forensics

In today's digital world, it is difficult to exist without having some level of digital profile existing throughout a broad range of technologies. Because of this, the information available during an investigation can allow for patterns to be captured, modeled, and used, so that behaviors and the potential of impending security events or incidents can be anticipated.

In the early days of technologies, the vision of what machine learning could become was realized through tools such as decisions trees and mathematical algorithms. With the significant advancement made to technologies from the 1980s and beyond, a new generation of machine-learning capabilities was realized with the evolution of clustering and link or text analysis. In this new paradigm of machine-learning capabilities, where a variety of techniques are applied in different combinations, organizations are moving farther away from being reactive and are increasingly customizing their targeted security monitoring capabilities based on deductive learning.

Deductive reasoning works by taking generalized information and making it more specific, a technique often referred to as a top-down approach. It begins

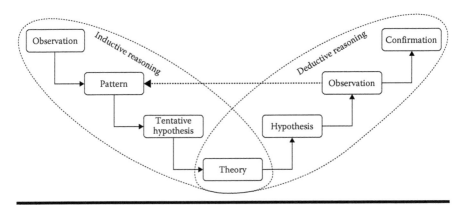

Figure 14.7   Phases of deductive and inductive reasoning.

by developing a theory and moves into a hypothesis that is testable or verifiable through fact-based observations and evidence. In Figure 14.7, the phases of both inductive and deductive reasoning are illustrated in how inductive and deductive reasoning work simultaneously to form a continuous cycle.

For example, what was traditionally used as the underlying process for enabling digital marketers to push products and services, the same behavioral technologies— also known as user and entity behavior analytics (UEBA)—are now applying a variety of extractive and inductive machine-learning techniques to track and identify security events as a component of enterprise-security and digital forensic programs. UEBA solutions are designed to identify and baseline the behavior of users and entities (i.e., systems, applications) to detect deviations from normal behavior. This is much like the concept of baselining information systems to detect deviations with file integrity monitoring (FIM) technologies, where profiles are built based on several factors, including work hours, logical and physical access, and business roles.

Machine-learning forensics can be strategically deployed throughout the organization to react and take appropriate actions to mitigate security events or incidents from happening, and to reduce the overall business-risk posture. However, it is important that organizations remember that the use of any machine learning tool or technique during an investigation still requires the involvement of digital forensic practitioners. For the time being, human guidance, experience, and contributions are the key success criteria in establishing evidence-based facts and conclusions during any digital forensic investigation.

Summary

The overlap between digital forensics and information security and cybersecurity capabilities has been widely acknowledged by industry specialists, academic professionals, and government agencies. Naturally, this resulted in digital forensic capabilities being incorporated as a vital component of an organization's overall enterprise-security program. This realization led to the close alignment of digital forensics with enterprise security to ensure that, when required, digital evidence is readily available.

Resources

ISF Standard of Good Practice for Information Security. https://www.securityforum.org/tool/the-isf-standardrmation-security/
ISO 27001. https://www.iso.org/isoiec-27001-information-security.html
NIST Cybersecurity Framework. https://www.nist.gov/cyberframework
OWASP Open Cyber Security Framework Project. https://www.owasp.org/index.php/OWASP_Open_Cyber_Security_Framework_Project

Glossary

1. **Electronically stored information (ESI)** is information created, manipulated, communicated, stored, and best utilized in digital form, requiring the use of computer hardware and software.
2. **Best practice** is a method or technique that has consistently shown results superior to those achieved with other means, and that is used as a benchmark.
3. **Crawling** is the means of browsing readily available content to search for, locate, and collect desired content.
4. **Taxonomy** is the name given to describe a controlled grouping of terms and language used to find and provide consistency within a specific subject field.
5. **Threat actors** identify and/or characterize the malicious adversary with intent and observed behaviors that represent a threat.
6. **Data-at-rest** refers to the protection of inactive data that is physically stored in any digital form (i.e., database, enterprise data warehouse, tapes, hard drives, etc.).
7. **Data-in-transit** is the flow of information over any type of public or private network environment.
8. **Data-in-use** applies to data that is actively stored in a nonpersistent state, such as memory, for consumption or presentation.
9. **Common body of knowledge (CBK)** is the complete concepts, terms and activities that make up a professional domain.
10. **Supervised learning** is a machine-learning task to which datasets with labelled responses are used to train and obtain desired outputs.
11. **Unsupervised learning** is a machine-learning task used to draw inferences from datasets that consist of input data without labeled responses.

APPENDIXES IV

Digital forensics has been a discipline of information security for decades. Since the digital forensic profession was formalized as a scientific discipline, the principles, methodologies, and techniques have remained consistent despite the evolution of technology and can ultimately be applied to any form of digital data. Within a corporate environment, digital forensic practitioners are often relied upon to maintain the legal admissibility and forensic viability of digital evidence in support of a broad range of different business functions.

This section contains supplemental information that expands on specific topics and subject matter discussed throughout the book. While these materials can be used as part of a digital forensic program, they have been included as stand-alone materials and can be referenced independently.

Appendix A

Investigative
Process Models

When technology was first involved with criminal activities, investigators did not follow any guiding principles, methodologies, or techniques when it can time to collect and process digital evidence. It was only in the 1980s when law enforcement agencies realized that there was a need to have an established set of processes that could be consistently followed to support their forensic investigations and guarantee the legal admissibility of digital evidence.

Over the years, there have been several authors who have taken on the task of developing and proposing a process model to formalize the digital forensic discipline and transform ad hoc tasks and activities into tested and proven methodologies. Displayed in Table A.1 is a list of different process methodologies that have been developed and proposed for digital forensic investigations.

Table A.1   Investigative Process Models

ID	Year	Author(s)	Model Name	Phases
P01	1995	M. Pollitt	Computer Forensic Investigative Process	4
P02	2001	U.S. Department of Justice	Computer Forensic Process Model	4
P03	2001	Palmer	Digital Forensic Research Workshop Investigative Model (Generic Investigation Process)	6

(Continued)

Table A.1 Investigative Process Models (*Continued*)

ID	Year	Author(s)	Model Name	Phases
P04	2001	Lee et al.	Scientific Crime Scene Investigation Model	4
P05	2002	Reith et al.	Abstract Model of the Digital Forensic Procedures	9
P06	2003	Carrier and Spafford	Integrated Digital Investigation Process	5
P07	2003	Stephenson	End-to-End Digital Investigation	9
P08	2004	Baryamureeba and Tushabe	Enhanced Integrated Digital Investigation Process	5
P09	2004	Ciardhuáin	Extended Model of Cybercrime Investigation	13
P10	2004	Beebe and Clark	Hierarchical, Objective-Based Framework for the Digital Investigations Process	6
P11	2004	Carrier and Spafford	An Event-Based Digital Forensic Investigation Framework	5
P12	2006	Kent et al.	Four Step Forensic Process	4
P13	2006	Kohn et al.	Framework for a Digital Forensic Investigation	3
P14	2006	K. Roger et al.	Computer Forensic Field Triage Process Model	12
P15	2006	Leong	FORZA: Digital forensics investigation framework	6
P16	2006	Venter	Process Flows for Cyber Forensics Training and Operations	3
P17	2007	Freiling and Schwittay	Common Process Model for Incident and Computer Forensics	3
P18	2007	Bem and Huebner	Dual Data Analysis Process	4
P19	2008	Selamat et al.	Mapping Process of Digital Forensic Investigations Framework	5

ID	Year	Author(s)	Model Name	Phases
P20	2009	Perumal S.	Digital Forensic Model Based on Malaysian Investigation Process	7
P21	2010	Pilli et al.	Generic Framework for Network Forensics	9
P22	2011	Yusoff	Generic Computer Forensic Investigation Model	5
P23	2011	Agarwal et al.	Systematic Digital Forensic Investigation Model	11
P24	2012	Adams et al.	Advanced Data Acquisition Model (ADAM)	3

It is important to note that while this listing may not be complete, the inclusion of a process methodology does not suggest it is better or recommended over other methodologies that were not included in the table.

[P01] Computer Forensic Investigative Process (1995)

Consisting of four phases, this model was proposed as a means of assuring evidence handling during a computer forensic investigation followed scientifically reliable and legally acceptable methodologies. The four phases are:

- *Acquisition* requires that digital evidence is collected using acceptable methodologies only after receiving proper approval from authorities.
- *Identification* interprets digital evidence and converts it into a readable human format.
- *Evaluation* determines the digital evidence's relevancy to the investigation.
- *Admission* documents relevant digital evidence for legal proceedings.

[P02] Computer Forensic Process Model (2001)

Consisting of four phases, this model was proposed in the *Electronic Crime Scene Investigation: A Guide to First Responders* publication and focused on the basic components of a digital forensic investigation. The four phases are:

- *Collection* involves searching for digital evidence sources and ensuring its integrity is maintained while gathering.
- *Examination* evaluates digital evidence to reveal data and reduce volumes.

- *Analysis* examining the context and content of digital evidence to determine relevancy.
- *Reporting* includes presenting digital evidence through investigation documentation.

[P03] Digital Forensic Research Workshop (DFRWS) Investigative Model (2001)

Consisting of six phases, this model was proposed as a general-purpose process for digital forensic investigations. The six phases are:

- *Identification* involves detection of an incident or event.
- *Preservation* establishes proper evidence gathering and chain of custody.
- *Collection* gathers relevant data using approved techniques.
- *Examination* evaluates digital evidence to reveal data and reduce volumes.
- *Analysis* examines the context and content of digital evidence to determine relevancy.
- *Presentation* includes preparing reporting documentation.

[P04] Scientific Crime Scene Investigation Model (2001)

Consisting of four phases, this model was proposed to strictly address scientific crime scene investigations and not the entire investigative process. The four phases are:

- *Recognition* identifies items or patterns seen as potential evidence.
- *Identification* classifies evidence and compares it to known standards.
- *Individualization* determines evidence uniqueness in relation to the investigation.
- *Reconstruction* provides investigative details based on collective findings.

[P05] Abstract Model of the Digital Forensic Procedures (2002)

Consisting of nine phases, this model enhances the DFRWS model by including three additional phases. The nine phases are:

- *Identification* involves detection of an incident or event.
- *Preparation* includes activities to ensure equipment and personnel are prepared.

- *Approach strategy* focuses on maintaining evidence integrity during acquisition.
- *Preservation* establishes proper evidence gathering and chain of custody.
- *Collection* gathers relevant data using approved techniques.
- *Examination* evaluates digital evidence to reveal data and reduce volumes.
- *Analysis* examines the context and content of digital evidence to determine relevancy.
- *Presentation* includes preparing reporting documentation.
- *Returning evidence* includes, where feasible, returning evidence to its original owner.

[P06] Integrated Digital Investigation Process (2003)

Consisting of five phases, this model was proposed with the intention of merging the various investigative processes into a single, integrated model. This model introduced the idea of a digital crime scene created as a result of technology where digital evidence exists. The five phases are:

- *Readiness* includes activities to ensure equipment and personnel are prepared.
- *Deployment* enables the detection and validation of an event or incidents.
- *Physical Crime Scene* involves the collection and analysis of physical evidence.
- *Digital Crime Scene* involves the collection and analysis of digital evidence.
- *Review* assesses the entire investigative process to identify opportunities for improvement.

[P07] End-to-End Digital Investigation (2003)

Consisting of six phases, this model was proposed as a general-purpose process for digital forensic investigations.The six phases are:

- *Collecting evidence* involves acquiring and preserving digital evidence.
- *Analysis of individual events* examines digital evidence to assess relevancy.
- *Preliminary correlation* assesses events to determine when events occurred and what technology is involved.
- *Event normalizing* duplicates and standardizes events into a unified structure.
- *Event deconfliction* consolidates multiple common events into a single event.
- *Second-level correlation* assesses the normalized events to further refine when events occurred and what technology is involved.
- *Timeline analysis* builds the chronological sequence of events.

- *Chain of evidence construction* establishes the correlation based on sequential events.
- *Corroboration* validates evidence and events against other evidence and events.

[P08] Enhanced Integrated Digital Investigation Process (2004)

Consisting of five phases, this model is based on the Integrated Digital Investigation Process. This model introduces the Traceback phase, which allows investigators to backtrack to the actual technology used in the crime. The five phases are:

- *Readiness* includes activities to ensure equipment and personnel are prepared.
- *Deployment* enables the detection and validation of an event or incidents.
- *Traceback* tracks back to the source crime scene including technology and location.
- *Dynamite* involves conducting investigations at the primary crime scene with intentions of identifying the potential offender(s).
- *Review* assesses the entire investigative process to identify opportunities for improvement.

[P09] Extended Model of Cybercrime Investigation (2004)

Consisting of 13 phases, this model was proposed as a generalized approach to the investigative process to assist in the development of new tools and techniques. The 13 phases are:

- *Awareness* allows the relationship with an investigation event to be identified.
- *Authorization* involves obtaining approval to proceed with the investigation.
- *Planning* scopes out how and where evidence will be collected.
- *Notification* informs stakeholders of the investigation.
- *Search for and identify evidence* locates and identifies evidence sources.
- *Collection of evidence* involves acquiring and preserving evidence.
- *Transport of evidence* includes moving evidence into a secure location.
- *Storage of evidence* includes placing evidence in protective custody.
- *Examination of evidence* evaluates evidence to reveal data and reduce volumes.
- *Hypothesis* constructs a theory based on the events that occurred.
- *Presentation of hypothesis* allows for a decision on the appropriate course of action.
- *Proof/defense of hypothesis* involves demonstrating the validity of the theory.
- *Dissemination of information* distributes information to stakeholders.

[P10] A Hierarchical, Objective-Based Framework for the Digital Investigations Process (2004)

Consisting of six phases, this model was proposed as a means of addressing all phases and activities described in preceding process models. The six phases are:

- *Preparation* includes activities to ensure equipment and personnel are prepared.
- *Incident response* detects and acknowledges an event or incident.
- *Data collection* gathers digital evidence in support of the response and investigation.
- *Data analysis* validates the detected against using collected digital evidence.
- *Presentation of findings* communicates findings to stakeholders.
- *Incident closure* includes acting upon decisions and assessing the investigative process.

[P11] Event-Based Digital Forensic Investigation Framework (2004)

Consisting of five phases, this model proposes following the processes for investigating physical crime scenes while considering the digital crime scene investigation as a subset. The five phases are:

- *Readiness* includes activities to ensure equipment and personnel are prepared.
- *Deployment* involves the detection of an incident and notification of investigators.
- *Physical crime scene investigation phase* is a series of steps and activities to search for, identify, and collect physical evidence to reconstruct physical events.
- *Digital crime scene investigation phase* is a subset of the physical crime scene investigation that involves a series of steps and activities to examine digital evidence.
- *Presentation* includes preparing reporting documentation.

[P12] Four Step Forensic Process (2006)

Consisting of four phases, this model proposes that forensics investigations can be conducted by even nontechnical persons through increased flexibility of steps and activities performed. The four phases are:

- *Collection* involves searching for digital evidence sources and ensuring its integrity is maintained while gathering.
- *Examination* evaluates digital evidence to reveal data and reduce volumes.

- *Analysis* examines the context and content of digital evidence to determine relevancy.
- *Reporting* includes presenting digital evidence through investigation documentation.

[P13] Framework for a Digital Forensic Investigation (2006)

Consisting of three phases, this model proposes merging existing process models into a broader and more adaptable model. The three phases are:

- *Preparation* includes activities to ensure equipment and personnel are prepared.
- *Investigation* involves all steps and activities performed to preserve, analyze, and store evidence.
- *Presentation* includes preparing reporting documentation.

[P14] Computer Forensic Field Triage Process Model (2006)

Consisting of six primary phases and six subtasks, this model proposes performing investigative tasks onsite, in a short timeframe, without seizing technology or acquiring forensic images. The six primary phases are:

- *Planning* includes activities to ensure equipment and personnel are prepared.
- *Triage* identified evidence and determine its relevance to the investigation.
- *User usage profile* focuses on analyzing user activity and behavior.
- *Chronology timeline* established a date/time sequence of digital evidence events.
- *Internet* examines artifacts from Internet related service activities.
- *Case specific* places focus on digital evidence relating directly to the investigation.

[P15] FORZA: Digital Forensics Investigation Framework (2006)

Consisting of six layers, this model proposes linking the eight practitioner roles and their associated procedures together throughout the investigative process. The six layers are:

- *Contextual investigation layer* understands the background details of the event.

- *Contextual layer* recognizes the involvement of business elements to the event.
- *Legal advisory layer* determines the legal aspects of the event.
- *Conceptual security layer* explores the design of systems and relevant security controls.
- *Technical presentation layer* determines the strategies and steps required of the digital forensics investigation.
- *Data acquisition layer* involves executing the identified digital forensic strategies and steps to collect evidence.
- *Data analysis layer* involves executing the identified digital forensic strategies and steps to examine evidence.
- *Legal presentation layer* involves discussing legal components as a result of the investigation.

[P16] Process Flows for Cyber Forensics Training and Operations (2006)

Consisting of three phases, this model proposes one workflow to govern general behavior on an electronic crime scene. The three phases are:

- *Inspect and prepare scene* contains the preparation actions to survey the scene, equipment to be seized, and evidence to be collected.
- *Collect evidence and evidence information* contains the elements involved in the collection of information related to evidence.
- *Debrief scene and record seizure information* contains the actions to record the existence and handling of evidence.

[P17] Common Process Model for Incident and Computer Forensics (2007)

Consisting of three phases, this model proposes the combination of incident response and computer forensics into an overall process for investigations. The three phases are:

- *Preanalysis* contains all steps and activities that are initially completed.
- *Analysis* includes all steps and activities performed during evidence examination.
- *Postanalysis* documents all steps and activities completed throughout the investigation.

[P18] Dual Data Analysis Process (2007)

Consisting of four phases, this model proposes following parallel investigative streams—the first stream with a less-experienced computer technician and the second stream with a professional investigator. The four phases are:

- *Access* locates and identifies evidence sources.
- *Acquire* involves collecting evidence and ensuring its integrity is maintained.
- *Analysis* examining the context and content of digital evidence to determine relevancy.
- *Report* includes presenting digital evidence through investigation documentation.

[P19] Digital Forensic Investigations Framework (2008)

Consisting of five phases, this model proposes:

- *Preparation* involves becoming familiar with the investigations and activities to ensure equipment and personnel are prepared.
- *Collection and preservation* involves the gathering and storage of digital evidence.
- *Examination and analysis* evaluates the context and content of digital evidence to determine relevancy to reveal data and reduce volumes.
- *Presentation and reporting* includes preparing and presenting digital evidence through investigation documentation.
- *Dissemination* distributes information to stakeholders.

[P20] Digital Forensic Model Based on Malaysian Investigation Process (2009)

Consisting of seven phases, this model is based on the Malaysian Investigation Process focusing on data acquisition and fundamental phases in conducting analysis. The seven phases are:

- *Planning* involves obtaining authorization and associated documentation to conduct an investigation.
- *Identification* identifies evidence to be seized while considering data volatility.
- *Reconnaissance* involves the gathering and storage of digital evidence.
- *Analysis* examines the context and content of digital evidence to determine relevancy.

- *Result* includes preparing reporting documentation.
- *Proof and defense* proves hypothesis with supporting evidence.
- *Archive storage* maintains evidence for future reference.

[P21] Generic Framework for Network Forensics (2010)

Consisting of nine phases, this model was proposed to specifically formalize a methodology for network-based digital investigations. The nine phases are:

- *Preparation and authorization* includes activities to ensure equipment and personnel are prepared.
- *Detection of incident/crime* indicates that an incident or event has occurred.
- *Incident response* consists of acknowledging and responding to an event or incident.
- *Collection of network traces* acquires data from sensors that collect network traffic data.
- *Preservation and protection* involves the gathering and storage of digital evidence.
- *Examination* evaluates digital evidence to reveal data and reduce volumes.
- *Analysis* examines the context and content of digital evidence to determine relevancy.
- *Investigation and attribution* reconstructs the event or incident using collected evidence.
- *Presentation* includes preparing reporting documentation.

[P22] Generic Computer Forensic Investigation Model (2011)

Consisting of five phases, this model was proposed as a means of generalizing the investigative process. The five phases are:

- *Preprocess* includes obtaining approval to proceed and activities to ensure equipment and personnel are prepared.
- *Acquisition and preservation* involves the gathering and storage of digital evidence.
- *Analysis* examines the context and content of digital evidence to determine relevancy.
- *Presentation* includes preparing reporting documentation.
- *Postprocess* includes returning evidence, where feasible, and identifying opportunities for improvement.

[P23] Systematic Digital Forensic Investigation Model (2011)

Consisting of 11 phases, this model was proposed with the goal of aiding in establishing appropriate policies and procedures in a systematic manner. The 11 phases are:

- *Preparation* involves becoming familiar with the investigations and activities to ensure equipment and personnel are prepared.
- *Securing the scene* secures the crime scene from unauthorized access and mitigates evidence tampering.
- *Survey and recognition* involves assessing the crime scene for potential evidence sources and establishes an appropriate search plan.
- *Documenting the scene* ensures crime scene documentation is recorded including photographs, sketches, etc.
- *Communication shielding* terminates all data exchange capabilities from technology.
- *Evidence collection* focuses on gathering of relevant data using approved techniques.
- *Preservation* establishes proper evidence gathering and chain of custody.
- *Examination* evaluates evidence to reveal data and reduce volumes.
- *Analysis* examines the context and content of digital evidence to determine relevancy.
- *Presentation* includes preparing reporting documentation.
- *Result* identifies opportunities for improvement.

[P24] Advanced Data Acquisition Model (ADAM) (2011)

Consisting of three phases, this model was proposed to function as an accepted standard for the acquisition of digital evidence. The three phases are:

- *Initial planning* involves becoming familiar with the investigations and activities to ensure equipment and personnel are prepared.
- *Onsite plan* involves learning additional specific details about the investigations to facilitate the acquisition of evidence.
- *Acquisition* involves the gathering and storage of digital evidence.

Appendix B

Education and Professional Certifications

Digital forensics requires that individuals have strong information technology knowledge as well as formalized training of digital forensic principles, methodologies, techniques, and tools. These are essential for maintaining the integrity, relevancy, and admissibility of digital evidence.

Professional Certifications

Internationally, there are a number of professional organizations that have established certifications and accreditations specific to the digital forensic profession. Predominantly, these certifications are provided by professional organizations with an industry-wide perspective on the digital forensic profession. However, there are a small number of certifications provided by merchants who sell digital forensic products and services.

It is important to keep in mind that while professional certification provides the assurance that an individual meet the required level of knowledge in digital forensics, these accreditations do not provide the in-depth level of education that formal academic program teach.

Although there may be some certification missing in the list below, the following are examples of digital forensics accreditations grouped, and alphabetically ordered, by professional organization. It is also important to note that the inclusion of these certifying bodies does not suggest that they are better or recommended over other professional organization that were not included in the list below.

Industry Neutral Certifications

- 7SAFE
  - *Certified MAC Forensics Specialist*
  - Certified Forensic Investigation Practitioner
  - Certified Forensic Investigation Specialist
- American Society for Industrial Security (ASIS) International
  - *Professional Certified Investigator (PCI)*
- Digital Forensics Certification Board (DFCB)
  - *Digital Forensics Certified Practitioner*
- International Council of Electronic Commerce Consultants (EC-Council)
  - *Computer Hacking Forensic Investigator (CHFI)*
- High Tech Crime Network (HTCN)
  - *Certified Computer Crime Investigator (CCCI) Basic*
  - Certified Computer Crime Investigator (CCCI) Advanced
  - Certified Computer Forensic Technician (CCFT) Basic
  - Certified Computer Forensic Technician (CCFT) Advanced
- Information Assurance Certification Review Board (IACRB)
  - *Certified Computer Forensics Examiner (CCFE)*
- International Association of Computer Investigative Specialists (IACIS)
  - *Certified Forensic Computer Examiner (CFCE)*
  - Certified Advanced Windows Forensic Examiner (CAWFE)
- International Information Systems Forensic Association (IISFA)
  - *Certified Information Forensics Investigator (CIFI)*
- International Society of Forensic Computer Examiners (ISFCE)
  - *Certified Computer Examiner (CCE)*
- SysAdmin, Audit, Networking, and Security (SANS)
  - *Global Information Assurance Certification (GIAC)—Certified Forensic Analyst (GCFA)*
  - Global Information Assurance Certification (GIAC)—Certified Forensic Examiner (GCFE)

Vendor Specific Certifications

- AccessData
  - *AccessData Certified Examiner (ACE)*
  - AccessData Mobile Phone Examiner (AME)
- BlackBag Technologies
  - *Certified BlackLight Examiner (CBE)*
  - Macintosh & iOS Certified Forensic Examiner (MiCFE)
- Guidance Software
  - *Encase Certified Examiner (EnCE)*

Formal Education Programs

At the highest level of training, a working and practical knowledge of all digital forensics must be achieved. Individuals who require this level of knowledge are those who must have the skills and competencies necessary to ensure that all principles, methodologies, and techniques are upheld in support of an organization's digital forensic program.

Working directly in digital forensics requires individuals to have a significant amount of training and technical skills to comprehend and consistently apply the profession's well-established scientific fundamentals. The information provided at this level is extremely detailed and requires individuals to have strong working and practical knowledge.

The number of higher/postsecondary institutions offering education programs focusing specifically on digital forensics has grown considerably. While each education program might be slightly different in the curriculum offered, they all cover the fundamental principles, methodologies, and techniques of digital forensics as required for individuals who are directly involved in the investigative workflow.

While there might be some higher/postsecondary institutions absent, the following is a list of digital forensic education programs grouped/ordered by geographical location and then ordered by the educational institute's name. It is important to note that inclusion of these digital forensic education programs does not suggest that these are better or recommended over other digital forensic education programs that were not included.

Australia

- Charles Sturt University
  - *Graduate Certificate Information Systems Security (Digital Forensics)*
  - Master Information Systems Security (Digital Forensics)
- Edith Cowan University
  - *Master of Digital Forensics*
- Macquarie University
  - *Postgraduate Diploma in Computer Forensics (PGDipCFR)*
  - Postgraduate Certificate in Computer Forensics (PCertCFR)
- Melbourne University
  - *Graduate Certificate in Digital Forensics*
  - Master of e-Forensics and Enterprise Security
- Murdoch University
  - *Cyber Forensics and Information Security (BSc)*

- University of South Australia (UniSA)
  - *Graduate Certificate in Science (Forensic Computing)*
  - Master of Science (Information Assurance)
- Swinburne University of Technology, Melbourne
  - *Graduate Certificate in eForensics*

Canada

- Algonquin College
  - *Computer Systems Technology—Security, Advanced Diploma (CST8606 Introduction to Digital Forensics)*
- BCIT Centre for Forensics and Security Technology Studies
  - *Bachelor of Technology (BTech)—Computer Crime Studies Option*
  - Forensic Investigation Advanced Specialty Certificate (ASC)—Computer Crime Studies Option
- Canadian Police College Technological Crime Learning Institute
  - *Advanced Internet Child Exploitation (AICE)*
  - Canadian Internet Child Exploitation (CICEC)
  - Cell Phone Seizure and Analysis (CSAC)
  - Computer Forensic Examiner (CMPFOR)
  - Digital Technologies for Investigators (DTIC)
  - Internet Evidence Analysis (IEAC)
  - Live Analysis Workshop (LAW)
  - Network Investigative Techniques (NITC)
  - Using the Internet as an Intelligence Tool (INTINT)
  - Advanced Computer Forensic Workshop (ACFW)
  - Registry Analysis Workshop (RAW)
  - Wireless Networks Workshop (WNETW)
- Ecole Polytechnique, University of Montreal's Engineering School
  - *Certificat en cyberenquête*
- Fleming College
  - *Computer Security and Investigations program*

England

- University of Bedfordshire
  - *(MSc) Computer Security and Forensics*
- Birmingham City University
  - *BSc (Hons) Forensic Computing*
- University of Bradford
  - *MSc Forensic Computing*
- Canterbury Christ Church University
  - *BSc (Hons) Forensic Computing*
  - MSc Cybercrime Forensics

- Coventry University
  - *Forensic Computing MSc*
- Cranfield University (based at the Defence Academy of the UK)
  - *Forensic Computing MSc/PgDip/PgCert*
- De Montfort University
  - *Forensic Computing BSc (Hons)*
  - Forensic Computing MSc/PG Dip/PG Cert
- University of Derby
  - *BSc (Hons) Computer Forensic Investigation*
  - MSc Computer Forensic Investigation
- University of Gloucestershire
  - *Forensic Computing Honours degree (3-year or 4-year sandwich)*
- University of Greenwich
  - *BSc (Hons) Computer Security and Forensics*
  - Computer Forensics and Systems Security, MSc
- Kingston University
  - *Cyber Security and Computer Forensics BSc (Hons)*
- University of Central Lancashire
  - *Forensic Computing BSc (Hons)*
- Leeds Metropolitan University
  - *BSc (Hons) Computer Forensics*
  - BSc (Hons) Computer Forensics & Security
  - MSc Digital Forensics & Security
- Liverpool John Moores University
  - *Computer Forensics BSc (Hons), BSc*
- University of East London
  - *Information Security and Computer Forensics (ISCF) Block Modem, MSc*
- London Metropolitan University
  - *Computer Forensics and IT Security (BSc Hons—Single)*
  - Computer Networking and Computer Forensics (BSc Hons—single)
  - Computer Forensics and IT Security (MSc)
- University of London—Royal Holloway
  - *Computer Forensics and IT Security (BSc Hons—Single)*
- Manchester Metropolitan University
  - *BSc (Hons) Computer Forensics and Security*
- Middlesex University
  - *BSc Honours Forensic Computing*
- Northumbria University
  - *Digital and Computer Forensics BSc (Hons)*
- The Open University
  - *M889 Computer Forensics and Investigations*
- University of Portsmouth
  - *BSc (Hons) Forensic Computing*
  - MSc Forensic Information Technology

- Sheffield Hallam University
  - *BSc (Honours) Computer Security with Forensics*
- Staffordshire University
  - *Digital Forensics BSc (Hons)*
  - Digital Forensics and Cybercrime Analysis, MSc, Postgraduate Certificate (PgC), Postgraduate Diploma (PgD)
- University of Sunderland
  - *BSc (Hons) Computer Forensics*
- Teesside University
  - *BSc (Hons) Computer and Digital Forensics*
- University of the West of England
  - *BSc (Hons) Forensic Computing*
- University of Westminster
  - *MSc Computer Forensics*

Germany

University of Erlangen, University of Munich, University of Applied Sciences Albstadt-Sigmaringen (joint program)

- *Digitale Forensik (Master)/Masters in Digital Forensics*

India

- Gujarat Forensic Sciences University
  - *M.S. Digital Forensics & Information Assurance*
- University of Madras
  - *Cyber Forensics and Information Security, MSc*
- Institute of Forensic Science, Mumbai
  - *Postgraduate diploma in Digital and Cyber Forensic and Related Law*
- The National Law Institute University, Bhopal
  - *Master of Science in Cyber Law and Information Security (MSCLIS)*

Ireland

- Blanchardstown Institute of Technology
  - *Bachelor of Science in Computing in Information Security and Digital Forensics*
  - Bachelor of Science (Honours) in Computing in Information Security and Digital Forensics
  - Master of Science in Computing (Information Security & Digital Forensics stream)

- University College Dublin
  - *Forensic Computing and Cybercrime Investigation (FCCI) Programme*
  - MSc Digital Investigation and Forensic Computing
- Dublin City University
  - *MSc in Security and Forensic Computing*
- Letterkenny Institute of Technology
  - *Bachelor of Science in Computing with Computer Security and Digital Forensics*
  - Bachelor of Science (Hons.) in Computer Security and Digital Forensics
- Waterford Institute of Technology
  - *BSc (Hons) in Computer Forensics*

Italy

- University of Bologna
  - *Forensic Computer Science*
- University of Milan
  - *Computer Forensics*
- University of Piemonte Orientale
  - *Corso di Informatica Forense*

Mexico

- Instituto Politecnico Nacional
  - *Maestría en Ingeniería en Seguridad y Tecnologías de la Información (Master of Security and Information Technology)*

Netherlands

- Universiteit van Amsterdam (UvA)
  - *Computer Forensics (part of Master's in Artificial Intelligence and Master's in Forensic Science)*
- Hogeschool Leiden
  - *Forensisch ICT*

New Zealand

- AUT University
  - *Master of Forensic Information Technology*

Norway

- Norwegian Police University College
  - *Digital forensics further education*

Scotland

- Abertay University (Dundee)
  - *BSc (Hons) Digital Forensics*
- Edinburgh Napier University
  - *Computer Security & Forensics BEng/BEng (Hons)*
- University of Glasgow
  - *Computer Forensics & E-Discovery*
- Glasgow Caledonian University
  - *Digital Security, Forensics and Ethical Hacking BEng/BEng (Hons)*

South Africa

- University of Cape Town (UCT)
  - *Postgraduate Diploma in Management in Information Systems (CG022)—INF4016W: Computer Forensics*

Sweden

- Högskolan Dalarna
  - *Digitalbrott och eSäkerhet, 180 högskolepoäng*
- Högskolan i Halmstad
  - *IT—forensik och informationssäkerhet, 120/180 hp*

United Arab Emirates (UAE)

- Zayed University
  - *Graduate Certificate in High Technology Crime Investigation Master of Science (M.S.) in Information Technology (Specialization in Cyber Security)*

United Kingdom

- Bournemouth University
  - *Forensic Investigations BSc*
  - Forensic Computing and Security BSc

United States of America

- American InterContinental University
  - *Bachelor of Information Technology (BIT): Specialization in Digital Investigations*
- American Public University System
  - *Undergraduate Certificate—Digital Forensics*
  - Graduate Certificate—Digital Forensics

- Anne Arundel Community College
  - *Cybercrime Degree Program, Cybercrime Certificate*
- Bloomsburg University of Pennsylvania
  - *Digital Forensics (B.S.)*
- Boston University
  - *Digital Forensics Graduate Certificate*
- Bristol Community College
  - *Associate Degree in Science in Computer Information Systems (Computer Forensics)*
- Bunker Hill Community College
  - *Digital and Computer Forensics and Investigations Option—Computer Information Technology Program—(Associate in Science Degree)*
- Butler County Community College
  - *Computer Information Systems—Computer Forensics and Security, A.A.S.*
- California State University, Fullerton
  - *Certificate in Computer Forensics I*
- Carnegie Mellon University
  - *Master of Science in Information Security Technology and Management (MSISTM)—Cyber Forensics and Incident Response*
- Catawba Valley Community College
  - *Cyber Crime Technology*
- Central Piedmont Community College
  - *Digital Evidence Training*
- Century College
  - *Computer Forensics—Associate in Applied Science Degree, Computer Forensics—Certificate*
- Champlain College
  - *Bachelor of Science, Computer & Digital Forensics*
  - Bachelor of Science, Computer Forensics & Digital Investigations (online)
  - Computer Forensics & Digital Investigations Certificate (online)
  - Master of Science in Digital Forensic Management
  - Master of Science in Digital Forensic Science
- Chestnut Hill College
  - *Certificate in Computer Forensics and Electronic Discovery*
- College of Lake County
  - *Computer Information Technology (CIT) program with various computer forensics courses*
- College of Western Idaho
  - *Information Technology: Information Security and Forensics*
- Colorado State University-Pueblo
  - *Bachelor of Science (BS) degree in Computer Information Systems (CIS)— CIS 462/562, Computer Forensics and Investigations*
- Community College of Philadelphia
  - *Computer Forensics Courses*

- Dakota State University
  - *MSIS Information Assurance (Forensics Classes)*
- Defiance College
  - *Digital Forensic Science (Bachelor of Science)*
- DelMar College
  - *Associate of Applied Science (AAS) degree—Information Systems Specialization - Digital Media Forensics Associate Emphasis (pdf)*
- DeSales University
  - *Master of Arts in Criminal Justice Online with a concentration in Computer Forensics*
- DeVry University
  - *Bachelor of Science, Computer Information Systems with a Specialized Track in Computer Forensics*
- Dixie State University
  - *BS in Criminal Justice—Digital Forensics Emphasis (PDF file)*
- Drexel University
  - *Minor in Computer Crime*
  - B.S. in Computing and Security Technology - Concentration: Computing Security - CT 212 Computer Forensics (Elective)
- Edmonds Community College
  - *Digital Forensics Certificate Information Security and Digital Forensics Associate of Technical Arts Degree (pdf)*
- Florida State College
  - *Computer Forensics Technician (6947)*
- Fountainhead College of Technology
  - *Network Security and Forensics*
- George Mason University
  - *MS in Computer Forensics*
- Herkimer County Community College
  - *Cybersecurity A.S.*
- Highline Community College
  - *Data Recovery/Forensic Specialist (Certificate and AAS options)*
- Illinois Institute of Technology
  - *Computer and Network Forensics, IT 538*
- Indian Hills Community College
  - *Digital Forensics Associate of Applied Science Degree (A.A.S.)*
- International Academy of Design & Technology
  - *Bachelor of Science in Computer Forensics (BS)*
- Iowa State University
  - *CprE 536: Computer and Network Forensics*
- James Madison University
  - *Master's Degree in Computer Science concentration in Digital Forensics*

- Johns Hopkins University
  - *MSc Security Informatics (650.457 Computer Forensics, 650.657 Advanced Topics in Computer Forensics)*
- John Jay College of Criminal Justice
  - *Master of Science in Digital Forensics and Cybersecurity, Certificate in Applied Digital Forensic Science*
- Kaplan University—Hagerstown Campus
  - *Bachelor of Science in Criminal Justice*
  - Master of Science in Criminal Justice
  - Associate of Applied Science in Criminal Justice
  - Computer Forensics Post Baccalaureate Certificate
- Kennesaw State University
  - *ISA 4350. Computer Forensics. 3-0-3.*
- Lamar Institute of Technology
  - *ITDF 1300 Introduction to Digital Forensics 3:3:0*
- Las Positas College
  - *Computer Networking Technology—Introduction to Computer Forensics and Computer Forensics II*
- Lawrence Technological University
  - *Graduate Certificate in Information Assurance Management (MIS5213 High Tech Cyber Crime)*
- Marshall University
  - *Computer and Information Technology Major—Computer Forensics Area of Emphasis*
  - Graduate Certificate in Digital Forensics
  - Master of Science Degree Program—Emphasis on Digital Forensics
- Metropolitan State University
  - *Computer Forensics (BAS)*
  - Computer Forensics Minor
  - Computer Forensics Certificate
- Middlesex Community College
  - *Certificate and Associate Degree Programs in Computer Forensics*
- Missouri Southern State University
  - *Bachelor of Science in CIS—Computer Forensics*
- Northcentral University
  - *Business PhD Computer and Information Security Specialization*
- Pittsburgh Technical Institute
  - *Network Security and Computer Forensics Concentration*
- Purdue University Cyber Forensics Lab
  - *CIT 420/556 Computer Forensics*
  - CIT557 Advanced Research Topics in Computer Forensics

- Regis University
  - *Information Assurance Certificate (options available in Computer Forensics and Network Forensics)*
- Rich Mountain Community College
  - *Computer Forensics Certificate*
- Richland College
  - *Digital Forensics AAS Degree*
  - Digital Forensic Analyst Advanced Technical Certificate
  - Digital Forensics Certificate Programs in Information Security/ Information Assurance
- Rochester Institute of Technology (RIT)
  - *BS in Information Security and Forensics (ISF)*
- St. Ambrose University
  - *BA in Computer Investigations and Criminal Justice*
- St. Petersburg College
  - *Digital Forensics and Computer Investigations (A.S. degree and certificate)*
- Sam Houston State University
  - *Digital Forensics (various classes)*
- Solano Community College
  - *Certificate and Associate Science Degree in Criminal Justice: Computer Forensics*
- Stanly Community College
  - *Cyber Crime Technology*
- Stark State College
  - *Cyber Security and Computer Forensics Technology*
- Stevenson University
  - *Master's in Cyber Forensics*
- The George Washington University
  - *Master of Science in High Technology Crime Investigation (HTCI)*
- Tompkins Cortland Community College
  - *Computer Forensics A.A.S. Degree*
- University of Alabama at Birmingham (UAB)
  - *Master of Science in Computer Forensics and Security Management (MSCFSM)*
- University of Advancing Technology
  - *BS in Technology Forensics*
- University of Central Florida
  - *Certificate Program*
  - Master of Science in Digital Forensics (MSDF)
- University of Nebraska Omaha (UNO)
  - *CSCI-4380 (Computer and Network Forensics)*

- University of New Haven
  - *Digital Forensics focus area (various degrees)*
- University of New Orleans
  - *Information Assurance Program*
- University of Northwestern Ohio
  - *Computer Forensics Associate Degree (pdf)*
- University of Rhode Island
  - *Digital Forensics Minor*
  - Digital Forensics Professional Certificate (online)
  - Digital Forensics Graduate Certificate (online)
  - Computer Science Master's degree with a concentration in Digital Forensics
  - PhD with a concentration in Digital Forensics
- University of Southern California
  - *Information Technology Program—Digital Forensics Specialization Computer and Digital Forensics Minor*
- University of Texas at Arlington
  - *CRCJ 3320 Cybercrime (pdf)*
- University of Texas at San Antonio
  - *M.S. I.T. and Infrastructure Assurance—6363 Computer Forensics class*
- University of Washington in Seattle
  - *Certificate in Digital Forensics*
- Utica College
  - *Online Cybersecurity and Information Assurance Bachelor's program (Cybercrime Investigations and Forensics Concentration Courses)*
- Walsh College
  - *Digital Forensics Certificate*
- Waynesburg University
  - *Bachelor of Science in Computer Security (Computer Forensics)*
- West Virginia University
  - *Certificate in Computer Forensics*
- Westchester Community College
  - *Computer Security and Forensics Certificate*
  - Computer Security and Forensics A.A.S.
- Westwood College
  - *Major in Computer Forensics*
  - Major in Computer Forensics (online)
- Wilmington University
  - *Computer and Network Security Bachelor of Science (credits in Electronic Discovery and Computer Forensics)*

Wales

- Cardiff University
  - *Computer Science with Security and Forensics (BSc)*
  - Computer Science with Security and Forensics with a year in industry (BSc)
- University of Glamorgan
  - *BSc (Hons) Computer Forensics*
  - MSc Computer Forensics
- Newport University
  - *Forensic Computing—BSc (Hons)*
  - Cyber-Crime Forensics, MSc

TEMPLATES

V

This section includes all template materials that are representative and supportive of both digital forensic readiness and business-process documentation. The templates provided in this section contain instructions to the author, standardized text, and fields that should be modified and replaced with values specified at the time of writing, including:

- Blue italicized text enclosed in square brackets (e.g., [text]) provides instructions to the author or describes the intent, assumptions, and context for content included in the template document. These fields must be deleted prior to finalizing the template document.
- Blue italicized text enclosed in angle brackets (e.g., <text>) indicates a field that should be replaced with information specific to a particular section of text within the template document.
- Text and tables in black are provided as standardized examples of wording and formats that may be used or modified as needed. These are provided only as references and suggestions to assist in developing the template document; they are not mandatory formats.

When using a template document, the following steps are recommended to perform modifications:

1. Replace all text enclosed in angle brackets (e.g., <Project Name>) with the correct field values. These angle brackets appear in the body of the template document, as well as in headers and footers.
2. Modify standardized text as appropriate for the template document's specific topic.
3. To update the table of contents, right-click on it and select "Update field," and then choose the option "Update entire table."
4. Before submission of the first draft of this document, delete all instructions to the author throughout the template document.

TEMPLATE A

Investigator Logbook

Case/Incident	Date:	Description:	Investigator:

Time	Action(s) Taken

Time	Action(s) Taken

Prepared By: _____   Signature: _____

Chain of Custody

Case/Incident: _____ Exhibit/Property Number: _____

Date Acquired (mm/dd/yy): _____ Time Acquired (24hr): ___ : ___

Location of Seized: _____ Seized By: _____

Description of Item (e.g., Model, Quantity, Serial #, Condition, Markings, etc):

Notes/Additional Comments:

Chain of Custody			
Date/Time	Released By (Name & Signature)	Received By (Name & Signature)	Comments:

Authorization for Evidence Disposal

This item is no longer needed as evidence and is authorized for disposal through the following method:

☐ Return to Owner ☐ Destruction ☐ Donation ☐ Other_____

Release By: _____ Signature: _____ Date: _____

Witness to Evidence Disposal

I, _____, witnessed on the _____ day of
_____ 20__ the disposal of this item as performed by _____
_____ in my presence.
Witness: _____ Signature: _____
Date: _____

Evidence Release to Lawful Owner

This item is no longer needed as evidence and has been released by me, _____
_____, to its lawful owner
Owner _____
_____
Address: _____
_____
Telephone Number: (_____) _____
Signature: _____ Date: _____

Bibliography

Adams, Richard; Hobbs, Val; Mann, Graham. The advanced data acquisition model (Adam): A process model for digital forensic practice. *Journal of Digital Forensics, Security and Law*, 8(4), Article 2, 2013, 25–48. http://ojs.jdfsl.org/index.php/jdfsl/article/download/110/198

Ahmad, Atif. The Forensic Chain-of-Evidence Model: Improving the Process of Evidence Collection in Incident Handling Procedures. *Proceedings of the 6th Pacific Asia Conference on Information Systems*, Tokyo, Japan, 2002.

Association of Chief Police Officers. *Good Practice Guide for Computer-Based Electronic Evidence*. 2007. https://www.7safe.com/docs/default-source/default-document-library/acpo_guidelines_computer_evidence_v4_web.pdf

Australian Signal Directorate. *Strategies to Mitigate Cyber Security Incidents*. Australian Government—Department of Defense, 2017.

Ayers, Rick; Brothers, Sam; Jansen, Wayne. *Special Publication 800-101 Revision 1: Guidelines on Mobile Device Forensics*. Virginia: National Institute of Standards and Technology (NIST), 2014.

Ballou, Susan. *Scientific and Technical Working Groups: An Overview*. 2009.

Barymureeba, Venansius; Tushabe, Florence. The Enhanced Digital Investigation Process Model. *Digital Forensics Research Workshop (DFRWS)*, 2004.

Beebe, Nicole; Clark, Jan. A Hierarchical, Objectives-Based Framework for the Digital Investigations Process. *Digital Forensics Research Workshop (DFRWS)*, 2004.

Bem, Derek; Huebner, Ewa. Computer forensic analysis in a virtual environment. *International Journal of Digital Evidence*, 6(2), 2007, 1–13.

Bennett, Brian T. *Understanding, Assessing, and Responding to Terrorism: Protecting Critical Infrastructure and Personnel*. John Wiley & Sons, 2007.

Bradley, Jaron. *OS X Incident Response: Scripting and Analysis*. Cambridge: Syngress, 2016. ISBN# 9780128045039.

Bretherton, F.P.; Singley, P.T. *Metadata: A User's View*. Institute of Electrical and Electronics Engineers (IEEE), 1994.

Bunting, Steve. *EnCase Computer Forensics—The Official EnCE: EnCase Certified Examiner Study Guide*. John Wiley & Sons, 2012.

Business Dictionary. *Jurisdiction*. WebFinance Inc, 2017.

California Department of Health Care Services. Health Insurance Portability and Accountability Act. State of California, 2016.

Campagna, Rich; Iyer, Subbu; Krishnan, Ashwin. *Mobile Device Security for Dummies*. Hoboken, NJ: John Wiley & Sons, 2011.

Canadian Criminal Law Notebook. Section 487: Search Warrants. 2017.

Carminati, F.; Betev, L.; Grigoras, A. *Grid and Cloud Computing: Concepts and Practical Applications*. IOS Press, 2016.

Carrier, Brian D.; Spafford, Eugene H. An Event-Based Digital Forensic Investigation Framework. *Digital Forensics Research Workshop (DFRWS)*, 2004.

Casey, Eoghan. *Digital Evidence and Computer Crime: Forensic Science, Computers and the Internet.* Boston, MA: Academic Press, 2004.

Casey, Eoghan. *Digital Evidence and Computer Crime: Forensic Science, Computers and the Internet,* 3rd Edition. Boston, MA: Academic Press, 2011.

Ceresini, T. *Maintaining the Forensic Viability of Log Files.* System Administration, Networking, and Security Institute (SANS)—Global Information Assurance Certification (GIAC), 2001.

Charters, Ian. *The Evolution of Digital Forensics: Civilizing the Cyber Frontier.* 2009.

Choksy, Carol. E.B. Ph.D. 8 Steps to develop a taxonomy. *The Information Management Journal,* 2006. http://www.guerilla-ciso.com/wp-content/uploads/2009/01/the-evolution-of-digital-forensics-ian-charters.pdf

Chow, Kam-Pui; Shenoi, Sujeet (Eds.). *Advances in Digital Forensics VI.* New York, NY: Springer, 2010.

Ciardhuáin, Séamus Ó. An extended model of cybercrime investigations. *International Journal of Digital Evidence,* 3(1), 2004, 1–22. https://www.utica.edu/academic/institutes/ecii/publications/articles/A0B70121-FD6C-3DBA-0EA5C3E93CC575FA.pdf

Cichonski, Paul; Millar, Tom; Grance, Tim; Scarfone, Karen. *Computer Security Incident Handling Guide.* Gaithersburg, MD: National Institute of Standards and Technology (NIST), 2012.

Cloud Security Alliance. *Quick Guide to the Reference Architecture: Trusted Cloud Initiative.* 2011.

Cloud Security Alliance. *Security Guidance for Critical Areas of Focus in Cloud Computing V3.0.* 2011.

Computer Ethics Institute. The Ten Commandments of Computer Ethics. 1992.

Conlan, Kevin; Baggili, Ibrahim; Breitinger, Frank. Anti-Forensics: Furthering Digital Forensic Science through a New Extended, Granular Taxonomy. *Digital Forensics Research Workshop (DFRWS)—Proceedings of the 16th Annual USA Digital Forensics Research Conference,* 2016.

Contesti, Diana-Lynn; Andre, Douglas; Henry, Paul A; Goins, Bonnie A; Waxvik, Eric. *Official (ISC)2 Guide to the SSCP CBK.* Cambridge: CRC Press, 2007. ISBN# 9780203331576.

Cornell Law Review. Evidence—Admissibility of evidence—Frye standard of general acceptance for admissibility of scientific evidence rejected in favor of balancing test. *Cornell Law School* 64, 1979.

Daluz, Hillary Moses. *Fingerprint Analysis Laboratory Workbook.* CRC Press, 2014.

Dawson, Maurice. *New Threats and Countermeasures in Digital Crime and Cyber Terrorism.* Pennsylvania, PA: IGI Global, 2015.

Digital Forensics Association. *A Word on Education.* 2017.

Digital Forensics Association. *Associate Level Programs.* 2017.

Digital Forensics Association. *Bachelor Level Programs.* 2017.

Digital Forensics Association. *Certificate Programs.* 2017.

Digital Forensics Association. *Doctoral Programs.* 2017.

Digital Forensics Association. *Master Degree Programs.* 2017.

Digital Forensics Certification Board. *Code of Ethics and Standards of Professional Conduct.* 2016.

Duke Law Center for Judicial Studies. *Electronic Discovery Reference Model.* 2016.

Duke Law Center for Judicial Studies. *Project Management Guide.* 2017.

Duke Law Center for Judicial Studies. *Technology Assisted Review.* 2012.

Dykstra, Josiah; Sherman, Alan. Acquiring Forensic Evidence from Infrastructure-as-a-Service Cloud Computing. *Digital Forensics Research Workshop (DFRWS),* 2012.

EC-Council. *Computer Forensics: Investigating Network Intrusions and Cybercrime (CHFI).* Nelson Education, 2016.

eLaw Exchange. *What Are the Different Types and Locations of ESI Should I Request.* Law Partner Publishing, 2010.

EUR-Lex. Directive 2013/40/EU. European Union, 2013.

EUR-Lex. Directive 2002/58/EU. European Union, 2014.

EUR-Lex. General Data Protection Regulation (GDPR)—Directive 95/46/EC. European Union, 2016.

Eilam, Eldad. *Reversing: Secrets of Reverse Engineering.* John Wiley & Sons, 2011.

Federal Bureau of Investigations. Forensic science communications. *Digital Evidence: Standards and Principles,* 2(3) 2000. https://archives.fbi.gov/archives/about-us/lab/forensic-science-communications/fsc/april2000/swgde.htm

Federal Register of Legislation. Cybercrime Act. Australian Government, 2001.

Fenu, Gianni; Solinas, Fabrizio. Computer Forensics Investigation an Approach to Evidence in Cyberspace. Society of Digital Information and Wireless Communications (SDIWC), 2013.

Fernando, A.C. *Business Ethics and Corporate Governance.* New Delhi: Pearson Education India, 2010.

Flynn, Nancy. *The Social Media Handbook: Rules, Policies, and Best Practices to Successfully Manage Your Organization's Social Media Presence, Posts, and Potential.* Hoboken, NJ: John Wiley & Sons, 2012.

Forensic Focus. *Computer Forensics Education.* 2017.

Forensic Science Laboratories Facilities Technical Working Group. *Handbook for Facility Planning, Design, Construction, and Relocation.* National Institute of Standards and Technology (NIST), 2013.

Fowler, Kevvie. *Data Breach Preparation and Response: Breaches are Certain, Impact is Not.* Syngress, 2016.

Freiling, Felix C.; Schwittay, Bastian. *A Common Process Model for Incident Response and Computer Forensics.* Laboratory for Dependable Distributed Systems, New York, NY: University of Mannheim, Germany, 2007.

Garrison, Clint P. *Digital Forensics for Network, Internet, and Cloud Computing: A Forensic Evidence Guide for Moving Targets and Data.* Syngress, 2010. ISBN# 9781597495387.

Gogolin, Greg. *Digital Forensics Explained.* CRC Press, 2012.

Goodwin, Richard. *The History of Mobile Phones From 1973 To 2008: The Handsets That Made It ALL Happen.* Know Your Mobile, 2016.

Graves, Michael W. *Digital Archaeology: The Art and Science of Digital Forensics.* Addison-Wesley, 2013.

Gricks, Thomas C. III; Ambrogi, Robert J. *A Brief History of Technology Assisted Review.* Law Technology Today, 2015.

Grobler, C.P.; Louwrens, C.P. *Digital Forensic Readiness as a Component of Information Security Best Practice.* Boston, MA: Springer, 2007.

Grobler, M.M.; Dlamini, I.Z. Managing digital evidence–the governance of digital forensics. *Journal of Contemporary Management,* 7, 2010, 1–21.

HG Legal Resources. *Information Technology Law.* HGExperts, 2015.

Harrington, Sean. Professional Ethics in the Digital Forensics Discipline: Part 1. 2014.

Harrington, Sean. Professional Ethics in the Digital Forensics Discipline: Part 2. 2014.

Herzig, Terrell W.; Walsh, Tom; Gallagher, Lisa A. *Implementing Information Security in Healthcare: Building a Security Program.* Chicago, IL: HIMSS, 2013.

Holt, Thomas J.; Bossler, Adam M.; Seigfried-Spellar, Kathryn C. *Cybercrime and Digital Forensics: An Introduction.* New York, NY: Routledge, 2015.

Hoog, Andrew. *Android Forensics: Investigation, Analysis, and Mobile Security for Google Android.* Elsevier, 2011.

Hrycko, Oleh. *Electronic Discovery in Canada: Best Practices and Guidelines.* Canada: CCH Canadian Limited, 2007.

Hutchins, Eric M.; Cloppert, Micheal J.; Amin, Rohan M Ph.D. *Intelligence-Driven Computer Network Defense Informed by Analysis of Adversary Campaigns and Instrusion Kill Chains.* Lockheed Martin Corporation, 2011.

IFSEC Global. *The Forensic Technologist: Data Privacy and Digital Forensics.* UBM, 2012.

IT@Cornell. *Cornell Project Management Methodology (CPMM) Guidebook.* Cornell University, 2005.

Ieong, Ricci Sze-Chung. FORZA: Digital Forensics Investigation Framework that Incorporate Legal Issues. *Digital Forensics Research Workshop (DFRWS)*, 2006.

Imperial War Museums. *How Alan Turing Cracked the Enigma Code.* 2017.

International Association of Computer Investigative Specialists (IACIS). *Code of Ethics.* Austin, TX: University of Texas, 2017.

International Information System Security Certification Consortium (ISC)2. *Certified Cyber Forensics Professional.* 2017.

International Information System Security Certification Consortium (ISC)2. *Code of Ethics.* 2016.

International Society of Forensic Computer Examiners (ISFCE). *Certified Computer Examiner (CCE) Certification.* 2017.

International Society of Forensic Computer Examiners (ISFCE). *Code of Ethics and Professional Responsibility.* 2017.

Jarrett, H. Marshall; Bailie, Michael W. *Searching and Seizing Computers and Obtaining Electronic Evidence in Criminal Investigations.* Washington, DC: Department of Justice—Computer Crime and Intellectual Property Section Criminal Division, 2009.

Johnson, Leighton. *Computer Incident Response and Forensics Team Management: Conducting a Successful Incident Response.* Newnes, 2013.

Kabay, M.E.. Ph.D. *A Brief History of Computer Crime: An Introduction for Students.* 2008.

Kanellis, Panagiotis; Kiountouzis, Evangelos; Kolokotronis, Nicholas. *Digital Crime and Forensic Science in Cyberspace.* Idea Group Inc, 2006.

Karake-Shalhoub, Zeinab; Al Qasimi, Lubna. *Cyber Law and Cyber Security in Developing and Emerging Economies.* Edward Elgar Publishing, 2010.

Kent, Karen; Chevalier, Suzanne; Grance, Tim; Dang, Hung. *Special Publication 800-86: Guide to Integrating Forensic Techniques into Incident Response.* National Institute of Standards and Technology (NIST), 2006.

Kershaw, Anne. *Automated Document Review Proves Its Reliability.* Pike & Fischer, 2005.

Kissel, Richard; Stine, kevin; Scholl, Matthew; Rossman, Hart; Fahlsing, Jim; Gulick, Jessica. *Special Publication 800-64 Revision 2: Security Considerations in the System Development Life Cycle.* National Institute of Standards and Technology (NIST), 2008.

Kohn, Michael; Eloff, J.H.P.; Olivier, M.S. *Framework for a Digital Forensic Investigation.* Information and Computer Security Architectures Research Group (ICSA), Department of Computer Science, University of Pretoria. 2006

Kruse, Warren G II; Heiser, Jay G. *Computer Forensics: Incident Response Essentials.* Indianapolis: Pearson, 2001.

Law Crossing. *Information Technology Attorney Job Description.* Employment Research Institute, 2015.

Lawson, Ben. *The Data Centric Security Model.* 2012.

'Lectric Law Library. *Precedent.* 2017. https://www.lectlaw.com/def2/p069.htm

Legal Information Institute. *Brady Rule.* Cornell Law School, 2015.

Legal Information Institute. *Daubert Standard.* Cornell Law School, 2015.

Legal Information Institute. *Federal Rules of Evidence.* Cornell Law School, 2015.

Legal Information Institute. *Federal Rules of Civil Procedure (FRCP).* Cornell Law School, 2016.

Legal Information Institute. *Best Evidence Rule.* Cornell Law School, 2017.

Lim, Sungsu; Yoo, Byeongyeong; Park, Jungheum; Byun, KeunDuck; Lee, Sangjin. *A Research on the Investigation Method of Digital Forensics for a VMware Workstation's Virtual Machine.* Elsevier, 2012.

Lloyd, Ian. *Information Technology Law.* Oxford University Press, 2014.

Marcella, Albert Jr; Menendez, Doug. *Cyber Forensics: A Field Manual for Collecting, Examining, and Preserving Evidence of Computer Crimes*, Second Edition. CRC Press, 2007.

Masys, Anthony J. *Disaster Forensics: Understanding Root Cause and Complex Causality*. Springer, 2016.

MathWorks. Unsupervised Learning. 2017.

McKemmish, Rodney. *When is Digital Evidence Forensically Sound. Advances in Digital Forensics IV*. Springer, 2008.

Mell, Peter; Grance, Timothy. *Special Publication 800-145: The NIST Definition of Cloud Computing*. National Institute of Standards and Technology (NIST), 2011.

Mena, Jesus. *Machine Learning Forensics for Law Enforcement, Security, and Intelligence*. CRC Press, 2016.

Microsoft TechNet. Secure Boot Overview. Microsoft, 2014.

Microsoft TechNet. *Responding to IT Security Incidents*. Microsoft, 2017.

Ministry of Justice. *Civil Procedure Rules (CPR)*. Government of the United Kingdom, 2017.

Mohay, George M. *Computer and Intrusion Forensics*. Artech House, 2003.

Murphy, Cynthia A. *Developing Process for Mobile Device Forensics V3*. System Administration, Networking, and Security Institute (SANS), 2013.

National Crime Victim Law Institute. *What are the Differences between the Civil and Criminal Justice System*. Lewis & Clark, 2010.

Nelson, Bill; Phillips, Amelia; Enfinger, Frank; Steuart, Chris. *Guide to Computer Forensics and Investigations*. Boston, MA: Thomson Learning, 2004.

Nelson, Bill; Phillips, Amelia; Steuart, Christopher. *Guide to Computer Forensics and Investigations*. Nelson Education, 2009.

Neto, Maximilliano Destefani. *A Brief History of Cloud Computing*. IBM, 2014.

Nikkel, Bruce J. The Role of Digital Forensics within a Corporate Organization. *IBSA Conference*, 2006.

NIST Cloud Computing Forensic Science Working Group Information Technology Laboratory. *NIST Cloud Computing Forensic Science Challenges*. National Institute of Standards and Technology (NIST), 2014.

NIST Cloud Computing Security Working Group Information Technology Laboratory. *Special Publication 500-299: NIST Cloud Computing Security Reference Architecture*. National Institute of Standards and Technology (NIST), 2013.

Office of the Auditor General of British Columbia. *Guide for Developing Relevant Key Performance Indicators for Public Sector Reporting*. Government of British Columbia, 2010.

Ontario Bar Association. Checklist for Preparing a Discovery Plan V2.1. 2010.

Overill, Richard E. *Digital Quantum Forensics: Challenges and Responses*. 2011.

O'Loughlin, Mark. *The Service Catalog: Best Practices*. Van Haren, 2010.

Pajek, Przemyslaw; Pimenidis, Elias. *Computer Anti-Forensics Methods and Their Impact on Computer Forensic Investigation*. Springer, 2009.

Pangalos, Georgios; Vasilios, Katos. Information Assurance and Forensic Readiness. *Technological and Legal Issues—Third International Conference*, 2009.

Parinita Bahadur. *Difference between Guideline, Procedure, Standard and Policy*. HR Success Guide, 2014.

Parliament of the United Kingdom. Computer Misuse Act. 1990.

Payment Card Industry (PCI) Security Standards Council, LLC. PCI Data Security Standards (DSS). 2016.

Peterson, Gilbert; Shenoi, Sujeet. Advances in Digital Forensics V. *5th IFIP WG 11.9 International Conference on Digital Forensics*. Springer, 2009.

Peterson, Gilbert; Shenoi, Sujeet. Advances in Digital Forensics XII. *12th IFIP WG 11.9 International Conference on Digital Forensics*. Springer, 2016.

Philips, Amelia; Godfrey, Ronald; Steuart, Christopher; Brown, Christine. *E-Discovery: An Introduction to Digital Evidence*. Nelson Education, 2013.

Pilli, Emmanuel S.; Joshi, R.C.; Niyogi, Rajdeep. A generic framework for network forensics. *International Journal of Computer Applications*, 1(11), 2010.

Pollitt, Mark; Shenoi, Sujeet. Advances in Digital Forensics. *IFIP International Conference on Digital Forensics, National Center for Forensic Science*, Orlando, FL, Spring 2006.

Porterfield, Jason. *File Sharing: Rights and Risks*. The Rosen Publishing Group, 2014.

Ray, Daniel A.; Bradford, Phillip G. *Models of Models: Digital Forensics and Domain Specific Languages*. Department of Computer Science—University of Alabama, 2007.

Republic of the Philippines, Official Gazette. Republic Act No. 10175. 2012.

Rowlingson, Robert Ph.D. A Ten step process for forensic readiness. *International Journal of Digital Evidence*, 2(3), 2004, 1–28.

Ruan, Keyun; Carthy, Joe; Kechadi, Tahar; Crosbie, Mark. *Cloud Forensics, Advances in Digital Forensics VII* Springer, 2011.

Sachowski, Jason. *Implementing Digital Forensic Readiness: From Reactive to Proactive Process*. Syngress, 2016.

Sammons, John. *Digital Forensics: Threatscape and Best Practices*. Syngress, 2015.

Schjolberg, Stein. *The History of Global Harmonization on Cybercrime Legislation—The Road to Geneva*. 2008. http://www.cybercrimelaw.net/documents/cybercrime_history.pdf

Schmitt, Veronia; Jordaan, Jason. Establishing the validity of MD5 and SHA-1 hashing in digital Forensic practice in light of recent research demonstrating cryptographic weaknesses in these algorithms. *International Journal of Computer Applications*, 68(23), 2013, 40–43.

Schroader, Amber; Cohen, Tyler. *Alternate Data Storage Forensics*. Elsevier, 2011.

Selamat, S.; Yusof, R.; Sahib, S. Mapping process of digital forensic investigation framework. *International Journal of Computer Science and Network Security*, 8(10), 2008.

Shaler, Robert C. *Crime Scene Forensics: A Scientific Method Approach*. Taylor & Francis, 2011.

Smallwood, Robert F. *Information Governance: Concepts, Strategies, and Best Practices*. John Wiley & Sons, 2014.

Smith, Ashley. Mobile Device Management: What's Legal, What's Not?. *Tom's IT Pro*, 2016.

mith, Fred Chris; Bace, Rebecca Gurley. *A Guide to Forensic Testimony – The Art and Practice of Presenting Testimony as an Expert Technical Witness*. Addison-Wesley, 2002.

SOX Law. The Sarbanes-Oxley Act. 2006.

Speaker, Paul J. Key Performance Indicators and Managerial Analysis for Forensic Laboratories. *Forensic Science Policy & Management: An International Journal*. Taylor and Francis, 1, 2009, 32–42.

Spreitzenbarth, Michael Dr.; Uhrmann, Johann Dr. *Mastering Python Forensics*. Packt Publishing, 2015.

Stephenson, Peter. *A Comprehensive Approach to Digital Incident Investigation*. Elsevier, 2003.

Stephenson, Peter. *(ISC)2 Official Guide to the CCFP CBK*. CRC Press. 2014.

Sule, Dauda. Importance of forensic readiness. *ISACA Journal*, 1, 2014.

Sutton, Jennifer Hyman. BYOD, CYOD, COPE: What Does It All Mean. *Business 2 Community*, 2014. https://www.isaca.org/Journal/archives/2014/Volume-1/Pages/JOnline-Importance-of-Forensic-Readiness.aspx

Tan, John. *Forensic Readiness*. 2001.

Techtarget. *Principle of Least Privilege (POLP)*. 2017.

The Sedona Conference. The Sedona Canada Principles 2015.

The Sedona Conference. The Sedona Conference Commentary on Rule 34 and Rule 45 "Possession, Custody, or Control." 2016.

The Sedona Conference. The Sedona Principles. 2017.

Thompson, Kevin Ph.D. *How to Estimate Capacity for Work in Agile Teams: Learn How to Estimate How Much Work Your Team Can Accomplish*. cPrime, 2012.

Tipton, Harold F. *(ISC)2 Official Guide to the ISSAP CBK*. CRC Press. 2011.

Tipton, Harold F. *(ISC)2 Official Guide to the ISSMP CBK.* CRC Press. 2011.

US Department of Justice. Electronic Communications Privacy Act. 2013.

US Department of Justice. *Principles on Transborder Access to Stored Computer Data.* 2004.

US Legal. *Binding Precedent.* 2016.

US Legal. *Frye Test Law & Legal Definition.* 2016.

US Legal. *Persuasive Precedent.* 2016.

United States District Court. *United States of America v Joseph Schmidt, III.* United States Government Publishing Office, 2009.

University of Rochester. Mobile Device User Agreement. 2016.

Vacca, John R.; Rudolph, K. *System Forensics, Investigation, and Response.* Jones & Bartlett Publishers, 2010.

van der Molen, Fred. *Get Ready for Cloud Computing,* 2nd edition. Van Haren, 2012.

Venter, JP. *Process Flows for Cyber Forensics Training and Operations.* CSIR Defencetek, 2006.

Volonino, Linda; Redpath, Ian. *E-Discovery for Dummies.* John Wiley & Sons, 2009.

Von Solms, Sebastiaan; Louwrens, Cecil; Reekie, Colette; Grobler, Talania. A Control Framework for Digital Forensics. In *Advances in Digital Forensics IV.* Springer, 2008. https://link.springer.com/content/pdf/10.1007/0-387-36891-4_27.pdf

Whitcomb, Carrie Morgan. An historical perspective of digital evidence: A forensic scientist's view. *International Journal of Digital Evidence,* 1(1), 2002. https://www.utica.edu/academic/institutes/ecii/publications/articles/9C4E695B-0B78-1059-3432402909E27BB4.pdf

Whitman, Michael E. Dr.; Mattord, Herbert J. *Principles of Information Security.* Thomson Learning, 2003.

Wilson, Mark; Hash, Joan. Special Publication 800-50: Building an Information Technology Security Awareness and Training Program. National Institute of Standards and Technology (NIST), 2003.

Yasinsac, A.; Manzano, Y. Policies to Enhance Computer and Network Forensics. *IEEE Workshop on Information Assurance and Security,* 2001.

Yusoff, Yunus; Ismail, Roslan; Hassan, Zainuddin. Common phases of computer forensics investigation models. *International Journal of Computer Science & Information Technology (IJCSIT),* 3(3), 2011. http://airccse.org/journal/jcsit/0611csit02.pdf

Zeltser, Lenny. *The Many Fields of Digital Forensics and Incident Response.* System Administration, Networking, and Security Institute (SANS) Digital Forensics and Incident Response, 2014.

Index

Business code of conduct policy, 72, 112–113,
139–140
Business continuity planning, 228
Business ethics, 72
Business risk scenarios, 206–208
BYOD, *see* Bring your own device

C

CALEA, *see* Communications Assistance for
Law Enforcement Act
Canada
civil procedure rules, 246–247
forensic education programs, 310
Sedona Principles, 245–246
CART, *see* Computer Analysis Response Team
Cause and effect, natural law of, 186–187
CAWFE, *see* Certified Advanced Windows
Forensic Examiner
CBK, *see* Common body of knowledge
CCE, *see* Certified Computer Examiner
CEI, *see* Computer Ethics Institute
Central storage system, 43
Certificate-based encryption, 163
Certified Advanced Windows Forensic
Examiner (CAWFE), 74
Certified Computer Examiner (CCE),
74, 76
Certified Forensic Computer Examiner
(CFCE), 73, 74
CFCE, *see* Certified Forensic Computer
Examiner
Chain-of-evidence model, 187
Chip-off analysis, 111
Choose your own device (CYOD), 117
CIA Triad (Confidentiality, Integrity, and
Availability), 175, 272
Civil justice system, 64
Civil law, 56
Civil litigation, 259
Click-wrap agreement, 146
Cloud computing, 6, 44
brief history of, 133–134
characteristics of, 135
consequences of organizations, 154
definition, 134–135
delivery models, 136
enterprise management strategies, 141
contractual agreements, 145–146
data-centric security, 146
reference architectures, 143–145
security and configuration standards, 142

evolution and creation of, 134
governance, 139
acceptable use policy, 140–141
business code of conduct policy,
139–140
isolation models, 136–137
legal considerations, 153–154
model dimensions, 137
process methodology, *see* Cloud computing
process methodology
service models, 135–136
threats and challenges, 137–139
evidence gathering and processing, 139
first responders, 138–139
hyperscaling, 138
Cloud-computing ecosystems, 6
Cloud computing process methodology
gathering, 150
collection and preservation, 151–152
identification, 150–151
preparation, 147
formal education, 149
general awareness, 148
high-level digital forensic model, 147
technology and toolsets, 149–150
presentation, 153
processing, 152–153
Cloud forensics, 147–150
Cloud service provider (CSP), 145, 152, 153, 181
Cloud settings, mobile device management, 119
Cloud storage, 110
COBIT, *see* Control Objectives for Information
and Related Technology
COBO, *see* Corporate-owned business only
Commercial off-the-shelf (COTS) technologies,
93, 94, 118
Common body of knowledge (CBK), 19,
73, 284
Communications Assistance for Law
Enforcement Act (CALEA), 58
Communication skills, 46
Community cloud, 136
Compliance, 84, 250
Computer Analysis Response Team (CART), 4
Computer ethics, 71–72
Computer Ethics Institute (CEI), 71
Computer forensic field triage process model, 302
Computer forensic investigative process, 297
Computer forensic process model, 297–298
Computer forensics, 4–5, 303
Computer law, 57
Computer security events, 41, 44